HEGEL'S INTRODUCTION TO THE SYSTEM

Encyclopaedia Phenomenology and Psychology

T0341924

As an introduction to his own notoriously complex and challenging philosophy, Hegel recommended the sections on phenomenology and psychology from *The Philosophy of Spirit*, the third part of his *Encyclopaedia of the Philosophic Sciences*. These offered the best introduction to his philosophic system, whose main parts are Logic, Nature, and Spirit.

Hegel's Introduction to the System finally makes it possible for the modern reader to approach the philosopher's work as he himself suggested. The book includes a fresh translation of "Phenomenology" and "Psychology," an extensive section-by-section commentary, and a sketch of the system to which this work is an introduction. The book provides a lucid and elegant analysis that will be of use to both new and seasoned readers of Hegel.

ROBERT E. WOOD is a professor in the Institute of Philosophic Studies at the University of Dallas.

Hegel's Introduction to the System

Encyclopaedia Phenomenology and Psychology

G.W.F. HEGEL

Introduction, Translation, and Commentary by
Robert E. Wood

Foreword by William Desmond

UNIVERSITY OF TORONTO PRESS
Toronto Buffalo London

© University of Toronto Press 2014
Toronto Buffalo London
www.utppublishing.com

ISBN 978-1-4426-4829-6 (cloth)
ISBN 978-1-4426-2605-8 (paper)

Library and Archives Canada Cataloguing in Publication

Hegel, Georg Wilhelm Friedrich, 1770–1831
[Philosophie des Geistes. English]
Hegel's introduction to the system: encyclopaedia phenomenology and
psychology / G.W.F. Hegel; introduction, translation, and commentary
by Robert E. Wood; foreword by William Desmond.

Includes bibliographical references and index.
ISBN 978-1-4426-4829-6 (bound). – ISBN 978-1-4426-2605-8 (pbk.)

1. Philosophy of mind. 2. Spirit. 3. Hegel, Georg Wilhelm Friedrich,
1770–1831. Philosophie des Geistes. I. Wood, Robert E., 1934–, writer
of introduction, translator II. Title. III. Title: Philosophie des Geistes.
English IV. Title: Introduction to the system.

B2918.E5W55 2014   193   C2014-903760-0

University of Toronto Press acknowledges the financial assistance to its
publishing program of the Canada Council for the Arts and the
Ontario Arts Council, an agency of the Government of Ontario.

**Canada Council   Conseil des Arts
for the Arts   du Canada**

ONTARIO ARTS COUNCIL
CONSEIL DES ARTS DE L'ONTARIO
an Ontario government agency
un organisme du gouvernement de l'Ontario

University of Toronto Press acknowledges the financial support of the
Government of Canada through the Canada Book Fund for its
publishing activities.

Assistance was provided by the Provost's and the Constantine Dean's
offices at the University of Dallas.

To my Father and my Mother
Whose dedicated care
Permanently shaped my life.

Contents

**Part IV: Overview of the Concluding Sections of
"Philosophy of Spirit"**

Foreword

It is always a difficult thing to introduce the thought of Hegel. There is the sheer difficulty of Hegel's thought, a difficulty of dimensions that many adept philosophers quail at even attempting an understanding. There is also the extensiveness of Hegel's great published books, his *Phenomenology of Spirit*, *Science of Logic*, and *Encyclopaedia of the Philosophical Sciences*, each of which asks immense effort and patience from any reader. And yet despite such difficulty, Hegel has not only been read but has exercised huge influence on philosophical thought, and in a larger cultural sense, in the centuries since he wrote. Even those who proclaim themselves as his enemies show themselves to be defined deeply by their antagonist. Hegel is almost impossible to introduce, yet in a sense nothing is more needed. Robert Wood's engaging book seeks to meet that need in his own distinctive way.

Wood has all the scholarly credentials needed to aid us in the reading of Hegel, but his purpose is to open up the richness of Hegel's thought, and to answer in his own way Hegel's claim that "the true is the whole." This claim too is a source of difficulty, since it seems one must know everything to know anything. And yet this view can also be a source of enabling rather than hindering. If the true is the whole, in a sense one can start anywhere, one can start wherever one happens to be, and traverse the pathways of connection revealed by attentive thinking. It is to the latter approach that Wood fruitfully resorts. He offers an accessible and nuanced introduction to Hegel's thought by setting out from the midst of the *Encyclopaedia*, where we find Hegel's philosophy of spirit. Hegel's views of the human being as embodied spirit are there articulated in terms of his anthropology, phenomenology, and psychology. The *Encyclopaedia* gives us the circle of the sciences, and as with any circle, wherever we start, if we but continue to traverse, we will pass along the entire circumference and get some sense of the whole. By starting where he does, Wood's emphasis is on what is closest to us, namely, our own being, as mindfulness emerges in our embodied being, and extends beyond itself. In Hegel's language, this is subjective spirit waking up to itself in the human being in a form beyond the immediacy of animal consciousness, and in all the mediated forms that carry it from its own particularity up to the level of absolute spirit itself.

Wood's point of entry is undoubtedly well chosen, especially when his reader sees that perhaps the major point of the book is to present Hegel's thought in a pedagogically accessible manner. Wood's solution to the problem of gaining access to the difficult richness of Hegel's thought makes persuasive sense. The structure of what he does is well laid out. A brief outline of Hegel's view is followed by a presentation of his relevant texts, selected also with reference to pedagogical usefulness, and here newly translated and accompanied with a helpful and illuminating commentary. Hence, the unfolding of Wood's book works well with a back and forth conversation between Hegel's own texts and the commentary shedding light for the student of Hegel on sometimes dense and enigmatic writings.

There is also something very fitting about this pedagogical strategy in the following sense. The *Encyclopaedia* is the only published text of Hegel's where he presents us with an account of the system as a whole, and so indeed it tries to live up to the claim that the true is the whole. But interestingly, perhaps its chief purpose was to serve as a kind of handbook for Hegel's own teaching, as a kind of textbook for his lectures. This is evident from the compositional structure: a set of numbered and interrelated paragraphs progressively unfold and constitute the main body of the work. With some paragraphs there are remarks by Hegel himself. But Hegel in his own teaching would speak on the text and its theme, sometimes extemporizing in very interesting ways. Versions of many of these oral additions are preserved for us from student notes. Of course, these have to be treated with scholarly caution, since they might not be exactly Hegel's own words. But though slips always were possible, indeed unavoidable, many students were adept in the art of accurate transcribing. The end results are an interesting combination of the written texts plus transcriptions of what Hegel was taken to deliver in a more oral form. One sees something of the pedagogical complexity in all of this – the interplay of written thought and oral reflection, plus the more extemporized supplementation, producing a work that is multilayered. One gets some sense of the practice of Hegel as a teacher.

What Wood impressively does can be seen in its own way as mirroring this complex pedagogical practice of Hegel. While he does not include these students' additions in his translation, he does make use of them in his commentary and in the interplay of the judicious guide with the primary texts. The result is a book that will be very effective for students newly coming to Hegel. One can recommend it as an excellent pedagogical tool, taking into account the translation of judiciously chosen texts with the lucid and helpful commentary. The whole work is written in a compact and engaging way, a great aid to the beginner as well as satisfying to the more adept. It is also written with an attractive lucidity, and though Wood could easily display impressive erudition, the important goal is the intelligible communication of Hegel's central insights. The result is a very worthy introduction to Hegel.

William Desmond
Professor of Philosophy, Institute of Philosophy
Katholieke Universiteit Leuven, Belgium
David Cook Visiting Chair in Philosophy
Villanova University, USA

PART I

Introduction

Preface

It is not that Hegel's philosophy has broken down. Rather, his contemporaries and successors have not ever yet stood up so that they can be measured against his greatness.

Martin Heidegger, *Hegel's Phenomenology of Spirit*

Hegel is notoriously difficult to read. The text easiest to read is the Introduction to his *Philosophy of History*, which is, consequently, frequently used in philosophy courses. However, Hegel himself warned that its basic presupposition, that Reason rules the World, is here assumed, but is demonstrated by his System.[1] Hegel famously said, "The True is the Whole."[2] The Philosophy of History has to be grounded ultimately in the Whole. Its premises lie proximately in the Philosophy of Objective Spirit as the developed institutional matrix for rational development, which, in turn, presupposes the Philosophy of Subjective Spirit, which deals with the structure of being a human individual. The proximate roots lie in the Philosophy of Nature, while the ultimate grounds of both Nature and Spirit are found in the Logic.

The book you have in your hands is an introduction to *Hegel's* view of the Whole in the System found in the *Encyclopaedia of the Philosophic Sciences*. It *follows his own recommendation* regarding the best way into his thought. The System consists of three parts: Logic, Philosophy of Nature, and Philosophy of Spirit. As his introduction to the System,

---

1 *Lectures on the Philosophy of World History: Introduction*, trans. H. Nisbet trans. (Cambridge: Cambridge University Press, 1975), 27.

2 *Phenomenology of Spirit*, trans. A. Miller (Oxford: Oxford University Press, 1977), §20, 11.

Hegel wrote the 1807 *Phenomenology of Spirit*. He later recommended the pared-down version of its first three parts on Consciousness, Self-Consciousness, and Reason that appears as the section on Phenomenology in the *Encyclopaedia*'s *Philosophy of Spirit*; later still, he recommended as well the Psychology section that follows the Phenomenology.

These sections recommend themselves because they are focused, not upon the highly abstract considerations presented in his Logic, but upon readily identifiable features present in the field of experience. They have immediate verifiability focused upon the always already given character of those features; they present materials experientially closest to us. So, following Hegel's own recommendation, the current work is centred upon the Phenomenology and Psychology sections in the Philosophy of Spirit, for which we are providing a translation and extensive commentary. That is the central focus. It has a setting.

We first provide an existential setting by an overview of Hegel's life and thought. Then, as an introduction to the System, the sections selected will be set within the general framework of the System itself. We will therefore provide, as the setting for the Phenomenology and Psychology within the System, an introduction to the Logic and the Philosophy of Nature as well as the general layout of the Philosophy of Spirit within which the sections appear.

The specific locus of our key texts is the treatment of the general structure of Subjective Spirit. The central of three subsections is the Phenomenology, which, as the field of the subject–object relation, the relation of awareness to the regularly appearing world surrounding it, provides an inventory of the general features involved. The field of awareness is rooted downwards in the Anthropology, a consideration of the ways in which embodiment affects human awareness. The field of awareness is also suspended from above in the Psychology as an inventory of the hierarchy of capacities operative in wakeful life. Consult the following diagrams for a visually clear presentation of the relations involved.

We will begin the translation and commentary with the closing sections of the Anthropology as transition to the Phenomenology. For each of the three translated sections I will first provide an overview. In the Philosophy of Spirit, Subjective Spirit is followed by Objective Spirit. I will outline that after the translation and commentary, concluding with a sketch of the apex of the System in the region of Absolute Spirit: the spheres of Art (in its highest mission), Religion, and Philosophy.

Diagram 1. Phenomenology and Psychology within the System

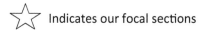 Indicates our focal sections

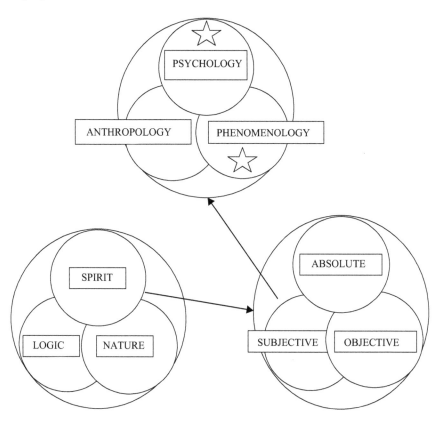

The thumbnail sketch of the Logic is necessary to understand the technical vocabulary that Hegel uses throughout. We will refer back to the terminology of the Logic at the end of our treatment of Subjective Spirit in order to underscore the technical terms Hegel uses throughout his thought. And in commenting upon each section, I re-explain the terms as they appear. Armed with these more technical considerations, we should be in a better position to be able to read the third volume of the *Encyclopaedia*, Hegel's *Philosophy of Spirit*, the fulfilment of the conceptual pattern laid out in the Logic.

It is important to underscore the translated texts as a single whole, since I have presented them by subdividing the various sections when paragraphs or particularly difficult sentences require some commentary. I have not followed the convention of placing the commentary after the text because I find it irritating to have to flip back and forth when meeting a section of particular difficulty.[3] Rather, I have chosen to place the commentary in tandem with the texts. The commentary stands under each such section, distinguished by a line space and a different typeface and font. I recommend attempting to read Hegel's texts together as a single whole before getting into the commentary. In fact, one might have a go at the texts even before my introducing and situating the text in the System. After one has worked through text and commentary, I recommend reading the whole text again to see how much progress the reader has made in comprehension. As I tell my students, there is no such thing as philosophical reading; there is only reading and rereading and rereading ... But I tell them that, with regard to Hegel, there is no such thing as reading, *only* rereading and rereading ... Hence this book and the way it is intended to be used.

* * *

Hegel published three progressively expanded versions of the *Encyclopaedia of the Philosophical Sciences*: in 1817, in 1827, and in 1830. The text of the *Philosophy of Spirit* I have worked from is the latest critical edition of the 1830 version edited by Lukas and Bonseipen.[4] It does not include the *Zusätze* or additions provided by Bouman in the 1843 edition based upon student notes from Hegel's lectures clarifying and expanding the Encyclopaedia text. I have used them as needed in my commentary. Omitting them has the advantage of reducing the size of

---

3 The convention of separating text and commentary appeared most recently in Michael Inwood, *A Commentary on Hegel's* Philosophy of Mind (Oxford: Clarendon Press, 2007) as a companion to his updating of the Wallace/Miller translation in G.W.F. Hegel, *Philosophy of Mind* (Oxford: Clarendon Press, 2007). It is regrettable that Inwood retains the translation of *Geist* by "Mind," which is more tepid than the rich associations the German word carries.

4 Georg Friedrich Wilhelm Hegel, *Enzyklopädie der Philosophischen Wissenschaften im Grundrisse* (1830), in *Gesammelte Werke*, ed. Wolfgang Bonsiepen and Hans-Christian Lucas (Hamburg: Meiner Verlag, 1992).

the current text for student readers. I have also not observed the practice of indenting remarks Hegel added to his original text and which we also find in the critical edition from which I have worked. They amount, in effect, to a new edition. Disregarding the indentation presents the text as a single whole.

* * *

The importance of Hegel continued into the movements subsequent to his thought, even into the present day. In the 1950s Maurice Merleau-Ponty observed that Hegel had spawned the major movements of thought that came after him. He was talking about Continental thought.[5] One decisive turning point was Alexander Kojéve's brilliantly one-sided lectures in the 1930s on Hegel's 1807 *Phenomenology of Spirit*.[6] Hegel has remained a significant force in Continental thought to this day.

In the Anglo-American world, John Dewey saw himself as a Hegelian minus the absolute standpoint, a Hegelian turned experimental.[7] In England during the first quarter of the twentieth century, Hegel had a decisive influence upon thinkers like Bosanquet, McTaggart, and Bradley, who stood in a line going back to T.H. Green in the late nineteenth century.[8] But Anglo-American thought in the final three-quarters of the twentieth century decisively repudiated Hegel.[9] At the same time, there occurred a split between Anglo-American thought and Continental thought as such.

The two hundredth anniversary in 1970 of Hegel's birth introduced a Hegel renaissance in the Anglo-Saxon world. John Findlay was one of the leaders who, along with Errol Harris, anticipated it.[10] Charles Taylor

---

5 *Sense and Non-Sense*, trans. H. and P. Dreyfus (Evanston: Northwestern University Press, 1964), 63.

6 *Introduction to the Reading of Hegel*, ed. A. Bloom, trans. J.H. Nichols (New York: Basic Books, 1969).

7 "From Absolutism to Experimentalism," *On Experience, Nature, and Freedom*, ed. R. Bernstein (Indianapolis: Bobbs-Merrill, 1960).

8 Hiralal Haldar, *Neo-Hegelianism* (London: Heath, Cranton, 1927).

9 Armand Maurer, in Étienne Gilson, Thomas Langan, and Armand Maurer, eds, *Recent Philosophy: Hegel to the Present* (New York: Random House, 1966), 454ff.

10 Beginning with *Nature, Mind, and Modern Science* (London: George Allen and Unwin, 1954), 228–55, Harris went on in several works to show the enduring relevance of Hegel's thought; see below, chap. 3, n. 2. Findlay wrote *Hegel: A Re-Examination* (New York: Collier Books, 1962).

turned from analytical philosophy to an extensive and systematic study of Hegel.[11] In his review of Taylor's *Hegel*, Richard Bernstein noted that the first part of Hegel's 1807 *Phenomenology of Spirit* was prophetic history of twentieth-century British philosophy, working out the internal logic of transition from sense-data positivism to the late Wittgenstein.[12]

In recent times, Robert Brandom began a sympathetic reading of Hegel's *Phenomenology*,[13] preceded by Willem de Vries.[14] The trend reached a certain culmination in *Mind and World* by John McDowell, who was decisively affected by Brandom's lectures on the *Phenomenology*.[15] McDowell traces the development of American thought from Quine, through Sellars, Rorty, and Davidson, to arrive at a position in which he claims that Hegel had completed the project initiated by Kant and addressed by the line of thinkers considered.[16] More recently, Thomas Nagel has called for a reconsideration of Hegel and Schelling over against mainstream neurological reductionism.[17] With the incipient healing of the gap that has yawned in America between the analytical and Continental traditions, it seems times are ripe for revisiting Hegel once more.

Alasdair MacIntyre, who edited a volume of studies on Hegel,[18] has reinvigorated at least aspects of this approach in his view of the progress of thought. He sees it as a matter of developing a tradition beyond itself

---

11 *Hegel* (Cambridge: Cambridge University Press, 1975).

12 "Why Hegel Now?" *Review of Metaphysics* 31 (September, 1977), 29–60.

13 Brandom has made available on-line at his own website his 2011 Munich Lectures, "Knowing and Representing: Reading (between the lines of) Hegel's Phenomenology": http://www.pitt.edu/~brandom/currentwork.html#munich.

14 *Hegel's Theory of Mental Activity* (Ithaca and London: Cornell University Press, 1988).

15 *Mind and World* (Cambridge: Harvard University Press, 1996). McDowell refers to Brandom's work on Hegel as "eye-opening" and states that *Mind and World* is a prolegomenon to a reading of Hegel's *Phenomenology* (ix).

16 Ibid., 111. Sellars, Brandom, and McDowell (with de Vries as a minor figure) constitute what has recently been called the Pittsburgh School of Philosophy by Chauncey Maher in his book by the same title (New York: Routledge, 2012). See also Paul Redding, *Analytic Philosophy and the Return of Hegelian Thought* (Cambridge: Cambridge University Press, 2010).

17 *Mind and Cosmos: Why the Materialist Neo-Darwinian Concept of Nature Is Almost Certainly Wrong* (Cambridge: Oxford University Press 2012), 17.

18 *Hegel: A Collection of Critical Essays* (Garden City: Doubleday, 1972).

by doing the same for a competing tradition and finding a position that can accommodate aspects of both traditions in a more rationally compelling whole. He presents Thomas Aquinas as an exemplar of this approach.[19]

* * *

One internal problem with Hegel is his formidable System, grounded in the Logic. But this is linked to an even greater external problem, that of a continual misreading, especially of his political work.[20] Linked to the problem of understanding each truth-claim that Hegel himself makes within the Whole is the problem of ideological approaches that both spawn and spontaneously latch onto the history of misreadings of Hegel. The difference between ideology and philosophy is that the former is not self-critical and hence cannot enter into sympathetic relation with what seems to oppose its ideological fixation. The problem is acute in religion and politics, where people tend, by the very nature of their commitments, to become locked into their dogmatic certitudes, unable to appreciate other positions from within.

And in general, aspects of Hegel's thought are interpreted without attending to his central claim, that "The truth is the whole," and to his central notion of *Aufhebung*.[21] An ordinary German term that carries three seemingly unrelated meanings – cancellation, preservation, and elevation – *Aufhebung* in Hegel's usage functions to indicate the way in which countervailing truth-claims should be treated. In looking at the history of philosophy, he notes that thinkers attain to classic status by reason of apprehending a central and, he thinks, *eternal* truth (so much for the attribution to Hegel of relativism, ordinarily understood). The problem is the articulation of that truth and its relation to other claims by other classic thinkers. Short of a systematic context in which each such truth can be situated, the articulation of a given truth has to be one-sided and has to entail rejection of other one-sidedly articulated basic truth-claims.

---

19 *Three Rival Versions of Moral Inquiry* (Notre Dame: University of Notre Dame Press, 1990).
20 See my "Misunderstanding Hegel," *Epoché*, Fall 2012.
21 *Phenomenology of Spirit*, trans. A. Miller (Oxford: Oxford University Press, 1977), §20, 11; *Philosophy of History*, 77; *The Encyclopaedia Logic*, trans. T. Geraets, W. Suchting, and H. Harris (Indianapolis: Hackett, 1991) §396, 154.

The task is to find a point of view that could do justice to the "eternal truths" contained in each great philosophy, shorn of the one-sided articulation in its original form, and rendered compatible with insights contained in other great philosophic systems. Hegel claims to have attained to a final systematic context that does justice to the whole history of philosophy. To that System we are providing an introduction.

* * *

I want to thank my colleague Philipp Rosemann and members of the Dallas DASEIN group, especially Charles Bambach, Rod Coltman, John Loscerbo, Rod Stewart, and Jeff Todd, for their careful critique of the translation. I want also to thank Dustin Wendland and Peter Antich for their careful reading and judicious suggestions, which led to greater clarity in the final version. I want especially to thank the reviewers for the University of Toronto Press for the most careful and helpful reviews that, as writer and editor, I have ever received. The present text is much better because of their advice.

Institute of Philosophic Studies
University of Dallas

Chapter One

Hegel's Life and Thought

Georg Friedrich Wilhelm Hegel was born in 1770 and died in 1831 of a stomach ailment. From 1788–93 he attended the Lutheran theological seminary at Tübingen. Astonishingly, his two roommates were to become as famous as Hegel himself: the future philosopher Friedrich Wilhelm Joseph Schelling and the future poet Friedrich Hölderlin. Wherever has something like that happened, that three famous thinkers were college roommates? They are rumoured to have planted a "freedom tree" to celebrate the beginning of the French Revolution; and every year thereafter until the end of his life Hegel toasted the storming of the Bastille. The trio produced a statement of a systematic approach to philosophy that was developed in different ways by Schelling and Hegel; but the poet Hölderlin was considered the heart of the group.

Schelling eventually took a position at the University of Jena and secured for Hegel his first teaching position there. For a time Schelling and Hegel collaborated on a philosophical journal in which Hegel produced two long articles, one a comparing the systems of Fichte and Schelling, the other dealing with the relationship of faith and knowledge.[1] At Jena in 1807 Hegel was completing his first major work, *Phenomenology of Spirit*, when Napoleon arrived in the city, having defeated the Prussian army in the battle of Jena. Hegel exclaimed that he "saw the World Spirit on horseback" riding through the streets of the city. The *Phenomenology* was a working through of Hegel's reading of

---

1 *The Difference between Fichte's and Hegel's Systems of Philosophy*, trans. H. Harris and W. Cerf (Albany: SUNY Press, 1977); *Faith and Knowledge*, trans. W. Cerf and H. Harris (Albany: SUNY Press, 1977).

the history of consciousness that culminates in the milieu of Absolute Knowing, where the conditions are ready for a systematic completion of the history of life and thought. But a break occurred between the two former friends that was to last a lifetime; in fact, Schelling was called to Berlin ten years after Hegel's death to battle the proponents of Hegel's philosophy.

After Jena, Hegel went on to become editor for a year of a pro-French newspaper in Bamberg. His next position was headmaster at a gymnasium or high school in Nuremburg from 1808–16. Here he worked on his massive and formidable *Science of Logic*, which came out in two instalments: in 1812 and 1816. He also developed the first edition of his *Encyclopaedia of Philosophical Sciences*, systematically covering the fields of Logic, Nature, and Spirit. Unbelievably, this work was an outline that he used to instruct students *at the gymnasium*! What kind of students must they have been! The Encyclopaedia went through three editions: in 1817, 1827, and in 1830.[2]

In 1816 Hegel received a professorship at the University of Heidelberg, and in 1818 was called to the newly founded University of Berlin. A special attraction of the university upon which Hegel remarked in his inaugural address was the academic freedom that was a hallmark of the vision of the founding father, Wilhelm von Humboldt, after whom the university was subsequently named. Humboldt was minister of education in the Prussian reform administrations of Stein and Hardenburg which, after the humiliating defeat of the Prussian army by Napoleon, strove to reform the entire Prussian military and political system from top to bottom. The pattern for the reform was provided by the development of the French constitution's overthrowing of serfdom and the privileges of the old divine-rights monarchies. Completing the revolutionary movements, Napoleon developed a legal code that he imposed on the countries he conquered. In many respects it became the model for the reform in Prussia.

The infamous Karlsbad Decrees of 1819 that followed the assassination in Prussia of the poet Kotzebue in 1817 put a halt to the Reform Movement and seriously infringed upon the academic freedom so

---

2 Posthumous editions have been expanded considerably by the addition of quite lengthy student notes. The current text is based on the 1831 edition and excerpts the sections on Phenomenology and Psychology, minus the student notes.

precious to Hegel. But Hegel saw in the Reform Movement the culmination of the historic process to build rational freedom in a more comprehensive sense into political life.[3]

Hegel's view of the rational follows Kant's distinction between abstractive Understanding (*Verstand*) and synthesizing Reason (*Vernunft*). As Hegel saw it, what is rational does not simply exist in some abstract realm, but is found always operative in history as well as in nature. In history the rational is the condition for the possibility of the long-term cohesion of the internal life of states which progresses through a set of institutions that guarantees individual rights but at the same time integrates individuals into the whole that is the nation state. The rational has progressively developed through history. And in his own age Hegel saw the kernel of actualized rationality in the Reform Movement that he attempted to present systematically in his *Philosophy of Right*, which appeared in 1821.[4] Some of his followers constituted a nucleus of reform-minded civil servants in the Prussian government. Hegel was elected rector of the University of Berlin in 1830 and died the next year.

In the approach Hegel recommended and that we are following in this book, the analysis of experience is the starting point. But he also taught us to think in terms of the truths contained throughout the history of philosophy. He attempted especially to bring the many-faceted truths laid hold of by Aristotle (384–322) into relation with the developments that have taken place since the advent of Christianity. Central to his endeavour was the Lutheran "witness of the Spirit," an appeal to what is deepest in each individual against merely external authority. But he saw this claim brought forward from an emotional "being touched" to an intellectual grasp of evidence in René Descartes's (1596–1650) appeal to the *cogito*, the "I think." Here, Hegel said, we reach land. Moderns influenced by this appeal expect to be given the evidence for what they are otherwise told simply by authoritative fiat. Modern science and modern philosophy as well as modern political thought live, each in its own way, under that appeal.

---

3 See Charles Sullivan and Robert E. Wood, "Rationality and Actuality: Hegel and the Prussian Reform Movement," *Existentia* 21, no. 1–2 (2011), 57–78.

4 *Elements of the Philosophy of Right*, ed. A. Wood, trans. H. Nisbet (Cambridge: Cambridge University Press, 1991).

In Hegel's thought, Baruch Spinoza's (1632–77) view of the cosmos as a single Substance of which everything individual is a completely determined accident – a view claimed by Einstein as the metaphysics most compatible with contemporary physics – is juxtaposed to and supplemented by Descartes's individualistic *cogito*. Though a kind of "accident," dependent upon the Whole in which it is inserted and destined to perish, the individual human for Hegel is nonetheless a centre of free initiative who can unveil more and more of the Whole through its search for evidence, and create political order along with space for creativity in the economy and the arts based upon its freedom to choose within the rational framework of the State. Hegel introduced the free Subject into Spinoza's encompassing Substance.

Immanuel Kant (1724–1804) inventoried experience as a coherent whole from the point of view of the "I think," which he called the *transcendental unity of apperception*, and which functions in terms of the categories of the understanding in the theoretical order. The categories are the basic principles, given with experience, for sorting out experience into a coherent whole. He also developed a theory of moral autonomy in which each rational subject legislates (gives *nomos*, or law) to itself (*autos*), but in a way that is morally obligated by reason of its rationality. In the latter case, Kant was following Jean-Jacques Rousseau's (1712–78) lead in viewing freedom as self-legislation that correlated with that of others in the rational will. Johann Gottlieb Fichte (1752–1814) followed by attempting to deduce the Kantian categories from what he called the "I = I," the self-awareness of the *cogito*, and to develop an ethics of perpetual striving to reach an ideal along with a politics of rational rule based upon the reciprocity of human subjects.

Hegel followed these directions, attempting in his Logic to "deduce" the categories, beginning with the most abstract and showing the insufficiency of each without its coordination with all the others. He attempted to display these categories as operative in one way in Nature and in another way in the history of the human Spirit. And the latter occurs on the basis of the structures of community that have become increasingly rational through the development of modern thought and life. Hegel thinks that the period in which he lived, that of the French Revolution and its aftermath, was a culmination of developments in the practical order that go back to the earliest foundation of States, and of developments in the theoretical order that go back to the beginning in Presocratic philosophy. These developments put his age in a position to gather the Whole together, now manifest in the main lines of its inherent rationality as the conditions for the possibility of an indefinite expansion in the theoretical and practical orders. His implicit basic question was: How must the cosmos be constituted so that the on-going development of human rationality – in science, technology, government, and art – is possible?

Throughout his life Hegel maintained that he was a devoted Lutheran, something orthodox Lutherans would strongly dispute. After all, in Hegel's System God as absolutely infinite must include the finite under penalty of not being *absolutely* infinite, and thus was not free to create or not to create. Furthermore, God comes to a fuller awareness of Himself through creation and especially through history. And finally, the immortality of the soul consists in its current relation to the eternal and encompassing region of the divine; but there is no individual survival after death.

Yet Hegel's claim to have been a devoted Lutheran was not a kind of social insurance at a time when religion was still linked to political control. It was a completely honest claim, for it was how he viewed the relation of Philosophy and Religion. Religion, especially Christian Religion, was the revelation of the Absolute, but in limited modes of representation. Philosophy translates the limited way of representing the truth characteristic of Religion into coherent conceptual form. In Hegel's view, he was simply raising Christian revelation to a fuller comprehension of its true content. After his death, this was one of the issues which split so-called Right Wing Hegelians, who followed a conservative political and religious direction, and Left Wing Hegelians (which included Karl Marx, 1818–83), who followed a revolutionary path.

PART II

Overview of the *Encyclopaedia of the Philosophic Sciences*

Chapter Two

Overview of "Logic"

1. Being
   a. Quality
      i.   Being-in-Itself
      ii. Determinate Being
      iii. Being-for-Itself
   b. Quantity
   c. Measure
2. Essence
   a. Essence as Ground
   b. Existence
   c. Actuality
3. Concept
   a. Subjective
      i.   Concept
      ii. Judgment
      iii. Syllogism
   b. Objective
      i.   Mechanism
      ii. Chemism
      iii. Teleology
   c. Idea
      i.   Life
      ii. Cognition
      iii. Absolute Idea

Overviews afford "nothing more than a picture for *ordinary thinking (Vorstel-lung)* ... to meet the subjective needs of unfamiliarity and its impatience."

Hegel, *Science of Logic*

One of the problems facing us as we begin to read Hegel is his for-midable terminology. Throughout his other texts he uses the technical terms forged in his Logic. In this chapter, we will locate and connect the various regions of the Logic in order to clarify the terminology.[1]

Hegel's central concern is the nature of rational existence and the con-ditions – logical-ontological, cosmological, anthropological, personal, and historical – for its existence and flourishing. To focus upon today's situation, we might say that he is providing insight into the conditions for the possibility of the scientist and the rationally free society.

The spelling out of these conditions appears in three interpenetrating realms: Logic, Nature, and Spirit as the eternal Trinity constituting the (famous or infamous) System. The Logic presents the interlocking set of presuppositions for the other two realms. It is actually *Onto-logic*, laying out "the thoughts of God before creation"; it is a philosophical transcription of the ancient doctrine of the Logos; and it includes for-mal logic as a subset. In Nature its categories operate within the over-arching principle of *exteriority* that involves things in space; in Spirit, within the principle of *interiority* that involves inter-subjective rational awareness developing in time.

Structured around the three domains of Being, Essence, and Concept, the Logic is developed with reference to the rational and free subject. Such a subject is directed to the Whole through the notion of Being. Thought thinks everything under the umbrella of Being, a founding notion that is initially empty. By reason of the essential embodiment of the rational subject, the categories of *Being* – in a technically narrow sense of the term – emerge first as immediately linked to sensory sur-face. They are the categories first introduced in ancient thought: Being

---

1 The most detailed treatment of the early parts of the Logic can be found in Stephen Houlgate, *The Opening of Hegel's* Logic (West Lafayette, IN: Purdue University Press, 2006). A treatment of the argumentation of select parts of the Logic can be found in John Burbidge, *On Hegel's Logic* (Atlantic Highlands, NJ: Humanities Press, 1981). More recently there is Burbidge's *The Logic of Hegel's "Logic"* (Peterborough, ON: Broadview Press, 2006).

(Parmenides), Non-Being (Buddha), Becoming (Heraclitus), Determinate Beings (Atomism), and the self-definition of a being as Being-for-Self involving sensory qualities, quantitative relations, and measure (Pythagoras).

The second set are what Hegel calls the categories of *Essence*; they underlie and are expressed through the sensory. The distinction between sensory surface and essential depth is available only to embodied rational beings. Initially, things *show up* within the sensory field having an *Essential Ground*; they begin to *show themselves* by developing in Existence; they *fully manifest themselves* in *Actuality*. The categories of Essence are also called "categories of Reflection" in that each term reflects its opposite.

The third set, the categories of the *Concept*, bring the rational subject into the picture, for such a subject is "the Concept entering into Existence," appearing among other beings as oriented towards the Totality. Rational activity presupposes Formal Logic and the Systems – Mechanical, Chemical, and Teleological (eco-systemic) – presupposed by life, with Life itself furnishing the basis for the distinctively human orientation towards the True and the Good aimed at the Absolute Idea, the Idea of the interlocking set of conditions for rational existence.

* * *

The Logic has a spiral structure that repeats the same three-fold relations in a set of the three progressively deeper levels: Being (*Sein*), Essence (*Wesen*), and Concept (*Begriff*). Typically, the third category in any section of the System is an *Aufhebung* of the first two that are typically opposites. As we noted previously, *Aufhebung* preserves, cancels, and elevates: each of the two opposites is *preserved* in its essential core, *cancelled* in its limited formulation, and *elevated* to compatibility with its opposite. To repeat: Being is simple immediacy, Essence entails the difference between surface and depth, while Concept joins the two of them by bringing in the human subject as "the Concept entering into existence." It is the human subject for which there is sensory surface and essential depth. The introduction of the Concept also involves the general logical and systematic natural presuppositions for human existence.

The Logic proceeds from the simplest categories to increasingly more complex notions. It begins with the empty notion of Being whose subcategories (Quality, Quantity, and Measure) apply in the first place, as we said, to sensory surface. In developing the category of Quality, we begin with Being (§§84–111).[2] As an initially empty notion, Being is indistinguishable from Nothing as sheer emptiness. The union of the two is the notion of Becoming (*Werden*), the first concrete concept: to become is no longer to be what one has been and not yet to be what one will be (§§86–8). But there is no Becoming without something that becomes. Hence, Becoming develops into Determinate Being (*Dasein*) (§§89–95) or the level of *beings*. Each such being is other than all the others. But each being also "returns to itself," defining itself against the others as Being-for-Itself (*Für sich*) (§§96–8). As a living being, it moves from initial potency to its completion in Actuality, where it becomes for itself what it was initially only in itself or in principle.

This basic articulation – Being as general principle, Determinate Being as the articulation of that principle, and Being-for-Itself as the gathering of the articulation into unity – gives the pattern at the sensory surface level for all subsequent development that goes beyond the sensory-based categories. The categories belonging to the immediately given are, first, *Quality* (§§99–106), the level at which the first Greek philosophers operated (sensory presentations of air, water, fire, and earth); then, intensive and extensive *Quantity* (§§107–11) (*intensive*: very loud; *continuous extensive*: four inches of red surface, and *discrete extensive*: four elements) and, finally, *Measure*, or the proportions of quantities determining the qualities given in experience. (The tension and thickness of vibrating strings in specific proportions produce the sounds that constitute the harmonic series – a Pythagorean discovery.) Though given immediately in sensory surface, these categories can be applied beyond the sensory – for example, to a determinate number of concepts: 3 sets of 3 or 9 basic categorical sets – or, most profoundly, to the divine Trinity, three-in-one.

The initial triad of Being, Determinate Being, and Being-for-Itself gets articulated at the level of Essence as Underlying Essence, Existence, and Actuality. As a subdivision of Underlying Essence there are

2 A note about the section numbers: Hegel viewed the *Encyclopaedia* as a single work with three parts and with the sections consecutively numbered. The Science of Logic goes from §1 to §244; the Philosophy of Nature from §245 to §376; and the Philosophy of Spirit from §377 to §577. At times he refers back in the sections of the Philosophy of Spirit we have selected from to section numbers from the other two parts.

the crucial categories of Identity, Difference, and Ground (Identity-in-Difference) (§§115–21), themselves repeating at this deeper level the initial categories of Being, Determinate Being, and Being-for-Itself.[3] Identity is the principle of abstract analytical Understanding; Ground as Identity-in-Difference is the basic principle of synthesizing, concretizing Reason. Each existent is a Determinate Being "coming out of its ground," a ground not suspected at the level of Determinate Beings. This shows the spiral or layering structure of the Logic: each more developed region repeats the earlier divisions in an enriched way by adding a new dimension.

Actuality is "the identity of Essence and Existence," that is, of underlying essential ground spelling itself out in Existence – the realm of determinate beings now viewed as standing out from their ground – until that essence has become fully developed (§§142–59). Hegel describes the basic characteristics of these categories of Essence as *Schein*, *Erscheinung*, and *Offenbarung* respectively. In the first place, I repeat, we have surface as a mere show (*Schein*) or *showing up* within the field of awareness wherein the underlying essential ground is not focused. A deeper focus attends to the surface as actually expressing Essence in Existence through how a thing *appears* in the various phases of its development (*Erscheinung*). Finally, in Actuality, a mature thing "makes open," *fully manifests* its essence (*Offenbarung*). The notion of Existence involves the relation of a Determinate Being expressing its Essence to other determinate beings that are now seen also as coming out of their grounds in their respective essences.

The subcategories of Actuality (*Wirklichkeit*) are Substance, Causality, and Reciprocity (§§150–9). As in Spinoza, Substance as a deeper articulation of encompassing Being refers in the first place to the all-encompassing Infinite that contains all existents as features necessarily inherent in it. Within the overarching Substance causal relations obtain, but as interrelated in a through-going Reciprocity. Actuality (*Wirklichkeit*) involves the full manifestation of this interrelated Totality. Further, Actuality contains Contingency that always accompanies the Necessity involved in the struggle of each essence to actualize itself in its existence

---

3 Some of these divisions are not present in the outline that begins the chapter. To include them would have involved parallel subdivisions in other categories that we will not treat. We have chosen the non-listed subdivisions when they are particularly illuminating.

in relation to others. Thus, there is a crucial distinction between the *existent* and the *actual* (*das Existierende* and *das Wirkliche*). The former is simply a matter of fact; the latter is a fulfilled essence. Nature itself is full of contingencies, but the freedom of human existence introduces a riot of contingencies through which Reason, nonetheless, is operative.

The distinction between Existence and Actuality is the key to understanding the much cited, little understood lines from the Philosophy of Right: "What is rational is actual and what is actual is rational." The first part opposes a utopian view of rationality as contained in some "realm beyond"; the rational is what holds actuality together in real existence. The second part indicates that not everything that exists is rational; the rational is where the actualization of an essence has occurred or is occurring in and through the existential contingencies and irrationalities that appear with it.

The language of manifestation involved in the level of Essence entails not only a showing *of* but a showing *to*; it entails one to whom showing happens. This is the third level, that of Concept (§§160–244), the *Begriff*, which, "when it has developed into a *concrete existence that is itself free, is none other than the I or pure self-consciousness*" (see §159).[4] The Concept makes its entry into existence in the self-consciousness of the individual human being when it rises above its particularity and bodily location to recognize its cognitive identity with the rational as such and therewith is able to determine itself.

In Hegel's peculiar usage of the term "Concept," what are otherwise called "concepts" are articulations by the human being, as the locus of manifestation, reaching out (*begreiffend*) towards the Whole and involving the development of the System of concepts as the conditions for the possibility of rational existence. The Concept as the third logical categorical set is divided into the Subjective Concept, the Objective Concept, and the Idea.

The Subjective Concept (initially Being as principle, then Essence as ground) (§§163–93) deals with formal logical considerations together with their ontological foundations. They are called "subjective," not because they are private opinions, but because they are the fundamental concepts employed by rational subjects in thinking through experience. Concepts are developed into definitional networks through Judgments and are causally interrelated through Syllogisms.

---

4 *The Science of Logic*, 583.

At this level, the triad of Being, Determinate Beings, and Being-for-Itself, re-inscribed at the level of Underlying Essence as Identity, Difference, and Ground, now appears in Hegel's explicit treatment of the first phase of the generic region of the Concept as Concept in the formal logical sense where it is distinguished and related to Judgment and Syllogism. Concept in the formal logical sense is divided into Universal, Particular, and Individual. Particularity is the articulation of the Differences within a universal essence, and Individuality is the unitary ground. The rational State, for example, is the unitary ground of the institutions and particular individuals with rights that safeguard rational Freedom. Individuals are embedded within the State, but are protected in their basic rights by mediating institutions.

As we said, all three formal notions – Concept, Judgment, and Syllogism – fall under the domain of the so-called *Subjective Concept*. However, Hegel attempts to show that these formal divisions have ontological correlates. Thus, each kind of real thing has its own "concept" to which it may or may not live up (an organism may be diseased and fail to reach its reproductive completion); each thing undergoes "judgment" (*Ur-teil* or primordial partition) represented by subject and predicate; and each thing is mediated, that is, joined together in terms of its concept to form a rational whole and is thus a "syllogism." The rational structure of a thing is situated within the fully mediated Whole that is the final Syllogism. One has to look past the formal logical meaning to its ground in things.

What the Self who operates in terms of the logical forms comes to understand is that it itself presupposes the *Objective Concept* (§§194–212). The Concept binds together the formal logical region of the Syllogism as principle of systematicity to that which is realized objectively in the systems within which the I is located, involving more than the plurality of Determinate Beings or Existents expressing their grounds. The systems are the level of Existence for the Concept, the appearance of the systematic ground, governed by principles that link their parts together, the higher subsuming the lower: *Mechanism* or the mechanical system of purely external relations, *Chemism* or the various chemical systems each component of which has an internal linkage to other elements through its valence bonds, and *Teleology* as the function of the organic ecosystem.

Material being "returns to itself" and is Being-for-Itself in the notion of Teleology. Teleology first appears as external where some things are taken as means to the ends of other things, like the elements for plants or the prey for predators, whether herbivores or carnivores. But that external teleology presupposes things which have ends in themselves, namely, the living: living things assimilate things external to themselves in order to develop and sustain their own lives.

The notion of teleology is crucial, for it is the locus of normativity. A teleological system implies interrelations among goal-oriented beings. Each such being is judged deficient insofar as it fails to meet its goals. Thus, we can speak of a sick organism and a dysfunctional State. The notion of Actuality presages teleology. It points to the achievement of a *telos* or end in the full development of an essence. In fact, *development* is the overriding character of the categories that fall under the Concept. At the level of the Objective Concept, the highest level is that of the systemic interrelation of things, within themselves and in relation to their ecosystem, that are goal-oriented, namely, organisms, which Hegel does not explicitly treat until the last categorical set: that of the Idea. So, the further Hegel goes, the more deeply he reaches into the grounds of what appeared earlier.

This leads us to the final level of the Idea (in terms of the spiralling structure, the Being-for-Itself, full Actuality, fully articulated as Ground, the paradigmatic Individual) as a union of Concept and Objectivity (§§213–44). The subcategories of the Idea are Life, Cognition, and the Absolute Idea. Teleological systems are possible because there is Life as an existent system distributed into its various genera and species. Mature organisms are completed individuals that began as seeds or eggs containing the principle of the organism, passed through particular levels of articulation according to that principle, and culminated in the mature, reproductively functioning organic individual systems in dialectic with their ecosystem. The human life-form, in turn, is completed in Cognition to establish unique, self-determining individuals oriented towards the True in the theoretical order and the Good in the practical order (§§223–35).

The development of the Whole culminates in what Hegel calls the "Absolute Idea," the knowledge of which is "Absolute Knowing" (*Absolutes Wissen*), the final For-Itself (§§236–44). This term might better be translated it as "Absolute Awareness," for it is always in some way involved in religious consciousness and in a full way in Christianity as Revealed Religion. Hegel's System claims to develop the conceptual System adequate to that awareness: to turn it from simple awareness to *Wissenschaft* or conceptual science based in Absolute Awareness.

Though "Absolute Awareness" sounds like omniscience, something much more "modest" is involved: it is the integrated display of all those structures, in the Logos, in Nature, in the structure of each individual human, and in the institutional interrelations of subjectivity that make intelligibility, understanding, and rational freedom concretely possible. That is what Hegel meant by turning *philo-sophia* from love of wisdom into the Science of Wisdom. This involves the human being as a living body, existing within and subsuming aspects of the chemical and mechanical systems operative in the ecosystem it presupposes, but oriented, at the cognitive level, towards the Whole of Being as the True and the Good. In Hegel's view, the Whole in turn is teleologically oriented towards its own display and development in human existence.

The rational State is the penultimate telos of the whole logico-cosmic-historical process. It provides the interlocking set of conditions in human institutions for the flourishing of rational and freely creative individuals. The State provides that matrix for the ultimate fruit of the System in the realm of Absolute Spirit, the realm of Art (considered in terms of its highest mission), Religion, and Philosophy.

* * *

Let us then recap: As the diagram on the following page indicates, the Logic follows a repetitive structure, with the pattern of *Aufhebung* operating throughout and the bald notions of Being, Determinate Being, and Being-for-Itself enriched by the upward turn of the structure at the next two levels, that of Essence and that of the Concept. Being, Determinate Being, Being-for-Itself are the surface categories attaining a fuller content through Essence as Ground, Existence, and Actuality.

In a final level, the previous two triads, those of Being and Essence, are surmounted by the categories of the Concept, that, entering into Existence, is the Self grasping towards the Totality. The level of Being, surmounted by underlying Essence, appears at the level of the Concept as the Subjective Concept or formal logic and its ontological correlates that rational subjects employ in thinking; the category of Determinate Being surmounted by Existence appears as the Objective Concept or the external systems that life and human existence presuppose; and the category of Being-for-Itself surmounted by Actuality appears as the Idea. The term "Idea" is used here in a very narrow technical sense as "the unity of Concept and Objectivity." The first level is the union of soul and body in Life-forms. The second is Cognition oriented towards the True

Diagram 2. Ascending Levels in the Logic

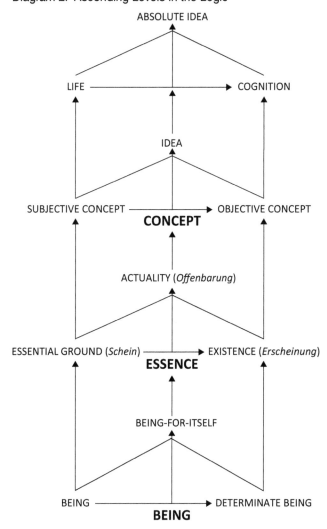

in the theoretical order and the Good in the practical order. Their final, in-principle completion is in Absolute Idea as the end of the logical process. The logical forms will be realized in the principle of exteriority as Nature and in the principle of interiority and intersubjectivity in Spirit.

As I said at the beginning of the chapter, this sketch and the diagram only introduces the terminology that will appear throughout our reading of Hegel's work. His application of these categories to the level of Spirit should gradually enrich our understanding of these terms and aid us in understanding the areas we will examine.

Chapter Three

Overview of "Philosophy of Nature"

1. Mechanics
   a. Space and Time
   b. Matter and Motion
   c. Absolute Mechanics
2. Physics
   a. Universal Individuality
      i.   Free Bodies
      ii. Elements
      iii. Meteorology
   b. Particular Individuality
      i.   Specific Gravity
      ii. Cohesion
      iii. Sound
      iv. Heat
   c. Total Individuality
      i.   Shape
      ii. Individual Particularization
      iii. Chemical Process
3. Organics
   a. Terrestrial Organism
   b. Plant Organism
   c. Animal Organism

In this second part of the Encyclopaedia Hegel attempts to show the way in which the Idea, whose basic structures he had exposed in the Logic, externalizes itself in the realm of Nature as the basis for its return to itself in the third part, the realm of Spirit. The divine Logos, eternally pre-containing the pattern of all possible types of existents outside Itself, expresses itself first in the medium of matter, the principle of externality and dividedness.

Hegel's treatment of Nature is focused upon overcoming the Newtonian view of Nature and the Cartesian view of Spirit aligned with it. Newton operated in terms of Descartes's separation of Nature, viewed in terms of the feature of Extension, from Spirit or Thought conceived of as a distinct kind of substance. In his typical procedure, Hegel returns these positions, as abstractions from full human experience, to their richer matrix in experience. Following Aristotle, whose works on the soul Hegel is expressly attempting to assimilate and develop, human existence as a psycho-physical whole is the high point and telos of Nature. As we said in regard to the Logic, one might here consider his view as pursuing the question regarding what conditions are necessary in Nature for the existence of the scientist who is exploring Nature.

Cartesian-Newtonian thought abstracts the lowest common denominator level of Nature: the mathematically treatable region operating according to the mechanistic laws of purely external relations. As we said, for Hegel Nature is the externalization of the Idea embedded in and governed by the principle of exteriority.

At this level, the opening triad of the Logic – Being, Nothing, Becoming – is instantiated in Space, Time, and Motion.[1] Under the generic heading of Being that plays in relation to Essence and the Concept and is divided into Quality, Quantity, and Measure, Hegel began the Logic with a more indeterminate notion of Being whose identity with Nothing is sublated into Becoming. The opening of the Philosophy of Nature shows these concepts appearing within the general principle of *exteriority*. Space is the encompassing realm of externalization, having aspects

---

1 Under the generic heading of Being that plays in relation to Essence and the Concept and is divided into Quality, Quantity, and Measure, Hegel begins with a more specific notion of Being whose identity with Nothing is sublated into Becoming. The opening of the Philosophy of Nature shows these concepts appearing in the general principle of *exteriority*.

outside of aspects, being sheer extension, but, like Being, sheer emptiness. It exhibits three dimensions – length, breadth, and depth – that
will become determinate through the things that exist in Space.

Time Hegel describes in terms that will be assimilated by Sartre to
speak of the self: "Time as the negative unity of being outside itself is …
being which, since it is, is not, and since it is not, is." Time is the triple
negativity: the no-longer of the Past, the not-yet of the Future, and the
non-temporally-extended, ever-flowing Now, moving out of the past
and into the future. Time is the same principle as the abstract I that
lives time from within in memory (oriented towards the past), attention (focused on the present), and fear and hope (projected towards the
future). Motion synthesizes Space and Time in Matter that composes
the determinate beings appearing in Space and Time.

Hegel goes on to deal with the elements that lie at the base of all
spatio-temporal things. He deals with them first in terms of the external
relations between them. It is this level that is explored in Newtonian
science as a science of mechanical principles. But one has to go beyond
Newtonism to reach the concrete. The level of Mechanics corresponds
to the first level of the Objective Concept in the Logic of the general
Concept.

In the human being, the level of Mechanics is assimilated first of all
by the level of Nature explored in Chemistry. Here the purely external
relations in Mechanics give way to the level of elements with "elective
affinities," native capacities to relate to each other so as to produce new
properties in things beyond the merely mechanical. So, for example,
hydrogen and oxygen each have the capacity to enter into relation with
each other so as to form water that exhibits different properties than
each of the elements in isolation from the other. This corresponds to
Essence in the Logic.

But whatever chemical processes are operating in the human being
as a living being, they are subsumed under the organic level, that is, the
level of instruments (organs) for the development and sustenance of
the organism as a system of instruments. This corresponds to the Concept as Idea in the Logic. The organic system integrates its organs into
a self-constructing, self-developing, self-sustaining, self-repairing, and
self-reproducing whole. Whatever chemical processes are involved, one
has to understand them not only in terms of mechanical and chemical
laws, but, more fundamentally, in terms of the inner teleology involved
in the organ-ism as a system of instruments. The analysis is parallel to
what goes on in human technology that develops instruments where

a complete empirical inventory of the object has to be supplemented by an understanding of what makes it an instrument, namely, its function or purpose that dictates the shape of its parts. However, in the organism the instruments are internally related to each other within an ever-flowing, comprehensive whole. The first level of the organic is plant life.

In the next level, that of the animal, aspects of the organism presuppose the metabolic functions common to plant life. Rising above that, special organs are developed for a function completely different from the non-conscious processes that underpin it: the function of the *manifestation* of things in the environment. Sensation reveals various manifest aspects of bodies, aspects that, synthesized over time, present those bodies that offer opportunities or threats to the well-being of the sensing organism. Sensation thus is inseparable from the appetites whose satisfaction sustains the organism. In Hegel's terms, the appetites reveal the awareness of lack in the organism that he considers an inner contradiction, a non-being within being. It drives the animal to fill the lack and overcome the contradiction by consuming or mating with or caring for the individuals in the environment to which the appetites are ordered.

Animals pass through various developmental stages driven by an initial lack of completion. In Hegel's terms, their "inner concept" is initially only *in itself* or potential and only gradually shows itself in existence until it becomes *for itself* or fully actualized, revealing itself as a reproductive adult member of its species. However, the individual animal cannot measure up fully to its concept insofar as, when it is fully unfolded, it is driven towards reproduction, a demand of the species upon the inadequacy of the individual. And the individual animal shows its inadequacy further by having to die as it is replaced by individuals of its own kind, keeping the species "eternal." Eros and Thanatos, sexual love and death, are thus tied together in organic being.

So the various levels in us recapitulate the hierarchy of the various kinds of bodies in the environment. Sensation presupposes the articulation of the organism that subsumes chemical processes which, in turn, presuppose mechanical processes. Distinctively human operations organize the sensory field and transcend it by introducing the universal concept and free self-determination. Spirit is both tied to and independent of, or – better expressed – in dialectical relation with what is Nature in us. In this dialectic, the two opposites, Spirit and Nature, are shown to require each other.

It is important to underscore that for Hegel the high point of the development of Spirit in human beings is the emergence of explicit rationality, of the sort that can uncover the immanent rationality of the System of Nature that it presupposes. Nature itself is a rational whole, a System composed of systems. So Hegel can say that Reason in us is not a separate faculty but is the unity of the psycho-physical whole, and indeed of the system of Nature within which it functions, come to self-presence as scientific knowing integrated in its fundamental presuppositions in the Hegelian System of Logic, Nature, and Spirit.

Distinctive humanness emerges with the notion of Being, what that great Aristotelian Thomas Aquinas had considered the first notion to arise in the mind. It involves an initially empty relation, beyond our animal dependency upon the environment, which allows us to say "I" and thus distance ourselves from all determinants, natural or cultural, in order to determine ourselves. And we do so as intellectual beings that can consider environmental beings and our own being purely speculatively, as they are, and not simply how they serve our natural appetites or appear within the thresholds of sensory perception that serves the appetites. This distance of the I also allows us the freedom to transform the environment and, in doing so, transform ourselves in virtue of our speculative understanding. This is what generates history as the field for the development of Objective Spirit, the locus of institutions of rational freedom, the second part of the Philosophy of Spirit.

So our intellectual operations depend upon sensations and appetites that present us with the theoretical and practical data that we learn to penetrate and transform. And those sensations and appetites depend upon the organs afforded by organic processes that assimilate things in the environment that nourish our organisms. Nonetheless, Hegel makes a sharp distinction between Nature and Spirit, as evidenced by his furnishing a separate volume for each. Spirit forms itself by rising above Nature; nonetheless, Spirit, forming and informing our natural bodies, is, as their soul, inseparably conjoined with Nature. So, as in Aristotle, we are not souls using or trapped in bodies, but Spirit-informed organic beings, psycho-physical wholes. As such, we belong in and to the world of Nature even as we transcend it by understanding and shaping it.

Just so, Hegel also considers the relation between Logic and these two realms as a kind of World-Soul informing both regions. Nature is the Idea in the realm of exteriority, divisibility, and dissolubility that is, nonetheless, Spirit's own matrix through which it "returns to itself" by developing over the millennia. It develops its Objective Spirit by accumulating and passing on its understanding and practices as the field within which it learns to catch up with its own basic orientation. It operates at its highest level in rising up to the contemplation of the eternal and encompassing Whole in Art, Religion, and Philosophy that each develop over time.[2]

A fuller understanding of Hegel's Philosophy of Nature along the lines indicated by some contemporary works would put us in position to be not so ready to dismiss it glibly as irrelevant to the sciences that have supposedly left it far behind by reason of their empirical and technological explosion. In fact, Hegel's view of Nature re-situates the scientist who has been implicitly absent from the reductionist tendencies that have dogged and now tend to dominate the thought in and of the sciences. Hegel's view of Nature would lead us to understand that what moves us in science is a free commitment to the True and the Good that essentially differentiates us from other animals with whom, nonetheless, we have an essential kinship.

---

2 A further exposition of Hegel's views on Nature would have to come to terms with the empirical sciences of our own time. This task was undertaken by Errol Harris in such works as *Nature, Mind, and Modern Science* (London: George Allen and Unwin, 1954), an examination of the interrelation of these three spheres from the early Greeks to mid-twentieth-century thought; *The Foundations of Metaphysics in Science* (Lanham, MD: University Press of America, 1983), a look at the fundamental categories involved in physics, chemistry, biology, and the behavioural sciences in the late twentieth century; and *Hypothesis and Perception* (London: George Allen and Unwin, 1975), a case study of crucial moments in the history of science. Harris has summarized his work in *Cosmos and Anthropos* (Atlantic Heights, NJ: Humanities Press International, 1991) and *Cosmos and Theos* (Atlantic Heights, NJ: Humanities Press International, 1992). See also S. Houlgate, ed., *Hegel's Philosophy of Nature* (Albany: SUNY Press, 1999).

Chapter Four

Overview of "Philosophy of Spirit"

1. Subjective Spirit
   a. Anthropology
   b. Phenomenology
   c. Psychology
2. Objective Spirit
3. Absolute Spirit

Philosophy of Spirit is the concluding part of Hegel's tripartite exposition dealing with Logic, Nature, and Spirit. It ends with a consideration of the three realms as constituting a circle (the study of it being an *en-cyclo-paedia*, an "en-circling study") in which each part implicates the other two. We could then begin with any one of them and show how the other two are presupposed. Spirit presupposes Nature, and Nature finds its end in Spirit; but both are expressions of the underlying realm of intelligibility that Hegel terms "Logic." Formal logic is a subset of Hegel's notion of Logic. The latter is linked to the Logos at the beginning of St John's gospel that has affinities with parallel notions in Philo and Plotinus. Since Hegel's treatment of Spirit employs the categories treated in the Logic, I have presented a preliminary introduction to the Logic where the reader can see them in their unity. In the commentary I will attempt, once again, to explain the terms as they occur.

Philosophy of Spirit explores the overall structure of the realm within which we humans live and is thus, in a sense, for us the most immediate realm of mediation between the other two realms that it presupposes,

Nature and Logic. Spirit (*Geist*) is sometimes translated as Mind, though that loses the rich connotations of *Geist* that is the root of the English "yeast." It is linked to fermented spirits that raise our spirits; it is found in *esprit de corps*, in the spiritedness of a race horse, in the spirit of an age, in the spiritual life, and in the Holy Spirit. Hegel draws upon all these meanings as he focuses them upon comprehensive human life penetrated by the Divine.

Philosophy of Spirit is divided, characteristically but not forcibly, into three parts: Subjective, Objective, and Absolute. The first is focused upon the general structure of what it is to be a human subject. It is divided, in turn – and arranged from lowest to highest levels, into Anthropology, Phenomenology, and Psychology. The terms are technical and not completely identical with today's common usage. Phenomenology presents the field of experience, while Anthropology explores its lower basis in Nature as Psychology explores its higher basis in explicit Spirit. Anthropology refers to the aspects of the human Spirit insofar as it is affected by embodiment, that is, insofar as it is – and necessarily so – the soul of an organic body. In logical terms, it is the realm of "Being," of what is immediate and implicit in relation to Spirit. Phenomenology concerns consciousness as the field of appearance, of immediate manifestation, the field of the subject–object relation. Logically, it is the realm of Essence, of correlation, coming out of the ground in Existence and Appearance.

Psychology analyses the hierarchy and interrelation of the faculties involved as conditions for the possibility of the field of immediate manifestation and its transcendence in relation to what underlies it, ultimately in relation to the encompassing Whole.[1] Logically, it is the realm of the Concept, Being-for-Itself, the return to self that encompasses everything. Relation to the Whole grounds the functional independence of the individual human subject and is expressly developed first in Objective Spirit and then in Art, Religion, and Philosophy together as the realm of Absolute Spirit that displays the meaning of the Whole.

When Hegel reaches the level of Spirit, the earlier triad of Being-in-Itself, Determinate Being, and Being-for-Itself is modified. The determinate Being of Spirit is its self-presence, its Being-for-Itself at a higher

---

1 Here, as throughout the commentary, we will refer back to the technical terminology developed in our treatment of the Logic. At this point the reader should reread the pertinent sections of the Logic to get used to the terminology. It will aid immensely in reading Hegel's texts.

level than Nature. The third triad thus becomes Being-in-and-for-Itself, that is, potentiality become actuality at the level of the human.

The Anthropology and the Psychology are the most developed sections in the Encyclopaedia, since Hegel had worked out his Phenomenology and both Objective and Absolute Spirit in other works. As we noted earlier, Phenomenology in the Encyclopaedia is a compression and modification of the first three parts of the 1807 *Phenomenology of Spirit*: Consciousness, Self-Consciousness, and Reason. In the 1807 Phenomenology, the other parts constituting the realm of Spirit – "the I that is a We and a We that is an I" – are Morality, Religion, and Absolute Knowing. Morality in the Encyclopaedia is now found in Objective Spirit, while Art, along with Religion and Philosophy, opens out to Absolute Knowing. The aim of the 1807 Phenomenology is to show the historical progression to the position developed systematically in the Encyclopaedia and thus to provide "a ladder to the Absolute standpoint."

Objective Spirit was given extensive treatment in the *Elements of the Philosophy of Right* (1821) and in *Philosophy of World History*, the latter a set of posthumously published lectures. As a consequence, Objective Spirit is presented in Hegel's text here only in outline. This section contains an analysis of those institutions called political in which, over time, subjective spirits have objectified themselves in such a way as to pass on that objectification to posterity. Such institutions are the conditions for the possibility of the fuller flowering of individual human subjects. As a matter of their ultimate telos, the institutions must be so structured as to allow for their transcendence in the direction of the Whole. The latter direction constitutes the realm of Absolute Spirit, that is, Spirit "absolved" from the non-freedom of its immersion in the passions, prejudices, and one-sided views that chain its fundamental freedom to move rationally in the direction of the encompassing Totality as the region of the Divine.

Absolute Spirit is constituted by three interrelated modes of expression: Art (in its highest mission as external manifestation of the Absolute), Religion (at its centre as the heart's rising up to the Eternal and Encompassing in concert with others), and Philosophy (at its deepest level as conceptual unfolding of what is intuited but not comprehended in Religion). In Hegel's tantalizing phrase: "Philosophy is the synthesis of Art and Religion."

Hegel's treatment of Absolute Spirit in the work we are considering, like his treatment of Phenomenology and Objective Spirit, is quite sketchy because he had given lengthy treatment to its three regions in his lectures (posthumously published) in *Aesthetics: Lectures on Fine Art*, *Lectures on the Philosophy of Religion*, and *Lectures on the History of Philosophy*. He also treated them, though significantly in a less extensive manner, in the later sections of the 1807 Phenomenology.

* * *

In what follows, for each of the three major parts of the *Philosophy of Spirit* we will provide an introductory summary. This is preliminary to our major focus upon Subjective Spirit in its three phases of Anthropology, Phenomenology, and Psychology. For the Anthropology, after the summary we will provide a translation of, and commentary upon, only the concluding two sections as Hegel's own transition to the Phenomenology. We will again provide a summary to our translation and commentary on the Phenomenology and on the Psychology. We will follow that and conclude the work with summaries of the treatment of both Objective Spirit and Absolute Spirit.

PART III

Hegel's Introduction to the System, Translation and Commentary: The Key Sections of "Philosophy of Spirit"

Chapter Five

Anthropology (Conclusion)

1. The Natural Soul
2. The Feeling Soul
3. The Actual Soul

Anthropology in Hegel's sense of the term is not, as the term is used today, the study of primitive human existence. Possibly he uses this term to focus on the human being as one animal species among others. More narrowly conceived, Hegel's Anthropology is the discipline that considers the human Spirit insofar as it ensouls a body and thus what effects embodiment has upon Spirit.

This is in the line of Aristotle, for whom a soul, as "first act of an organized body having life potentially," is named by its highest power. So the rational soul ("Spirit" in Hegel's sense of the term), requiring sensation as its materials, requires in turn the bodily instruments or organs for sensory experience. Hence, the rational soul forms and sustains the organism through its nutritive power. As soul, it pervades the organism – hence its universality, a one-over-many in relation to its plurality of organs, but not as explicitly rational. Spirit here is "immediate or implicit." "Immediacy" in Hegel is the phase to which the logic of Being applies. At this level Spirit is "natural," that is, it is not present to itself; it is "sunk in Nature," hence external to itself. Nature in general is such by reason of being governed by the principle of matter, the principle of exteriority and dividedness: a natural entity has parts outside of parts and can come apart and come together and is thus subjected to change; its Being is Becoming.

Hegel's treatment is, of course, in three phases: First of all, as *Natural Soul*, Spirit is "qualitatively determined by insertion into Nature." This is, to begin with, the level that involves what we would today call "genetic determination." It involves the articulation of the organism in the growth process and the corresponding states of mind the individual passes through by reason of the developmental process: infancy, youth, adulthood, old age. It involves the impact of the environment through climate and seasonal changes. It involves the impact of race and custom upon individual awareness. It involves the enduring alternation of waking and sleeping and the pubescent awakening and adult perdurance of sexuality and sexual differences. And it involves a consideration of the system of the senses that serves organically based desire, both rooted in the organism.

Second, as *Feeling Soul*, it can come into conflict with itself in insanity and somnambulism. Soul's linkage with Nature governed by the principle of exteriority opens up the possibility of its own interior division. Feeling already is divided from its organic ground. It is here that Hegel assimilates the science of his time dealing with psychopathology.

In the third phase, as *Actual Soul*, soul can become "at one with its immediacy by the reduction of corporeality to a sign." This is found in the development of skills where the body is effortlessly taken up into the expression of Spirit, as, for example, in speaking or participating in sports. This is embodiment as pervaded by Spirit and thus entails the development of the fully actual adult soul that, through its development, has taken on a "second Nature." We live in our bodies through the mediation of our "second Natures," the habit structures upon which we rely in our deliberate efforts.

* * *

Our task in the current work is to read the Phenomenology and the Psychology. In order to follow the transition from Anthropology to Phenomenology, we turn now to the final paragraphs of the Anthropology.

Note the clear distinction of Hegel's text from my commentary by separating it from the commentary with a line space as well as using a different typeface and font. This allows the reader to read Hegel's text as a continuous whole and reread it without its being broken up. In this work, the commentary runs below the text to get away from the usual placing of commentary at the end or in a separate volume. The usual practice involves the annoying and cumbersome flipping back and forth from text to commentary. If one needs explanation from the commentary while reading the text, one can read it without flipping back and forth.

With the exception of my indicating the German word for a translated word, the italics within Hegel's text are his own; the brackets are mine.

Conclusion to Hegel's Anthropology

The Actualized Soul

§411. The soul in its fully developed and fully appropriated embodiment exists for itself [is actualized] as *individual* subject. Embodiment is thus *exteriority* as predicate in which the subject only relates itself to itself. This exteriority does not represent itself [as body]; it represents the soul and is therefore the *sign* of the soul. As this identity of the interior with its subordinate exterior, the soul is *actualized*. In its embodiment it has its free form, in which it feels *itself* and gives *itself* to be felt, and which, as the artwork of the soul, has *human* pathognomic and physiognomic expression.

Mere existence involves an entity stepping forth from its ground in its underlying essence with various contingent accidents and standing in relation to other existents. Actuality (*Wirklichkeit*) involves an essence having come from being-in-itself (potential, *an sich*) to being-for-itself (actualized, *für sich*), becoming what it was meant to be, fulfilling itself and showing itself as such. For the living being, the soul as principle of life appropriates materials from the world around it in order to articulate its organ-system. The soul involves a pervasion of its body and is thus a universal over the particulars of its organs, but not an abstract universal, such as the *notion* of soul; it is rather what Hegel calls "a concrete universal." For the humanly living being, actualizing its essence involves, on top of organic articulation, the development of habits that turn its embodiment into an expression of itself as a freely choosing individual human existent. So human existence at the level of "soul" is aimed towards turning the body into a sign of the personality. The human body is not simply the object of natural science as something exterior, appearing as a thing among things with parts outside parts. In its body the conscious subject is aware of itself (is related to itself) as one with its embodiment. It feels itself and is able to be felt by others. In its bodily behaviour the human individual expresses himself or herself as a unique person to others.

Such exterior expression enables others to "read" the character of a person from his or her external comportment. Pathognomy and Physiognomy were the names at Hegel's time for a stage in the empirical inquiry into human beings. "Pathognomy" was the study of emotions through the exterior movements involved in voice, gesture, and overall comportment. It focused upon immediate emotions. "Physiognomy" was the art of discovering the more enduring temperament and character from outward appearance.

In its habituation the human being becomes at home with itself: it "in-habits" its body. ("This being-with-itself [*Beisichselbersein*] we call inhabitance [*Gewohnheit*].") Habit is "a universal mode of action constituting his individuality posited by him and become his own" (§410, *Zusatz* [henceforth Z], 188). As with native powers, so with habit, we orient ourselves *universally* towards all those *kinds* of individual things and situations correlative to the habit. Just as the soul is a concrete universal over against its body and in relation to all those kinds of individuals correlative to the kinds of things upon which it can act and that can act upon it, so through habituation the human being creates its own set of powers by taking over its native powers and establishing a second Nature. Such a second Nature is a set of developed spontaneities that support our focal efforts. The position of lips, tongue, teeth, and palate when I speak is not a matter of focal attention. Michael Polanyi [(1891–1976), physicist turned philosopher who emphasized "tacit knowing" or "know-how" that makes explicit knowing possible] speaks here of the "from-to" structure that involves "tacit knowing." We "know" how to articulate the features of our oral cavities, *from* which implicit knowing we give attention *to* what we are expressly articulating in speaking. Actually, unless we try to make it explicit, we do not know explicitly how we know how to do something.

Here and throughout, "for itself" or "being-for-itself" is how I translate *für sich*. Its correlative, *an sich*, I will translate as "in itself" or "being-in-itself." In order to link up Hegel's technical usage with their English equivalents, I will add in brackets ["explicitly" or "actually"] to "for itself" and ["implicitly" or "potentially"] for "in itself."

Upright posture generally, laughter, crying, formation of the mouth and especially of the hand as absolute tool, and so forth, are different types of human expression. So also is the spiritual tone suffusing the whole that presents the body immediately as the externalization of a higher nature. This tone is so slight, indeterminate, and ineffable a modification

since the form in its exteriority is something immediate and natural and thus can only be an indeterminate and wholly imperfect *sign* for the Spirit; it cannot represent how Spirit exists for itself [actualized] as *universal*. For the animal the human form is the highest mode in which the Spirit itself appears. But for the Spirit it is only its *first* appearance; *language* is its more perfect expression. The external form is indeed its most proximate mode of existence; but at the same time, in its physiognomic and pathognomic features, it is *accidental* to Spirit. To seek to elevate physiognomy, and ultimately cranioscopy, to the level of the *sciences* was thus one of the emptiest fancies, still emptier than a *signatura rerum* which supposed that one could recognize the healing power of plants from their shape.

One's carriage, gestures, mode of speech, and modes of manual dexterity exhibit an overall individual configuration that allows one who knows any particular individuals to recognize them immediately upon seeing or hearing them. On the other hand, as developed Spirit, the human being has hold of the universal as such. For this, language is the more adequate expression, for language is that which brings each of us out of our private idiosyncrasies and into the realm of the universal and public. Animals confront the gestural style of humans, but cannot penetrate to their hold on the universal. Language, as repository of the eidetic or universal notions, is the basic expression of "a We that is an I and an I that is a We" (1807 *Phenomenology of Spirit*, §177). It takes one out of one's privacy into a public space of meaning into which each individual subject has been inducted. At the same time, it requires in each human subject a reference to the Whole and thus the I as centre of both free self-disposal and recognition of what phenomenologists call "the eidetic" (after Plato's *eidos* or Form), the universal and necessary. Reference to the Whole makes the human individual itself a "concrete universal." In Aristotle's expression, it is, "in a way, all things." [Aristotle , pupil of Plato, divided up the field of experience to lay the basis for scientific inquiry in all distinct directions.] The way is by way of reference and thus as a question regarding the place of human being within the All. The conventions of language hold the places for the eidetic inventories established by various subjects within a given culture in communication with one another across space and time.

Because the I is freely self-disposing and universal-apprehending, the empirically descriptive properties it presents in its bodily shape are even less descriptive of its full reality as Spirit than either its overall gestural style or its language. Hence, the pseudo-sciences that attempted to understand the differences of humans from the differing structures of their bodies, especially by the shape of the head (cranioscopy), were without merit. Persons are recognized by their deeds of which speech is most basic.

The *signatura rerum* is an expression used by Jacob Böhme (1575–1624), whom Hegel otherwise appreciates. In his History of Philosophy, he devotes more space to Böhme than to Böhme's contemporary, René Descartes, the father of Modern Philosophy. The *signatura* followed a set of mystical experiences after which Böhme claimed he could see into the heart of things from their surface presentation.

§412. *In itself*, matter has no truth in the soul.

The expression "has no truth" seems odd. But Hegel regularly distinguishes between the *correct* and the *true* (*Encyclopaedia Logic*, §25, Z 2, p. 60). The former is factual, the latter involves teleological completeness. Matter in the life of the soul is an aspect within the whole and not an independent entity. Though it may be isolated in our attending solely to sensory description of its structures and motions in biology, in us – and, indeed for Hegel, in the cosmos – it is oriented towards Spirit. The telos or goal of matter in general is its serving as a matrix for Spirit's self-development. For Hegel this is true not only of the matter organized by the soul into an organ system in an individual organism; it is true for matter in the universe as a whole. Matter is the cosmic phase of exteriority that Spirit has to overcome and appropriate to itself in knowing and shaping. It is projected by the divine Spirit as Creator of heaven and earth.

As existing for itself [actualized], the soul separates itself from its immediate being and places itself over against itself as embodiment which can offer no resistance to the soul's formative power. The soul, in opposing itself to the body, has sublated it, determined it as its own, and abandoned the meaning of *soul* as the *immediacy* of the Spirit.

The soul is first of all (immediately) the life of the body. But in the development of the conscious I, this immediate phase of spirit is sublated (*aufgehoben*). Hegel calls attention to the speculative richness of the term *aufheben* in ordinary German: cancellation, preservation, and elevation. At the earliest phases of embryonic development there is no awareness. Spirit is one with its body in the mode of unconscious immediacy, unmediated by the pastness of memory involved in learning or the anticipation of future satisfaction implied in appetite. When consciousness emerges, the past and future emerge as other than the immediate and, at the phase of reflective consciousness, the organism appears as an other to the I. From the position of the free self-disposing I, Spirit is able to mould the body according to its choices. In learning skills – walking, talking, manipulating – one takes over one's body as a matter of habituation.

Material articulation is *cancelled* in its supposed self-sufficiency, *preserved* as an aspect, and *elevated* into the expression of Spirit. Indeed, in development from the fertilized ovum to the neonate and on to the adult, each early phase is itself sublated, a perfect example of a dialectical series.

The actualized soul, in the habituality of sensation and its concrete self-feeling, is in itself [potentially] the ideality of its determinations existing for itself [actualized]. In its exteriority it is inwardized in itself and is infinite relation to itself.

When the soul is actualized as Spirit through habits of perceiving and acting, it is not simply a fact but the "ideality" of the factual or "real" body that is transformed into an expressive instrument of Spirit. As it pours itself into its own embodiment, Spirit comes to inner possession of itself. The possession of skills is latent, but involves the permanent possibility of their exercise. Hegel describes this inner possession as "infinite self-relation" in the sense of unimpeded, unlimited access to itself. Hegel uses the term "infinite" in this odd sense when a potentiality has passed through the limitation of various phases of development and reaches the completion of its Nature and exists "for itself" as *actuality*. Prior to that completion it is finite in the sense of limited to not having reached its innate perfection. "Infinite" in another sense describes the field of operation of any power: it is oriented towards an *indeterminate* number of individual instances of the kind of thing or aspect of a thing correlative to the power. There is no specifiable limit to the number of individual instances that fall under the scope of a given power.

This being-for-itself [actuality] of the free universality is the higher awakening of the soul to the *I*, to abstract universality, insofar as it is *for itself* [actualized as] abstract universality. In this way it is thus for itself [actualized] *thinking* and *subject* and indeed determinately subject of a judgment, in which the I excludes the natural Totality of its determinations as an object, as a world *external to it*. And yet in doing so it relates itself to it, so that it is immediately at the same time reflected in itself. Thus it is *consciousness*.

"Abstract universality" here refers to the capacity each of us has to abstract from *every* content, to back off from *all* determinants because, as Spirit, each of us is referred to the Whole as encompassing concrete Universal. I might suggest that this is because the notion of Being, with which Thought is identical, as the first notion in Hegel's Logic, refers to absolutely everything, but in a completely empty manner. Being referred to the Whole, Spirit is pried loose from any part, even from the various aspects of itself, and is thus delivered over to itself. For Hegel this is the ability to say "I," to be other than any other, even within itself. From this position of abstract universality we possess "free universality," uncoerced by any finite determinant, and are thus free to choose, to take responsibility, to determine ourselves. Hegel calls this *formal* or *negative* freedom. The issue at this point is with what content one then fills this empty universality. The abstract universality of the I also enables one to isolate from the contingencies of their instances the abstract universalities involved in experience as such. That is why, in his Logic, Hegel identifies "the Concept" (*Begriff*) entering into Existence with the I: the I is the grasping after (*Begreiffen nach*) the Whole, which grounds the grasping of the universal natures, the concepts immanent in things.

The *Zusatz* to this section says pithily: "[T]he universal that relates itself to itself exists nowhere outside of the 'I' ... In the 'I' ... the ideality of natural being, and so the essence of the soul, becomes *for* the soul ... [Through habit the 'I' has] filled the initially empty space of its inwardness with a content appropriate to it through its universality" (198).

The division within the self between conscious, free subjectivity and the dark, determined organism is, according to Hegel's technical vocabulary, a *judgment* (*Ur-teil*) or "primordial partition" that joins what it separates. The world – including one's own embodiment – stands over against the conscious subject which relates itself to itself when it relates to what stands over against it as its object. The I is the other to whom the otherness of other things can be displayed. However, it is not other as a Cartesian spiritual substance in relation to its mechanical body; it is other as one pole in the dyadic relation of a psycho-physical whole. [*René Descartes* (1596–1650) viewed awareness (made famous as the *cogito* in the *cogito ergo sum*, the one absolutely indubitable truth) as a distinct substance externally conjoined with a mechanized body. It was a view satirized by twentieth-century British philosopher Gilbert Ryle as "the ghost in the machine." Cartesius, his Latin name, was applied to the *Cartesian coordinates* in the analytical geometry he invented.]

Phenomenology

The usual formal organization through triple division appears in this section as *Consciousness*, *Self-Consciousness*, and *Reason*. The whole section follows the logic of *Appearance* coming out of the ground of *Essence* into *Existence* and being completed in *Actuality*. Spirit, the end of the process, though at work in the beginning in the formation of the organism, first makes its appearance with the emergence of consciousness as the explicit coming to itself of living being. Spirit appears to itself as it manifests what is other than itself.

Consciousness is the region of the subject–object relation where the focus is first upon the object. The living object appears as rising up to appearance out of its hidden organic ground, both like and unlike the conscious subject. It is like because the sensory appearance is not simply descriptively *there* like the eyeball to the optometrist when he does his work; it is *expressive* of the hidden ground that both reveals and conceals itself in the descriptive "there-ness," like the face of the patient when doctor and patient speak to one another and the optometrist attends to the total expressive configuration of the face as the context of the expressivity of the eyes. But, of course, the appearance of a plant does not show the peculiar sense of self and of world-inhabitance that characterizes the look of the human Other because there is no self-awareness exhibited or involved. But there is a striving of the whole organic system to reach its adult, reproductive state; and each stage expresses this striving towards that end.

Self-consciousness arises out of desire stirred by the object. It is first of all an awareness of the biological needs of the self. Self-consciousness develops at the distinctively human level as the desire for the reciprocity of consciousnesses, as the desire for recognition, for confirmation by another I. When mutual recognition is grounded in the recognition of the identity of Reason in all humans, we have the stage of the explicitly conscious historical emergence of Reason that underpins the whole of reality.

In consciousness what is contained within the natural soul, the effect of things upon sensibility, is set over against the I. The latter is "absolute negativity," that is, the absolute other to any particular objects because, via the notion of Being, it includes them all in principle and thus "overreaches" any given object in its "absolute universality." In Hegel's view we have to think here also of soul as species-work, overarching the individual, and of species as articulated by the work of Life, the overarching World Soul, and of everything, all of Life and the material world upon and within which it operates, as the projection of the all-encompassing Absolute Spirit to which our finite Spirit is referred and which, for Hegel, reaches its own fulfilment in the development of human awareness in history. The I is the unmediated opposite of its universality, that is, individuality in the unique sense of the term: a free being, able to determine itself. It distinguishes itself from itself and is thus self-aware. Paradoxically, its absolute universality (though initially only by way of anticipation) is focused in unique individuality. It is this existent contradiction that sets in motion the task of filling its emptiness with rational content, reaching towards the Whole whose framework will be displayed in Absolute Knowing. Aware not just of individuals in the environment present through sensation, the human being is aware of species as universal types through the ability to abstract the universal. The individuality of the human I involves, in its abstractive function, freedom from all determination and thus freedom for self-determination. Pried loose from any determination by being referred to everything via the notion of Being, the I is free with regard to any particular.

Consciousness has three phases. Its first and immediate aspect is *sensation* as presentation of individual sensory properties located in a particular point in space and at a particular moment in time. Its second phase is *perception* as the apprehension of the pervasive "universality" of the thing, the underlying unity of the diverse properties, the underlying force causing the properties and displayed through time. Here the immediacy of sensation is mediated by past experience. There is a correlation between the manifestation of the underlying thing and the self-presence of the perceiver: both endure through all the changes brought about in and by them through time. In the third phase, *intellection*, there is an advance to the universality of law, of abstract universal correlation between differing aspects. Consciousness attains a deeper insight when it grasps living process as underlying substance developing its differences through articulating its organs, each of which requires all the others, and yet annulling the differences by holding them in the functional wholeness of a single organism. Here consciousness advances further in recognizing an inwardness like itself, at least at the organic level.

However, we are not purely theoretical observers. Before we are thinkers we must be eaters; and before there can be eaters, there has to be their origination through sexual union between their parents. The appearance of sensorily given individuals evokes appetite tied to sustenance and reproduction as a first level of self-consciousness. For Hegel, appetite is an existent contradiction, a non-being within being, an intrinsic lack come to self-consciousness. But all contradiction is driven to its own overcoming: we strive to fill the lack by consuming the other – though the contradiction continues to emerge ever again in the eventual re-emergence of appetite – an example of what Hegel calls "the bad infinite," the indefinite repetition of the same. bodily based appetite is what Socrates called "a leaky vessel" that empties each time we fill it.

At the distinctively human level, an I – implicitly at a distance from all otherness, even within itself and thus even in relation to its own organic being – through its body confronts another bodily present I. Each I is such because it is projected towards Being as a whole and thus, as Aristotle has it, is, "in a way, all things," in the light of which it attends to any particular. It is "a light" that encompasses all and thus finds any other I, also all-encompassing in principle, to be a contradiction to itself. Indeed, the all-encompassing character of its orientation and the unique particularity of the I is itself a contradiction. In the encounter with another I, a struggle ensues. In its extreme form, it is a struggle between freedom and life. One, unafraid to risk its life for the sake of its own willing, overcomes the other who succumbs because of the fear for its own life. The Master overcomes the Slave because the thought of death has already overcome the Slave but not the Master.

However, there is a dialectical reversal. The Slave, forced to work for the Master, focuses his energies, discovers properties of Nature only available through working with them, and in the process develops skills that would otherwise lie fallow. The Master as such knows nothing of this development and remains the passive recipient of the fruits of the Slave's labour. Work frees both the theoretical and practical capacities of the Slave; non-work keeps the Master chained through his appetites to ignorance and lack of skill except for the employment of physical power over the Slave.

But then a higher level was reached in Stoicism when the abstract freedom of the I was realized: whether a Slave or a Master, whether Epictetus or Marcus Aurelius, in chains or on the throne, man as man is free. That means that each I has the ability to abstract from his circumstances, both external and internal, and to take up his own relation to those circumstances. This is the discovery of Reason surmounting Master and Slave and in principle joining all humans as rational beings.

For Hegel, this is a central insight:

> This universal reflection or reciprocity (*Wiedererscheinen*) of self-consciousness is the Concept. It is aware of itself in its objectivity as subjectivity identical with itself and is thus universal. It is the shape of consciousness forming the *substance* of all essential spirituality in the family, the fatherland, and the state as it is the substance of all the virtues, of love, friendship, courage, honour, and fame. (§436)

The human being rises to an awareness that Reason, operative in him/ herself, is, at the same time, the permeating principle of the Whole. Reason not only encompasses the Master/Slave relation, it encompasses the general subject–object relation as well. The reciprocity of consciousnesses is the central notion in Hegel's thought, the identification of the self with the other, the identity-in-difference of the self and the other that defines love and friendship and the wider relations of family and country as well as the virtues operative in these relationships.

We turn now to Hegel's text and to the paragraphs that constitute the Phenomenology section of the Philosophy of Spirit.

Hegel's Phenomenology: Introduction

§413. *Consciousness* **constitutes the level of reflection or the** *relationality* **of Spirit, its** *appearance.*

Consciousness, unlike a plant, exists in a sui generis type of relation, that of the *manifestation* or *appearance* of what is other than itself. It is a manifestation at the logical level that Hegel calls Essence. In the Logic, the phase preceding Essence, mere Being, deals with the categories directly related to sensory surface: Quality, Quantity, Measure, Becoming, Something and Other, Atoms and the Void, Finite and Infinite, and the like. Essence, the level appropriate to reflection that folds back from surface to underlying depth, introduces the basic relation between inner and outer. The inner in relation to sensory appearance is Essence; the outer is Existence, rising to the appearance of the Essence through the outer sensory surface made possible by the conditions provided by surrounding existents, and culminating in full identity between Essence and Existence in the Actualization of all the powers of the Essence to reach its mature form in relation to its surroundings. Applied to the human Spirit, consciousness as the sphere of the subject–object relation is first of all the realm of Appearance proper. It is through the existence of the human being that something can appear expressively out of its ground as a being in its own right and not simply as object of appetite.

The I is the unhindered (*unendlich*, "infinite") relation of the Spirit to itself, but as *subjective*, as *certainty of itself.* The immediate identity of the natural soul is elevated into this pure ideal identity with itself. The contents of soul become *object* for this reflection that is for-itself. The being-for-itself of pure abstract freedom lets its determinateness, the natural life of the soul, go forth from itself, just as free as an *independent object.* At first the I is aware of this as *external to it* and is thus consciousness. The I as this absolute negativity is implicitly (*an sich*) identity in being other. The I is itself and overreaches the object sublated as an *in itself.* It is *one* side of the relation and the *whole* relation. It is *the light* that manifests itself as well as what is other than itself.

Life entails a form of self-relation, but as confined within the unconscious pervasion of the organic whole by the Soul as principle of life. In animal forms, the self-relation is in the field of manifestation, but only as focused upon the sensorily appearing other in function of organic need. At the human level these limits are overcome in the self-awareness of the I as an other to any appearing other, thus "absolute negativity," even in relation to its own body and its soul life. Being aware of its own soul life as external to it involves being present to itself. That is why Hegel says of such awareness of externality: *thus* it is consciousness.

In the Logic, Being is initially opposed by Non-Being. This relation is realized in one of its highest forms in the I as a Not to any Being. [This is the historical background and phenomenological insight focused in Jean-Paul Sartre's *Being and Nothingness*, where the Nothingness is consciousness that manifests Being. Sartre (1905–80), the twentieth-century thinker most identified with the Existentialist movement, made central the individually existent human being and its free self-determination. Many of Sartre's key notions derive from Hegel.]

What grounds the I is reference to the Whole via the notion of Being as the "light" in which anything that is encounters the I – indeed, in which the I is present to itself as an instance of Being. So referred, any I is beyond any limited mode of otherness. Each determinate being (*Daseyn*) is other than any other; however, the individual human being is *absolutely* other because it is projected beyond finite beings to Being as a whole. It is "absolute" in the sense of being implicitly "absolved" from the limitations of forms lower than it, being in this sense "infinite" or unrestricted. It is thereby free to take up its own relation to the Whole and to whatever finite modes appear within the Whole, even the finite modes of itself. The contents of the Natural Soul – its organs, functions, sensations, and desires – though belonging to the Spirit as its own base, can now nonetheless become *objects* for the I, taken up into the field of consciousness and thus cancelled in their limited mode of appearance, preserved in content, and elevated to the level of the universal as expressive of human being's inner inhabitance of a world of meaning. Standing back from everything as the locus of the light of Being, Spirit overreaches the barriers of finite sensory relation and reaches towards the thing-in-itself. There is a simultaneous freeing of the object from being subsumed under the needs of the organism and an elevation of the object to its own essence in reflective awareness.

The *Zusatz* reads: "As light is the manifestation of itself and of its other, *darkness*, and can only manifest itself in manifesting this other, so also the I is only manifest itself insofar as its other is manifest to it in the form of something independent of it" (201).

§414. The identity of the Spirit with itself, first established as I, is only its abstract, formal ideality. This identity was *Soul* in the form of *substantial* universality; it is now subjective reflection into itself, related to this substantiality as to its negative, as something dark lying beyond it. Consciousness is thus, as is relation generally, the *contradiction* of the independence of both sides and their identity in which they are sublated. Spirit as I is *Essence*; but since reality in the sphere of Essence is determined as immediately Being and at the same time ideal, it is as consciousness only the *appearance* of Spirit.

The I, possessed of the notion of Being, reflects back into itself, separating itself from its organic base, with which it is nonetheless identical. This is an instance of Hegel's fundamental principle of *identity-in-difference* or, as he sometimes puts it, "the identity of identity and non-identity." As an embryo, the self-conscious I was only a potentiality. Spirit at this level is implicit as "substantial universality" or Soul pervading the whole organism. Soul is not a thing over against Body as another thing; it is the principle of the wholeness of the organism, related to it as concrete universal to particulars. The whole organism as Soul-pervading-Body is a thing in itself, Substance but not yet Subject. When in the course of individual development Spirit as the power of reflection arises, its own Body and the life that immediately arises from it appears as a dark other, its continuing unconscious ground. Each side seems to contradict the other, but they are only constituted in their relation as sides of a single human being. This split between the two sides, inner and outer, is an instance of the logical sphere of Essence. *Appearance* is a subcategory of Essence when a being has come forth from its implicitness but has not yet reached the identity of underlying Essence with manifest Existence, Essence fully realized in the category of Actuality.

The I here is a kind of empty point of origin for knowing and choosing. It is abstract in the sense of not yet filled with concrete content. It is "ideality" as distinguished from "reality" or the materiality that anchors it; but at this stage the I is purely formal: it is an empty form without its proper content. It appears among other things from out of its ground, but has not yet reached its proper fulfilment as fully actual Spirit.

§415. Since the I *for itself* exists only as formal identity, the *dialectical* movement of the Concept, the further determination of consciousness, does not exist as its own activity, but is such merely *in itself* [potentially] and as alteration of the object for the same consciousness. Consciousness appears thus determined diversely according to the diversity of the given object and its further development appears as an alteration of the determinations of its object. The I, the subject of awareness, is thinking (*Denken*); the further logical determination of the object is what is *identical in subject and object*, their absolute interconnection, that whereby the object is the subject's own.

The filling of the empty I with appropriate content takes place in a series of developmental stages, a movement Hegel calls "dialectical." In a dialectical series an earlier phase is "sublated" (*aufgehoben*): *cancelled out* in its limitations, *preserved* in what is positive in it, and *elevated* to a higher phase. This happens in a paradigmatic way in the growth of an individual from fertilized ovum to articulated foetus, to developing infant, and on, through adolescence, to full adulthood. The earliest phases are cancelled, preserved, and elevated.

The Concept is a central notion in Hegel. It is the third and concluding phase of the Logic, preceded by the categories of Being and of Essence. The I who confronts sensory surface and learns to read essential depth is itself the Concept at the level of existence, the place where relation to the Whole opens up within the realm of beings. The level of Being contains the categories that apply in the first place to sensory surface, to what is immediately given. The categories of Essence reflect upon the basic relation of inner to outer, that is, of Essence to Existence as Appearance, culminating in Actuality as the full display of the identity of inner and outer through the Essence reaching its full actualization. The categories belonging to the Concept proper (*Begriff*) bring into the picture the relations to the Subject who thinks in terms of categories. So the *Begriff* (from *greifen*, to grasp) entering into existence is the embodied human Spirit who grasps after the Whole. Indeed, this level hearkens back to the beginning of the Logic, where the identity of Thought and Being is presupposed and Thought is the Not-being in relation to Being. It hearkens back as well to the beginning of the Philosophy of Nature, where the moving negativity of Time is identified with human awareness: "being what it is not and not being what it is."

Formal logic, the categories of the Systems in Nature (Mechanical, Chemical, and Ecosystemic) as Object for awareness, and the categories that underpin the subject – Life, Cognition, and Absolute Idea – are the subcategories of the Concept identified with Existence in the Idea. The introduction of the Concept as the region of the basic underlying subcategories brings Logic itself and the notion of the embodied Thinker into the picture. Consciousness, as the locus of manifestation for the Cosmos, is inclined to forget itself or view itself as outside the purview of scientific objectivity. In fact, it is the ground of such objectivity and, for Hegel, the telos of the Cosmos. Things are "there," manifest for a human subject who is the locus for their manifestation. Lower things are stages presupposed for the existence of the human subject. The human subject in its rational activity completes the hierarchy of Being. Knowing completes things as the display of the interconnection of their underlying essences within the cosmic Whole, and rational willing completes theoretical knowing to establish an institutional matrix for Spirit's development. The Concept is the relation of inner and outer realized in human awareness. It is in this sense that Hegel speaks of the I as the Concept entering into existence: the at first purely formal grasp (*Begriff*) after the Whole that finds its own completion in being filled with the inner essences, now understood as actualized in displaying their concepts to the developing I.

Kantian philosophy can be most specifically considered to have grasped Spirit as consciousness and to contain only determinations of phenomenology, not of [speculative] philosophy. It treated the *I* as a relation to something lying beyond, which, in its abstract determination, is called the Thing-in-itself; and only according to this limited mode does it grasp both intelligence and will.

Kant's philosophy centres upon a distinction between phenomena and noumena, or things appearing in accordance with the finite structure of human awareness and things in themselves apart from such appearance. *Immanuel Kant* (1724–1804) is guided in this view by a distinction, on the one hand, between how things would be displayed immediately to a Knower Whose knowing made them to be and Who knows them immediately and exhaustively (the hypothetical notion of God as Creator with direct intuitive understanding) and, on the other hand, how things appear to us having sense organs and possessing categories for discursively building up our knowledge of objects over time from what is given in sensory experience. For instance, our eyes filter off certain aspects of things in the environment to present us with coloured things appearing within a horizon as the limit to our field of vision; and things appear perspectively distorted, appearing larger as they stand closer to the viewer and smaller as they appear further away. Seeing only gives an aspect at a time, linked to other sensory aspects in order that things may present themselves more fully to us.

Kant made what is called the *transcendental turn* from focus upon objects to focus upon the conditions in the subject of awareness that make possible the appearance of objects. He referred to this turn as a *Copernican revolution in thought*. As the sun *appears* to move about the earth, so things appear to determine our knowing. And as the former happens, Copernicus contended, because of the movement of the earth upon which the viewer stands, giving the illusion of the sun revolving around the earth, so the position of the knower, his receptive and discursive structure, the "earth" upon which he stands, determines how things as such make their appearance, but not how they really are apart from that appearance. The upshot is that we do not know "things in themselves," but only things as filtered through our finite knowing apparatus.

Hegel's speculative philosophy claims to overcome this limited view of a mind trapped within its own categories with a view of mind that "overreaches" the ob-jectivity or "set-over-against-ness" of things by grasping their underlying intelligibility.

If indeed in the concept of the *reflective* power of judgment Kant arrives at the *Idea* of Spirit – subjectivity/objectivity, an *intuitive understanding* and so forth – as well as at the Idea of Nature, yet this Idea of Spirit itself is again demoted to the phenomenal realm as a merely subjective maxim. (Cf. §58, Introduction.) *Reinhold* thus possessed a correct understanding of this philosophy as a theory of *consciousness*, calling it the "*faculty of representation*" (*Vorstellungsvermögen*). *Fichtean* philosophy had the same standpoint: the Not-I exists only as *object* of the I, determined only in *consciousness*, and remains as constant impetus (*Anstoss*) that functions as *Thing-in-itself*. Both philosophies thus show that they had not attained to the Concept or to *Spirit* as it exists *in and for itself*, but only as it is in relation to an other.

Kant had initially fractured the world of experience into two irreconcilable halves. His *Critique of Pure Reason* presented Nature as a realm subjected to the categories of scientific mechanism. His *Critique of Practical Reason* introduced the notion of moral freedom as self-determination (autonomy) through concepts. His *Critique of Judgment* attempted to heal the gap. Judgment is the act of relating the individual to the universal. The overriding distinction Kant works with is that between two forms of judgment, determinative and reflective. *Determinative judgment* involves the application of innate or a priori categories to sensory experience: the universal category is given by the very structure of the mind that then finds the sensorily given individuals to fit under it. Presupposing that the conditions of objectivity furnished in determinative judgment have been realized, *reflective judgment* moves from the sensed individuals to seek the universal empirical concepts suitable to each type. Suppose we have apprehended a collocation of sensory experiences as enduring through the variation of its presentations, set in a context of antecedent and consequent causes, and reciprocally tied to its immediate context – what goes on in ordinary life spontaneously as objective presentations. But now such presentations, which instantiate the proper application of the a priori categories, come in different types. They divide into living forms and non-living and into natural and artificial. Granted such an objectively appearing multiplicity of types of individuals, how do we make sense of them? Kant here introduces, as the central notion for reflective judgment, the notion of *purposiveness* presented by art and applied to Nature. As art subsumes the mechanisms of Nature under human purpose, so living forms can be considered as subsuming mechanisms under natural purpose. Projected to the Whole, the Cosmos appears as an arena for human development and moral striving fashioned by a Divine Being.

This is what is involved in Hegel's referring to "the Idea of Nature" in Kant. The idea of an Intuitive Understanding that knows things-in-themselves by creating and sustaining them is involved in the notion of God presented here. But what is crucial is that Kant presented this only in the mode of *as if*. Viewed in terms of such projection, the universe appears to us *as if* its organisms act like artists do and *as if* the Whole were fashioned by a Divine Moral Artisan. Such a view is still phenomenal and a merely human way of making sense of things. The thing-in-itself remains unknown to us. Kant's disciple Fichte held the same view of an unknowable thing-in-itself, this time considered as impetus from without that awakens consciousness to itself.

[*Johann Gottlieb Fichte* (1762–1814) was a follower of Kant who focused upon the I as starting point and ultimately presented a moral view of the world. He was instrumental in stirring up patriotic fervour in Germany against the Napoleonic conquests. *Karl Leonhard Reinhart* (1757–1823) was also an interpreter of Kant who, unlike Fichte, was better known in his own time than he is currently. Hegel thinks his view of Kant's thought as a philosophy of *representation* (*Vorstellung*) is correct and coincides with Hegel's own view of Kant as focused only on the "being placed over-against-ness" (*Vor-stellung*) of things in relation to a finite knower.]

On the other hand, in relation to *Spinozism* it should be noted that Spirit itself emerges from Substance in the judgment [*Ur-teil* as "primoridial partition"] through which it constitutes itself as *I*, as free Subjectivity over against determinism, and philosophy emerges from Spinozism in that for [speculative] philosophy such judgment is the absolute determination of the Spirit.

Hegel said elsewhere that to philosophize is to think like Spinoza. What he meant was that one had to view Being as a single Whole with each thing understood as it fits within and, indeed, is grounded in the Whole. For *Baruch Spinoza* (1632–77), the Whole is a single *Substance* with the known *Attributes* of Thought and Extension, and things are *Modes* or accidents of that Substance. Everything is fully determined by the place it occupies within the whole System, so that one who would understand human beings should view them as determined within the world System in the same way one views lines and planes and triangles as determined by their places in the geometric System. For Hegel, Spinoza's thought was a necessary stage that had to be sublated. Substance had to be raised to the level of Subject because of the evidence of the I as self-determining, set over against what is already determined both in itself and in the cosmic context. What is determined are the subjective and cosmic conditions that make a self-determining I possible: that is presented in Hegel's System where – contrary to critics like Danish philosopher and father of twentieth-century Existentialism *Søren Kierkegaard* (1813–55) – self-determining Subjectivity is *located* rather than submerged. These observations are relevant to contemporary physics in that the Cosmos is treated as a single law-governed space-time-energy matrix within which individuals appear as enfoldings. Einstein remarked that Spinozism is the philosophy most compatible with contemporary physics. Hegel's further development shows how, among other things, the free choice scientists engage in by pursuing their research fits into his System where mechanisms, having been subsumed under organisms, are ultimately subsumed, in turn, under freedom.

Hegel uses the term "judgment" here in his own idiosyncratic way, resting upon the etymology of the German term for judgment, *Urteil* or primordial (*Ur*) partition (*Teil*). So the distancing of the I as conscious subject from the completely determined unconscious living Substance that is its ground is the "primordial partition" in human experience.

§416. The goal of Spirit as consciousness is to make its appearance identical with its essence, to raise *its self-certainty to truth*. The *existence* which Spirit has in consciousness is finite because it is only a formal relation to itself, mere certainty. Since the Object is only determined abstractly as *Spirit's own*, or in the Object Spirit is only reflected back into itself as abstract I, Spirit's Existence still has a content that it has not yet appropriated.

Certitude within Hegel's thought is a first step that sets in motion a development that leads to the fuller truth involved in the initial certitude. (Note again that "truth" in its fullest sense means teleological completion of an essence, as in the case of a "true man.") Hegel has said that Descartes's identifying the indubitable certitude of the I present to itself brings us to land, solid ground against the shifting waves of the history of philosophy. The solid ground lay in the certitude of the *cogito*, the "I think" that resists even the most stringent of doubts. Even if I am in doubt about the status of the objects of my awareness, there is no doubt that I am aware and thus indubitably exist. That is Descartes's Archimedean point. Hegel viewed Spinoza and Descartes as complementary. It is the self-presence of the I that resists subsumption under the merely substantial Whole of Spinoza; but it is the Spinozist Whole that rescues Descartes from the limitation of mere Subjectivity.

The indubitable self-presence of the *cogito* is the point of *Appearance* of the Thinker, the phase logically called Existence, an essence appearing out of its ground in relation to other existents but not yet having reached its full Actuality when Appearance is identical with its Essence, that is, when it fully manifests its completed Essence. The *truth* (in the sense of teleological completeness) of the I is the completion of its project as design upon the Whole. That occurs when historical developments in Thought and Life reach a certain high point. This makes possible the appearance to fully reflective awareness of the completed

System of categories presupposed in human understanding and free action. Such awareness is "absolved" from the finitude of all that blocks its completion in the System of concepts required for all intelligibility, so-called Absolute Knowing or Absolute Awareness (*absolutes Wissen*). At that level, all objectivity is understood as grounded in the divine Subjectivity in which we participate as knowers.

§417. The levels of Spirit involved in this raising of certitude to truth are three. Spirit is (a) *consciousness* as such which has an object as such, (b) *self-consciousness* for which the *I* is the object, and (c) the unity of consciousness and self-consciousness when Spirit views the content of the object determined like itself and views itself as determined in-and-for-itself [fully actual]. It is then *Reason, the very Concept of Spirit*.

Consciousness and Self-Consciousness are clear enough at this stage. It is the announcement of their reconciliation in Reason that is more difficult. Reason (*Vernunft*) has to be set against abstract analytical Understanding (*Verstand*). The distinction is central to Kant's thought. *Verstand* subsumes sensations under categories and thus divides up the field of experience into Objects for a Subject. *Vernunft* is the drive towards Totality, striving to extend and unify our hold upon things and upon ourselves as related to things. The Enlightenment as the Age of Reason is for Hegel really the Age of Abstract Analytical Understanding. Its abstractions have to be overcome by repositioning them within a more concrete view of the Whole.

Verstand operates in terms of the principle of *identity*, which in the history of thought first appears in *Parmenides* (fl. 500 BC). He separated the notion of Being from all that displays Non-Being, namely, the things that we find in experience characterized by plurality and change. Each thing is *not* any other and is composed of parts or aspects for which the same holds; and each thing passes from non-being to being and from being to non-being, while in between it is such that it is *not* what it was nor what it will be. Being Itself, considered apart from all things, is absolutely undivided and unchanging – prototype of "*onto-theo-logy*" or a view of God (*theos*) tied to the logic (*logos*) of the notion of Being (*tou ontos*).

["Onto-theo-logy" is a term coined by *Martin Heidegger* (1889–1976), himself often termed an Existentialist in the line of Kierkegaard and

Friedrich Nietzsche (1844–1900), but better understood as an ontologist or a thinker focused upon the question of Being and upon human reality as *Da-Sein*, the place where the question of Being as the question of the Whole occurs. (Nietzsche aimed at the reinsertion of Spirit into Life, renouncing the contempt for life exhibited by Platonism and by Christianity as "Platonism for the masses.")]

Following Parmenides, Greek Atomism held that being is found in the ultimate units or Atoms that are separated from each other by the non-being of the Void or Space in which they change external positions but remain internally changeless, indivisibly self-identical (*a-tomoi*, or un-cuttables). In Descartes, Thought is a self-identified region over against Extension as the basic attribute of Matter, posing the problem of the Mind–Body relation in its starkest form. In certain forms of epistemology, knowing is the transference of information from an exterior sphere into an interior sphere or from the surrounding world into the brain. In contractarian political theory, each individual is an atom of self-interest over against the larger whole that is formed out of external contractual agreement between individuals. In its crudest form, love is viewed as "the contact between two epidermises." Marriage therapists often work with a "marriage contract" in which each partner agrees to a list of "do's" and "don't's." Hegel considers marriage "a contract to transcend the point of view of the contract," based upon calculating self-interest, in genuine love. In each case the problem is how to compose a whole out of the originally isolated self-identical units. The same is true of the State.

Beyond Kant, for Hegel *Vernunft* or Reason as drive towards Totality operates in terms of the principle of *identity-in-difference*. Human beings as individuals can only be themselves on the basis of having been raised in an antecedent community with its institutional arrangements of systematic wholes, beginning with language. Humans are only completed through love as the overlapping of subjectivities, just as knowing involves the subject "overreaching" sensory appearance to identify with the thing known. Thought is related to Extension via the notion of Soul that is related to the Body, not as one thing external to another, but as a concrete universal principle to its instances. And the Divine, both immanent in and transcendent of Its creatures, is Itself the identity-in-difference of the Trinitarian life where the Father finds the Other of Himself in the Son (the Word as the Father's utterance) to which He is bound by the Spirit of love. It is through that internal Other that there is able to be an other to God as creation (all things being made through the divine Word). And indeed, for Hegel, as a self-styled orthodox Christian, that

Other, the Word, let the secret of the Whole out when He appeared in that creature who is open to the Whole, that is, when God announced His identity with Man in the appearance of Christ. Kierkegaard, Hegel's acerbic critic, basing himself upon the principle of identity, had his pseudonym Johannes Climacus view the God-Man as absurd and paradoxical, requiring a passionate "leap of faith" to accept Him. Hegel, basing himself upon the principle of identity-in-difference, viewed the God-Man as the revelation of the rational principle of the Whole. The working out of that principle historically is what Hegel's thought claims to complete. The Concept of Spirit as Ground and pervading Principle of the Whole comes to itself in the historical completion of Spirit.

Consciousness as Such

1. Sensory Consciousness

§418. Consciousness is, to begin with, *immediate* and its relation to the object is thus the simple unmediated certainty of it. The object itself is thus determined equally as immediate, as *in being* and reflected into itself, and as an immediate *individual*. This is *sensory* consciousness.

Again, immediate certainty is the starting point that has to be developed in order to reach the fuller truth involved. Sensation as such is direct awareness of individual features (this colour, sound, etc.) indubitably present to awareness as simply *there* and other, "reflected into itself" as over against consciousness. [The odd expression "reflected into itself" is the parallel, on the part of things, to spirit's own reflection into itself in thought. In immediate sensation, the I is "reflected into itself" out of sensory immediacy just as the thing sensed is at the same time "reflected into itself." Both are "defined" over against each other.] There is a two-fold indubitability involved: of the sensory feature and of the I as aware of it. Considered only as sensing, awareness does not bring the past or an awareness of types (the notions of red, high C, or colour, sound, and the like) to bear upon the immediate in order to mediate it, that is, to identify it or to interpret it. Of course, this is a highly abstract notion. Sensing as sheer immediacy has to be ingredient in experience as its enduring anchor, but it is always concretely mediated by past experience and by awareness of types. The features of the object *as immediate, in being* as well as *"reflected into itself,"* and as *individual* involves categories brought to bear by us who reflect upon it;

they are not, qua universal, features present to sensing as such. What is given sensorily is an "outside face" in relation to the selective power of our sense organs; but the thing appearing sensorily exists apart from its mode of appearance, turned back into itself, so to speak, hidden but expressing itself from out of its hiddenness.

Consciousness as relation contains only the categories that are determinations of objects for it and that belong to the abstract I or to formal thinking. Thus, sensory consciousness knows only of this as a *being*, as *something*, as an *existing thing*, as *individual*, and so forth. Although it appears as the richest in content, it is the poorest in thoughts. Sensory determinations (*Gefühlsbestimmungen*) constitute that rich filling. They are the *material* (*Stoff*) of consciousness (§414), that which is substantial and qualitative that the Soul *is* and finds *in itself* in the region of Anthropology. The I, as reflection of the soul into itself, separates this material from itself and gives it first the determination of *Being*. In my 1807 *Phenomenology of Spirit* (§§ 90–108) I have characterized the object of sensory consciousness as spatial and temporal individuality, *here* and *now*; but that belongs properly, not to sensing as such, but to immediate intelligent viewing (*Anschauen*). The object at the level of sensing proper is first to be taken only according to the relation it has to *consciousness*, namely, as something *external* to it. The object is still not determined as external to itself or as being outside itself.

Remember, the "region of Anthropology" refers to Spirit as affected by embodiment – that is, having sensations and organically based desires. Sensing is a mode of being affected, a feeling in the soul that is objectified through the separation of the reflective I from its own feelings. As it reflects, the I brings the a priori categories to bear upon the sensed object. Hegel lists them here in logical order from lower to higher categories: the lowest category is of simple *Being*, then the category of *Determinate Being* – that is, of being *Something* or rather *Somewhat* (*Etwas*) as distinct from what is Other, then the category of *Existence* as coming out of its essential ground under conditions provided by surrounding existents, and then being an *Individual* as opposed to an abstract universal. Spatio-temporal location pertains to the sensed object as a thing belonging to the external sphere of Nature. Sensing qua sensing does not present these categories, but the way it presents things exhibits instances of them. *Edmund Husserl* [1859–1938, father of contemporary phenomenology] noted the same thing: we observe things via the categories that we bring to bear upon sensing.

What does it mean to be a thing "external to itself"? Material things are capable of being sensed because they do not exist wholly in themselves. They have parts outside parts and display an outside without any self-presence – at least as material.

§419. The *sensible* as something becomes an *Other*. Reflection of *Something* (*Etwas*) into itself as a *Thing* (*Ding*) has many characteristics, and as an individual in its immediacy it has *manifold predicates*. The multiple individuality of the sensible realm thus becomes something *broad*: a manifold of *relations, determinations of reflection*, and *universalities*. These are logical determinations posited through the Thinker, that is, here through the I. But *for the same* I making its appearance, the Object itself has in this way changed. In this determination of the Object sensory consciousness is *Perception* [*Wahr-nehmen*, literally "truth taking"].

To repeat something that bears repeating, the first category we apply to whatever we encounter is that of simple Being. It develops through its own abstract emptiness into Becoming. It is followed by *Daseyn* or Determinate Being as Something other than others as well as other than itself in Becoming. Deepened further at the level of Essence, the encountered aspects become Properties of underlying Things. Experience is thus not merely sensory immediacy. Sensory features are recognized as clustering about *Things* that endure through the changing presentations they make in sensation, each thing being an underlying Force that appears through its Utterance in affecting the sensibility of an animal being. A thing "comes out of itself" in being sensed and yet withdraws into itself, is "reflected into itself" as exceeding any mode of sensory presentation. Through the organization of sensations we grasp things in perception or "truth taking" (*Wahr-nehmen*). Such things are experienced as "in front of" us and "to the right of x," as moving fast and then slowing down, as things of certain types with properties, not only of sensory types (red, stinking, loud) but also of behavioural types (intelligent, cruel, etc.). Bringing categories to bear upon the sensorily given allows us to view things as enduring through the variations in their presentations.

2. *Sense-perception* (Wahrnehmen)

§420. Consciousness that transcends the sensory intends to perceive or to *take* the object in its *truth* [*Wahr-nehmen*], not as merely immediate, but as mediated, reflected into itself, and universal. It is thus a combination of the sensible with broader thought-determinations of concrete relations and connections. Thus, the identity of consciousness with the object is no longer the abstract identity of [sensory] *certitude* (*Gewissheit*) but the *determinate* identity of *intellectual apprehension* (*Wissen*).

Certitude is in the mode of immediacy: the certitude of the I present to itself and present to the immediately given *sensum*. The "truth" of what is so encountered comes only through the mediation by reflection that learns to categorize and thus recognize the object as being, as an instance of a type, as something, as a determinate being, as an existent, as an accident of a substance, as reciprocally causing and being caused, and so on – that is, through categories that the thinking subject brings to bear upon mere sensations.

"Universal" is used here, in keeping with its etymology (Latin *unum versus alia*, one turned towards others), as the unity of the thing overarching the plurality of its modes of presenting itself sensorily.

Sense-perception is the more proximate level of consciousness at which *Kantian philosophy* fixes Spirit. It is the standpoint of our *ordinary consciousness* and more or less the standpoint of the *sciences*. It begins with sensory certitudes of single apperceptions or observations that are supposed to have been raised to truth so that they are considered in their relations and reflected upon to become at the same time something necessary and universal by means of definite categories: they become *experiences*.

Hegel's use of the term *experience* here follows Aristotle's usage at the beginning of his *Metaphysics* that parallels ordinary usage when we speak of someone as "a person of experience." A person of experience has been around, knows his way, has things sorted out – has, as a matter of fact, brought the categories to bear upon the successive mass of fleeting sensations.

§421. This linkage of the individual and the universal is a mixture since the individual remains the *ground* of being that lies there fixed against the universal, to which at the same time it is related. The thing perceived is thus a many-sided contradiction. There is a contradiction, generally speaking, between the *individual* things of sensory apperception, which should constitute the *ground* of the universal experience, and the *universality* that rather should have a higher claim to be the essence and ground. There is a contradiction between the *individuality*, taken in its concrete contents that constitute its *self-supporting character*, and the manifold *features* that, rather, free from this negative bond and from one another, are independent *universal materials* (§123ff.), and so forth. Here, insofar as something is determined as *object*, we really find in the most concrete form the contradiction of the finite that runs through all the forms of the logical spheres (§§194ff.).

In order for a sensation to become objective it has to be subsumed under a universal type and sorted according to the categories. Thus, the white and black, smooth, thin, flexible, rectangular object – the page you are currently reading – is experienced not only in terms of separate individual features, but in terms of the types of features identified and in terms of their unity in a single thing. The thing is what Hegel calls "the negative bond" between the features in that it is *not* any one of them.

There are two contrasts here. One is the contrast of the universality of the types together with the categorical orderings over against the individuality of the page with its individual sensory features. Should the individual entity ground the universal (Aristotle)? Or should the universal be the ground (Plato)? [*Plato*, the teacher of Aristotle, was himself taught by *Socrates* (470–399 BC). Plato is especially known for the separation of universal Forms as primary being from changing beings as derived participants in the Forms. Socrates was centrally concerned with ethical issues and carried on dialogues aimed at definitions. Aristotle focused upon empirical inspection as the enduring point of departure for human knowing and on the mind as the place of the Forms.] The other contrast is that between the differentiable character of the features that are capable of being considered apart from this page and the relative independence of the object that carries them. Pushing analysis in that direction leads to a reduction of things to aggregates of originally independent "matters" – an analysis that is appropriate to the inorganic but fails, at the level of the organic, to grasp the "spiritual bond" (Goethe) present only as a "not" in relation to sensory givenness.

[*Johann Wolfgang Goethe* (1749–1832) was a polymath: a poet, statesman, and amateur scientist who greatly influenced Hegel's views of Nature.] Both contrasts fall under what Hegel understands by contradiction because they both entail some form of not-being: the individual is and is not the universal, the multiple characteristics of a thing are and are not the thing. In fact, it is contradiction that leads speculative thought beyond the ordinary employment of the categories into the finally noncontradictory System that finds a place for them all. A perceived contradiction shows that we have not yet reached a sufficiently high synthetic viewpoint that can reconcile the elements in the original contradiction.

3. *Abstract Analytical Understanding* (Verstand)

§422. The most proximate *truth* of sense-perception is that the object is rather an *appearance* and its reflection into itself, on the contrary, is an *interior* and universal matter existing for itself. Consciousness of this object is *abstract analytical understanding*. On the one hand, *interiority* involves the *cancellation, preservation, and elevation* of the *manifold* of the sensible and is in this way abstract identity. In spite of this, however, it also contains the manifold, but as an *inner, simple distinction* that remains identical with itself throughout the alterations of appearance. This simple distinction is the realm of the *laws* of appearance, its tranquil, universal copy.

"Truth" again goes beyond correctness as a deepening of what is correctly apprehended. Here what is correct is the sensory presentation; but its deeper status is that of appearance in relation to what is interior, of the expression in the sensory surface of what goes beyond the sensory. This truth is "proximate" because there are deeper levels to be uncovered. The single individual appearing in the unity of the various sensory features as object of consciousness is an external appearance whose inner reality is its universal essence in two senses. The individual thing is a "concrete universal" as the one that holds together the multiplicity of its various aspects. But the individual also is an instantiation of its species as the abstract universal essence. However, for Hegel essences are not fabrications of the mind but overarching realities expressed in the individuals whose essences they are; to this extent Hegel is a Platonist. However, such universals require individual instantiation; to this extent Hegel, in a manner like *Plotinus*, synthesizes Aristotle and Plato. [Plotinus (AD 204/5–70) systematized previous

Greek thought in Neoplatonism. Its mystical and otherworldly tendencies were key influences upon both Eastern and Western Christian thought in the Middle Ages.] The essence abstracts from the individual features of its instantiations, but also delimits in a law-like fashion the sets of variations such instantiations can exhibit, for instance, size, specific colour, shape, and the like. The laws are laws of relations between several factors. Though the individual instances are subjected to time and thus change, the laws that govern their types remain unchanging: a "tranquil copy" of the ever-changing appearance.

§423. At first the law as the relation of fixed universal features has its necessity in itself insofar as its distinction is internal to it. One of the features, as not externally distinguished from the other, itself lies immediately in the other. However, in this way the inner distinction is what it in truth is, the distinction in its own self or *the distinction that is no* [absolute] *distinction*. In this determination of form generally, consciousness, containing as such the mutual *independence* of subject and object, is *in itself* [potentially] overcome. The judging I has an object that is not distinguished from it. Its object is *itself*; it becomes *self-consciousness*.

The viewpoint of consciousness is that of attending to objects independent of the conscious subject. Abstract analytical understanding grasps the necessary co-implication of the relations expressed by laws as the "interior" of the object appearing through sensation. The relations require one another and are thus not external and separable like parts of an aggregate body: they are internally related. The key claim here – not too clearly made (cf. the 1807 *Phenomenology of Spirit*) – is that when in reflection one "goes behind" the sensory curtain to grasp universal relations, one really is grasping oneself. This follows the old Aristotelian adage: "The intelligible in act is the intellect in act." We are not identical with our externally observable bodies but, as minds reaching towards the Totality, we encompass the spatio-temporal limitations of our own bodies and the sensations and desires that arise from them by "overreaching," through intellectual apprehension of universal relations, what is given in sensation. In a similar manner, sensed objects are not identical with their external representations as individual space-time occupants but are expressions of their own "interior," the realm of universals, of essences.

Hegel uses the odd expression "a distinction which is no distinction" elsewhere, but he explains that this means "no *absolute* distinction." It is distinction without separation and thus involves necessary internal relation.

Self-Consciousness

§424. The truth of consciousness is *self-consciousness*. The latter is the ground of the former so that in the existence of every consciousness of another object there is self-consciousness. I am aware of the object as mine (it is my representation) and I am thus aware of myself therein.

Once again, "truth" involves a movement to a higher level implicit in the lower, a move to teleological completion. The adult is the "true" man implicit in the child. Though consciousness is fixed upon objects as other than consciousness, implicitly it is aware of itself as other than the other or as "the same," other than which the other is presented. The other appears as other because I am present to myself, identical throughout my life, as other to that other. I know that it is I who know, even though I am focused upon what I know and not upon myself. In Sartre's terms, we always have pre-reflective awareness of ourselves in every explicit awareness of an other.

Consciousness, though presupposing self-consciousness, is treated first in accordance with Hegel's general move from most exterior (e.g., categories of Being) to the more interior (categories of Essence).

The expression of self-consciousness is I = I: *abstract freedom*, pure ideality. But here it is without reality since it itself is its own *object*. There is no object as such since there is no distinction between the self and its object.

The odd expression "I = I" was used by Fichte to express the identity of the I as an instance of the wider "A = A," the expression of logical identity (*Science of Knowledge*, 1, §1, 1–7, 94ff.). But self-identity is more than an instance of identity: it is reflective self-presence as focused on by Descartes in the *cogito*. The I is an other to every appearing other, free from all otherness, including what is within oneself, and thus free to determine itself. It is the *ideality* for which its embodiment is its most immediate *reality*. "Reality" here is used technically for what is other than awareness and its non-physical grounds (even though awareness's "ideality" requires the "reality" of embodiment as the instrumental complex needed for self-actualization).

The problem of self-consciousness is its non-objectifiability. Though we might reflect upon the I, it is I who do the reflecting and thus as a subject escape from the "object." In the Zen tradition, the self is like a hand that can grasp all objects but cannot grasp itself. Thinking of the I is thinking of a unique point of origin for the display of any kind of content and for self-determination. As such, the I is empty, free from all content as condition for self-determination, but only abstractly free. It moves from "ideality" to "reality" in embodied action through choice. It is free to choose, but it might easily choose to lose hold of itself through drunkenness or to close itself off from truth through groundless assertion. It moves from abstract freedom to substantial freedom through choosing the rational, that is, the true and the good.

Hegel sees the I = I as a modern discovery that is the basis for his own *Philosophy of Right*. Everything other than an I is only possible property; only an I – either one's own or that of others – has rights. The I develops through taking possession, first of its own body, and then of environmentally given things that it apprehends, marks as its own, and shapes. Through property one develops a relation to others, also I's, who recognize the right to property and enter into contractual relations regarding it.

§425. Abstract self-consciousness is the *first* negation belonging to consciousness, and thus is also burdened with an exterior object, formally with its negation. It is thus at the same time the previous level, consciousness, and is its contradiction of itself as self-consciousness and as consciousness. In the I = I, consciousness and negation in general have already been cancelled, preserved, and elevated in themselves [potentially]. As this certitude of itself against the object, self-consciousness is the *drive* to posit that which it is in itself, that is, to give content and objectivity to the abstract awareness of itself. It is also the reverse, the drive to free itself from its sensibility, to cancel, preserve, and elevate the given objectivity and to posit it as identical with itself. Both processes are one and the same: the identification of consciousness and self-consciousness.

Mere awareness of the I as non-object, as point of origin for all objectification, views the object as exterior to itself. Awareness is *not* the object and not itself an object: it is negation of exteriority. (Recall the

Nothing over against Being in the first triad of the Logic and Sartre's *Being and Nothingness*, found in things and consciousness respectively.) Hegel sees a contradiction between the I as point of origin for objectification (consciousness) and the I as freely self-determining (self-consciousness). Kant separated *the transcendental unity of apperception*, "the I think that must accompany any representation," from the self as the origin of free self-determination and thus of responsibility. The former was one pole in a field of phenomena; the latter "the sole noumenal fact." Hegel identifies the two, in spite of the difference in function of each. The abstract I is by its essence driven to give content to itself by what it comes to do, including coming to know. It is also driven to separate itself from immersion in its sense life in order to organize its impulses rationally and also to "go behind the curtain" of appearance to grasp the underlying truth of things that is one with the completed rational self. The I does and does not separate itself from its objects; it *identifies itself* with them *as other than* itself in a cognitive identity-in-difference that is completed in a loving identity-in-difference.

1. *Instinctive Desire* (die Begierde)

§426. Self-Consciousness in its immediacy is *singular* and *instinctive desire*. It is the contradiction involved in its abstractness that should be objective or in its immediacy that has the form of an exterior object and should be subjective. The object is determined as null for the self-certitude proceeding from the cancellation, preservation, and elevation of consciousness, just as in the relation of self-consciousness to the object its abstract ideality is null.

The initial phase of Self-Consciousness is awareness of oneself as an individual and as one with instinctive desire. A child spontaneously identifies itself with its impulses and is frustrated when not allowed to act upon them. Self-Consciousness is both abstract in that the I, though it is a drive to take on content, is implicitly other than any content, and yet not abstract but immediate as identified with an impulse that is other than the conscious I as a drive to assimilate content to itself. The body and its impulses lie in the sphere of objectivity, as other than the awareness thereof; but the body should become subjective, that is, imbued with the life of the conscious subject as its embodied expression. Reflective Self-Consciousness discovers the I as the capacity to abstract from all content, making the object meaningless in itself; but as so abstracted, the I is itself empty of all meaning.

§427. Self-Consciousness is aware of itself *in itself* [or implicitly] in the object that is correlate to appetite in this relation. This identity becomes explicit *for* the self in the negation of both one-sided moments by the I's own activity. The object can afford no opposition to this activity since it is in itself [potentially] and for self-consciousness [explicitly recognized as] what is lacking in the self. The dialectic whose nature is to cancel, preserve, and elevate itself exists here as the activity of the I. The given object is posited therein as subjective, while subjectivity is itself divested of its one-sidedness and becomes objective.

Because an appetite is a relation to an object – hunger for food, thirst for drink, sexual desire for mate – self-consciousness implicitly identifies with the object. The independent object and the I driven by desire are explicitly identified through the activity of the I. Thus, their initial separation is negated. The object has the passive potentiality to be assimilated by the I, which recognizes the lack in itself that can be filled by the object of desire. As the object is assimilated to subjectivity, subjectivity takes on objective content.

§428. The product of this process is that the I becomes something actual, is one with itself and satisfied *for itself*. According to its external side, in this return into itself it remains proximally determined as *individual* and has maintained itself as such, since it relates itself only negatively to the object that lacks a self and is thus merely consumed. In its satisfaction instinctive desire is thus generally *destructive* as in its content it is *self-seeking*. And since satisfaction happens only in individual cases that are transient, in being satisfied appetite arises again.

Experiencing a lack, the self is unfulfilled; filling the need, the self is actualized. Awareness goes outside itself and "returns to itself" to sustain its own external organic being as the immediate or proximate determination of itself as an individual. (Its ultimate determination as a rationally conscious self must go further and identify with the universal.) Through eating it grows and sustains itself; through sex it reproduces itself. At least in terms of eating and drinking, appetite destroys its object. And even in terms of sexual relations which do not destroy the object, appetite as such essentially seeks its own satisfaction and is indifferent to any enduring regard for the object that fulfils it. Though a universal orientation towards the kind of objects that could satisfy it, appetite is only satisfied by individuals in particular circumstances. Mozart's Don Giovanni is a perfect example of identification with an appetite: he is sexual desire incarnate. Universally oriented through sexual desire towards all women, he tries to conquer as many as possible: over 1000 in Spain and some 1800 altogether, all neatly recorded by his attendant, Leporello. Sexual appetite is in principle insatiable, arising again and again after its satisfaction, seeking ever new individual objects, using and abandoning women one after the other. In his *Republic* Plato refers to bodily appetites as "leaky vessels": filling them is only temporary since they readily empty again and require being filled anew. They exhibit what Hegel calls "the bad infinite," the indeterminate succession, *et sic ad infinitum*.

§429. But according to its internal side or *in itself* [implicitly], the self-feeling that arises for the I in being satisfied does not remain in abstract being *for itself* [explicitness] or only in its individuality. The result, as the negation of *immediacy* and of individuality, contains the feature of *universality* and the *identity* of self-consciousness with its object. The judgment or the diremption of this mode of self-consciousness is the consciousness of a *free* object, in which the I has the awareness of itself as I, but which is also still outside consciousness.

If the outer side of appetitive relation involves the individual related to other individuals, its inner side is a universal orientation towards individuals of the *type* that could satisfy it. As an individual identified with its desires, the I is aware of itself *in abstraction from* its founding orientation to the Whole. If it becomes aware of that orientation, it is able to negate or overcome its immediately manifest individuality, which only uses others to satisfy its appetites. It is able to be identified in knowing and loving with what is other as such. In such relations, the other is preserved in its otherness and seen as an instance of the universal. The relation the I has to it is also universal. Self-consciousness separates (*ur-teilt*, judges or "primordially separates") itself from the other and also from its own appetites, allowing the other to be freely manifest as existing in itself. This is most deeply the case when the other is another I, identification with which brings the I more fully to itself.

2. Recognitional (anerkennende) Self-Consciousness

§430. This is a self-consciousness for a self-consciousness, first *immediately* as an other for *another*. I see myself immediately in him as an I, but also therein as an immediately determinate object absolutely opposed to me as an independent other. The cancellation, preservation, and elevation of the *individuality* of self-consciousness was the *first* instance of sublating. It is thereby determined only as a *particular*. This contradiction provides the instinctive desire to *show* itself as a free self and to be *there* (*da zu sein*) for the other as free. Here we have the process of *recognition* [mutually, of free and intelligent human beings].

In the first phase the other is encountered as another I and not simply as an empirical object. The other person, by reason of its own reference to the Whole, is, like me, set at an infinite distance from any encountered and encountering other by being referred to the Whole. The otherness here is thus unlike the otherness of a subhuman entity. It is, as it were, *infinitely* other, but at the same time, in that respect, just like me. One might ask, How do "I see *myself* immediately in him"? We should think here of everyday usage where, for example, in a functional family, each finds him/herself in the others, is identified with them. But in a hostile situation that Hegel goes on to describe, the otherness of the I steps forward all the more in a relation of extreme difference.

The individuality of the I is subsumed under (cancelled, preserved, and elevated in) the awareness of my simultaneous universality, which is oriented towards the Whole and displays the I as a particular instance of I-ness. This simultaneous individuality and universality is another contradiction that has to be overcome.

In the *Zusatz*, Hegel distinguishes two phases of immediacy. The first involves the I identified with its appetites where the other is immediately encountered as object of appetite. At this level, humans as well as plants and animals could appear as food. The second involves the I having discovered its non-identity with appetite and being in immediate encounter with another I. Hegel then comments on the contradiction involved at the second level: "Since the I is completely *universal*, absolutely pervasive, *uninterrupted by any boundary*, the *same essence* in *all* men, both selves related here to one another are *one* identity; they constitute, so to speak, *one* light. On the other hand, at the same time they are *two*; they exist perfectly fixed and rigid over against one another, each as one *reflected into itself*, absolutely *distinguished* from and *impenetrable* by the other." The expression "reflected into itself" appeared earlier in the context of immediate sensing, where consciousness and the object are both "reflected into themselves" out of the immediacy of sensation. Here it is clearer, since each I is aware of its own otherness in relation to what appears over against it. What Hegel is working with here is what is involved in the long history of commentary on Aristotle's notion of *nous* (intellect), viewing it both as the possession of each individual human being and as a single, separate intellect for all humans.

The second claim, the otherness of each other, is easy to accept: each I is a conscious subjectivity necessarily related to and expressed in but clearly other than its embodiment, separated from all else not only by bodily enclosure but especially by the inescapable privacy of subjectivity that withdraws from its embodiment as it expresses itself in it.

The first claim, the identity of two or more persons, is not so obvious. There are two aspects here. On the one hand, the I pervades everything. It is separate from any given thing and freely self-disposable *precisely* because it is by its nature oriented towards *everything* via the notion of Being, which includes absolutely everything, albeit emptily. Metaphorically expressed, the notion of Being is the "light" that illuminates everything. This goes back to a line that runs from Parmenides, Plato, Aristotle, and Plotinus, on to Aquinas and Spinoza. For Parmenides *Being* as the changeless One is the region of light for the intellect; for Plato the Good as the One is the sun that illuminates the intellect and the Forms; for Aristotle, the light of the productive intellect (*nous poietikos*, translated one-sidedly into Latin as *intellectus agens* or acting intellect, which comes into English as *agent intellect*) "illuminates" sensory experience in order to raise its particularity to universality. The notion of Being is that empty orientation that leads the self to fill itself with increasingly more comprehensive intelligible content. On the other hand, though this orientation towards the Whole grounds subjectivity, it is the same light in all human beings.

This is the most difficult part of the claim. It is based upon the notion of intelligibility. As the Greeks noted, science is not based upon *similar* concepts in each scientist, but upon *identical* concepts. Though achieved by and in each I, science delivers concepts true of all objects and for all subjects of the same kind. Aristotle grounded intellection in *nous poi-etikos*, a fabricating intellect that was "separate, unmixed, coming from without." Islamic Aristotelian commentators such as Ibn Sina (*Avicenna*, 980–1037) and *Ibn Rushd* (*Averroes*, 1126–98), preceded by Neoplatonists like Plotinus, spoke of a single Intellect for all, a World Mind as the locus of the universal Forms exhibited by individual things. *Thomas Aquinas* (1225–74), who argued strongly against an Averroistic single Agent Intellect and in favour of the need for each human being to have his/her own agent intellect, nonetheless spoke of intellect as "a kind of participation in the one divine light" and thus as something trans-subjective. This is in line with his general teaching that every creature is enduringly grounded, "participates," in the Eternal God to Whom it is transparent. Sensing reveals each individual as separate from others because sensory presentation is a mode of actuality and what it cannot present is the underlying powers of sensorily given things. A fortiori, it cannot present the perpetual groundedness of each separately appearing thing in its Creator.

In modern times Spinoza re-invoked this notion. Hegel is here resurrecting this line. With Aquinas Hegel holds that each of us has *his/her own* interior "light of being"; but with the Neoplatonists he holds a single Intellect for all. Hegel's variation on the theme is that this Intellect develops over time through the activities of generations of human individuals. This consists in making explicit the implicit intelligibility or "rationality" of the Whole rooted eternally in the Logos and unveiled in the Logic.

The first step in this development has to be overcoming immediacy: the immediacy of the I identified with its appetites and the second immediacy of the I in its private inwardness. The implicit grounding of the second immediacy in the I's reference to the Whole drives it towards overcoming the separation from others involved in embodiment and subjectivity that contradict its universal orientation. But at the level we are here considering, the I only recognizes the other I immediately and tries to get the other to acknowledge oneself by displaying itself as a free and independent self.

§431. It is a struggle, for I cannot be aware of myself as myself in another insofar as the other is for me an immediately other determinate being. I am thus directed to the cancellation, preservation, and elevation of this immediacy. Likewise, I cannot be recognized as immediate; rather I

can be recognized only insofar as I sublate the immediacy in myself and through this give determinate being (*Daseyn*) to my freedom. But this immediacy is at the same time the bodiliness of self-consciousness, in which as in its signs and tools it has its own self-feeling, its being for others, and its relation mediating that self-feeling with them.

The problem of relations between I's Hegel expresses as a problem of immediacy. The first immediacy is sensation that has to be mediated, read intellectually as expressive of the underlying essence of what we encounter sensorily. In the case of another person, the expression of an I does not occur in the proper sense when the I is "sunk in Nature," identified with its appetites. It occurs through its freely refashioning itself and the world around it through the development and mastery of language together with the intelligibility available only through language and through the development of various modes of operation as well as those skills of transforming Nature involved in technology. All of this involves a primary mastery of one's own bodily movements. These refashioned structures are not given by Nature but created by human choice and intelligence and presuppose distance from appetite. One's own immediately encountered body becomes an expression, not of immediate appetite, but of free and intelligent subjectivity. Correspondingly, the other I calls out to be recognized as other than its immediately encounterable bodiliness, ultimately as the centre of free choice and intelligence, locus of the manifest intelligibility of the Whole.

432. The struggle for recognition is thus a matter of life and death. Each self-consciousness *imperils* not only the life of the other but also its own life; but it is only *in danger* that each is also directed to the maintenance of its life as the determinate being (*Daseyn*) of its freedom. From one point of view, the death of one of them dissolves the contradiction through the abstract and thus crude negation of immediacy. But, from the more essential point of view, this is a new contradiction, greater than the first, to the determinate being of recognition that is at the same time cancelled, preserved, and elevated therein.

The "thus" is not immediately apparent. Why should the struggle be "a matter of life and death?" One might understand the situation as one of being sunk in appetites such that the human other initially appears only, like other animals, as food. That would surely involve a life and death struggle. But what is at stake is subjectivity rising above identification with its own life, its embodiment, and its consequent immersion in appetites. Risking death, the I opts for the superiority of its own choice over life itself. Life is not valuable in itself but only as the embodied expression of the I's own freedom. "Better dead than a slave," as an old adage would have it.

There is a contradiction involved in more than one person being "in a way all things," that is, encompassing the Whole via the notion of Being. The killing of another eliminates the contradiction involved in two (or more) such encompassments. But the elimination of the other is an even greater contradiction to the essential *inclusiveness* of the I as oriented towards the Whole, since in this way it can only include the Whole by excluding parts. Only *recognition* of the other I – indeed, any other I – as free and rational can overcome the contradiction because Reason operating in each of us is the same for all.

In the *Zusatz* Hegel remarks that the struggle for recognition is here pushed to an extreme and can only occur where men exist as single, separate individuals. It is absent once humans organize themselves into the State. He further remarks that "although the State can also *originate in violence*, it does not rest on it," for "the Spirit of the people, custom, and law are what governs in the State. There man is recognized and treated as a *rational* being, as *free*, as a person."

§433. In that life is as essential as freedom, the struggle at first ends with inequality as a one-sided negation. One of the contenders gives the priority to its life, maintains itself as individual self-consciousness, but gives up its being recognized [as a free and intelligent human being]. The other maintains himself in relation to himself and is recognized as superior by the former as by the one who is subjected. Here we have the relation of *Master and Slave*.

There is an inescapable duality in human existence, not only between the body as such and awareness, but within awareness between those aspects that arise from embodiment (sensations and appetites) that are determined prior to choice and those involving the reciprocal interplay between understanding and choice. In the struggle between two "I"s, the one who sets freedom above life overcomes one who holds the opposite. "Better Red than dead" might read a more recent adage. The slavish mentality is that of one who is not willing to risk death for distinctive human existence as a free and intelligent person.

The struggle for recognition and subjection to a Master is the *appearance* in which the collective life of man arises as one origin of the *State*. The *power* which is the ground in this appearance is thus not the ground of *right*, although it is the *necessary* and *justified* moment in the transition from the *situation* of self-consciousness sunk in instinctive appetites and individuality to the situation of universal self-consciousness. It is the external *inception* of the State in the order of *appearance*, not its *substantial principle*.

The technical use of the category *Appearance* involves the display of a *developing* essence. The sprout is the first appearance of the essence of the seed that is oriented towards a fully actualized, reproductive plant. In the currently focused situation, the essence involved is the *human* essence, but not a fully *actualized* human essence. Even though, for Hegel, Slavery violates the essence of humanness, he yet sees the power relation between Master and Slave as a necessary moment in the development of humanness, but one that must be surpassed. The basis lies in the initial identification of oneself with one's appetites, acting on one's urges like an infant, and the subsequent identification with private subjectivity which learns to choose on the basis of its appetites or its arbitrary whims. Parents act as Masters to their children when they teach them to control themselves on the basis of command and principle, rising above infancy and adolescence, ideally to become free and intelligent adults. The latter involves the "substantial principle" of the State that emerges later in history, beyond the stage of infancy and adolescence for humankind. The substantial principle is a teleological principle, first in the order of intention, last in the order of execution. The human essence is realized when appetites are mastered and individual subjectivity directed to the universality of law – both of Nature and of social relations. This anticipates the notion of "free Spirit" at the conclusion of the Psychology.

The merely negative moment of free choice becomes positive in freeing one's possibilities for understanding the order of things and choosing in a way that corresponds with that order, that is, by respecting the conditions of universal, rational human flourishing. Individuals mature by rising to the level of functioning adults within their society, built to correspond to the requirements of Nature and Spirit and to the meaning of the Whole as that is understood in any given community. Humankind matures as comprehensive understanding moves from myth to philosophy, as technology and institutional construction develop human potentialities, as they create the conditions for ongoing development, and as philosophy itself becomes more comprehensive.

§434. First of all, since, as the instrument of mastery, the Slave must, at the same time as he is enslaved, be kept alive, this relation is one of a *communality* of need and care for the Slave's satisfaction. In place of the brutal destruction of the immediate object, there appears the acquisition, maintenance, and formation of it as mediating [between human individuals]. In this process both extremes of independence and dependence coalesce. The form of universality in the satisfaction of need is a *lasting* means and a provision looking to and securing the future.

Master and Slave form a communality of need based upon the provision of the necessities of life. The Slave is forced to work upon things, learning to refashion raw materials in order to produce and utilize the instruments for more efficient production. In the process, the Slave both learns more about the laws of Nature than the Master and develops his own abilities to refashion Nature. Working with Nature reveals aspects never discoverable by mere observation. Master and Slave become mutually dependent, but the Slave secures the independence of knowledge and skill. The repeatability of the processes in knowing and controlling Nature to satisfy human need establishes a humanly constructed universality parallel to and developed in terms of the laws of Nature, the world of technology, and the skills that sustain it. Like natural powers, skills are universal orientations towards the kinds of things upon which they regularly operate. But they do not come into being by Nature; they come into being by the interplay of human understanding and choice, grasping the regularities of Nature and projecting new forms through their combination in manipulating matter to fulfil human projects. Embedded in individuals, skills are passed on to others. Over time they are capable of being increasingly refined and multiplied. This process forms an aspect of what Hegel terms "Objective Spirit," the accumulated transfer of practices and the institutions that support them as enduring objects from the subjectivities that initiated them, developed them, and died, having passed them on to succeeding generations. We will consider that in summary after the last phase of Subjective Spirit presented in the Psychology as Hegel moves on to Objective Spirit.

§435. Second, according to the distinction of the two, by reason of the cancellation, preservation, and elevation of his immediate being-for-self, the Master sees in the Slave and his service the value (*Gelten*) of his own *individual* being-for-self. However, this sublation depends on another. The Slave, however, overcomes his individual self-will in service to the Master, sublates the inner immediacy of instinctive desire, and in this externalization and "fear of the Lord" finds "the beginning of wisdom." Here we have the transition to *universal self-consciousness*.

The Master sees in the Slave the mirror of his own individual superiority because he rose above his own life by mastering the fear of death to which the Slave succumbed. The Master's immediate identity with his own life is overcome and he is aware of his superiority over the other who yet remains other in a negative sense. However, the freedom the Master achieves by risking his life is only the lowest grade of freedom, that of the *natural will* that is dragged about by its whims. He is free to do what he feels like doing, but not free to determine what he feels like.

By contrast, the Slave has his identity with his appetites and his immediate subjectivity broken by external obedience to the Master, but rises to the universal through the knowledge and skill developed in manipulating Nature. For the realization of the human essence, the externality of this obedience has to become the internally free pursuit of knowing and community with all other free and intelligent humans. Through work upon Nature rational freedom emerges. In a perversion of this significant insight, Nazi slave-labour camps had over their entrances the motto *"Arbeit Macht Frei,"* roughly translated, "Freedom through Labour" (literally, "Work Makes Free")! In the *Zusatz* Hegel remarks: "This subjugation of the Slave's selfishness constitutes the *beginning* of true human freedom. This shaking of the singularity of the will, the feeling of the nullity of selfishness, the habit of obedience, is a necessary moment in the formation of every man. Without having experienced the discipline that breaks self-will, no one becomes free, rational, and capable of command. To become free, to attain to the capacity for self-regulation, every people must therefore go through the harsh discipline of subjection to a Master." He also adds (in the *Zusatz* to §433) that "in the history of peoples, slavery and tyranny are, therefore, a necessary stage and thus somewhat *relatively* justified." He underscores "relatively" (*beziehungsweise*) and adds "somewhat" (*etwas*) because, in his view, slavery is a violation of "eternal human rights" (*ewige Menschenrechte*).

3. Universal Self-Consciousness

§436. *Universal self-consciousness* is the affirmative awareness of one's self in another self in which each has *absolute independence* as free individuality. However, because of the negation of its immediacy [as subjective self-will] or instinctive desire, it does not separate itself from others. Each is universal and objective. Its universality is realized in that reciprocity wherein each consciously recognizes itself in the free other and is aware of that insofar as it recognizes the other and is aware of it as free.

Immediate awareness of the human other as another I is, in the case of the Master related to the Slave, negative. In consciousness of oneself as universal, any human other is included precisely as another free and intelligent I. By reason of rising above the first two levels of immediacy (being sunk in Nature or in subjective self-will), the I does not separate itself from others but appreciates each human being in its free self-disposability. Each rises out of mere individual subjectivity to form itself in accord with universality and objectivity. One recognizes oneself in the other, existing only as identified with the other as free and intelligent subjectivity.

This universal reflection or reciprocity (*Wiedererscheinen*) of self-consciousness is the Concept. It is aware of itself in its objectivity as subjectivity identical with itself and is thus universal. It is the shape of consciousness forming the *substance* of all essential spirituality in the family, the fatherland, and the state as it is the substance of all the virtues, of love, friendship, courage, honour, and fame. But all this *appearance* of the substantial can be separate from the substantial and be merely for itself in empty fame, vainglory, and the like.

The terminology here is admittedly difficult. We see again the use of the notion of "the Concept" which, recall, is, at the level of existence, the I itself, the "grasping" (*Begriff*) towards the Whole. This level of the Logic brings knowers into the categorial System rather than, according to our spontaneous inclination and ordinary scientific practice, keeping them outside as observers and manipulators. By reason of the way in which the I grasps the Whole, it is the region of logical categories. At a first level, Concept generically includes as its species concept, judgment, and reasoning, the region of formal logic. But if the Concept entering into existence is the I, the "grasping" (*Begriff*) towards the Totality that makes formal logic possible, it presupposes the Objective Concept of the mechanical, chemical, and organic Systems subsumed in the life of the human being, and is completed in the cognitive and volitional functions reaching the level of so-called Absolute Knowing.

The stages of self-consciousness, from the I as identified with desire to the I as separated from others and struggling with them, form the stage of the *Appearance* of the essence to be fulfilled. The process culminates in the *Actualization* of the essence through the recognition of all humans as other selves. In the Logic this is the transition from Essence to Concept. Fulfilled subjectivity is, objectively, aware of itself as all-inclusive. One could also say that it is identical with its fulfilled self only as it identifies with what is objective to itself as other selves. This is what is involved in familial relations: in the husband related to his wife, parents to children, siblings to one another. In a functional family, each finds itself in the others, is happy when they succeed, and is willing to sacrifice for their sake. In genuine patriotism, one identifies with one's country and its way of life, so much so that one is willing to put one's life on the line for it. In the relation of individuals to each other beyond institutions, this reciprocity of consciousness is the essence of love and friendship, of courage and honour. But the latter two states can be merely vainglory and provide only the appearance of real identity with others. The authentic identity-in-difference revealed in these relations is for Hegel the clue to all reality. In the *Zusatz* he refers to this finding of oneself in others as "the speculative or the rational and true [that] consists in the unity of the Concept or the subjective and objectivity." Beyond the sciences of Nature, inhabitance of a world together with others constitutes the basis for the higher view of Nature as itself the place where Spirit dwells.

§437. This unity of consciousness and self-consciousness contains first of all the individuals mutually illuminating (reflecting, *scheinende*) each other. But their difference in this identity is completely indeterminate differentiation or rather a difference that is no [absolute] difference. Their truth is thus the universality and objectivity of self-consciousness existing in-and-for-itself as *Reason*.

How do they mutually illuminate each other? Is it that one comes to understand him/herself in and through relations with a human other, recognizing and being recognized? This happens at one level when, for example, one tries out for a position and others recognize that one has or does not have what it takes to fill the position well. One discovers by trying out and being judged by competent judges whether one has the developed capacity or not and how one fares in relation to others competing for the same position. But since Hegel refers to love and friendship, family and fatherland, the recognition involved is one related to one's comprehensive functioning as a self. In the functional family, each is affirmed, accepted in a comprehensive way as the self one is. Affirmation by others in this way gives a certain identity to the self. Each thus "illuminates" the selfhood of the other, making each other aware of one's self-worth. Hegel sees this process as the exhibition of what he means by "Reason."

Reason is potential (in itself) in everything. That is to say, everything is potentially intelligible: it exhibits a rational character. But Reason exists in consciousness at a higher level of potentiality: as the potential to work at understanding all things and thus manifest the reason in them. Indeed, this is the cosmic purpose of things themselves: to establish in human beings the condition for the possibility of their own manifestation and consequent subsumption under consciousness as known objects. When consciousness awakens to Reason as its own ability to actualize the potential intelligibility in everything, that ability exists actually, though at this stage only as an awareness that it is this ability. So we have three, and eventually four or five, levels: (1) the potential intelligibility of everything; (2) consciousness as able to actuate that potentiality; and (3) consciousness as aware that it has this potentiality. That is where the analysis stands in the text at this point. Later we find (4) the history of thought as the progressive actualization of that potential when humans come to understand more and more through the development of philosophy. When that development is completed in principle, it involves (5) the actualization of a systematic understanding of the main lines of the Whole in an interlocking set of categories that is rightly called "absolute" or "absolved knowing" (*absolutes Wissen*), that is, absolved from the darkness and partiality that characterizes the prior stages. Such understanding is not omniscience, but an awareness of the interlocking set of conditions – ontological, psychological, cultural, and cosmic – for the possibility of rational existence.

But one has to remember that the principle of Reason in Hegel's sense is identity-in-difference, a concretizing and synthesizing power as distinct from abstract analytical Understanding that operates in terms of the principle of identity or separateness. The development of Reason involves living through and being aware of one's identity with the Whole and its principle, the trinitarian God, the Logos bound to the One by the principle of Love.

Reason as the unity of the Concept and Reality is the *Idea* (§213). As Reason appears here, the opposition between the Concept and Reality as such has attained the initial form of the Concept existing in the process of the for-itself [the activation] of consciousness and of the object present externally over against it.

In Kant "Idea" as a distinctive concept is the notion of encompassing Totality corresponding to Reason and distinguished from Understanding. Idea is articulated into the external Totality in the idea of World, the internal Totality in the idea of Soul, and, in the idea of God, the Ground of the Totality. Hegel's Idea is the third category under the Concept, after the categories of Being and Essence. The subcategories of the Concept are the Subjective Concept, the Objective Concept, and the Idea, or Formal Logic, Systems of externality (Mechanism, Chemism, and Teleology), and the union of the two. The three parallel, in a transformed way, Kant's Ideas of Soul, World, and God. Hegel reserves the term "Idea" for the ideas of Life, Cognition, and Absolute Idea as object of Absolute Knowing or "absolved knowing," the completion of the divine plan. A living thing is not a mere external conglomeration of parts, but a whole unfolding from within and defining itself against its environment. It is also an expression of its species whose power over it is exercised in reproduction and death. Each species, in turn, is an expression of encompassing Life that aims at the production of humans as the locus for the manifestation of the Whole.

The Concept as the unity of Being and Essence culminates in the Idea as the unity of Subjective and Objective Concept. The latter is here termed Reality as the externality of physical Systems for which the Concept is the Ideality or internality, parallel to the soul as the ideality of the body. *Being* is the region of categories involved in the immediacy of surface presentation; *Essence* involves the categories of what underlies and is expressed in that surface, moving from being implicit and developing through appearance to full actualization; and *Concept* involves the inclusion of the conditions of manifestation in subjectivity. That in turn involves the rational subject's employment of formal logical categories in attending to manifestations as well as the categories involved in things being "over against" such subjectivity. These categories culminate in the objective foundation of subjectivity in the organism living in its eco-System and the rising of cognition from such foundation to the comprehensive awareness of the interlocking system of all the categories involved in human development, that is, in "absolved knowing."

Notice that *absolutes Wissen* is not omniscience, even though Hegel talks of it as "thinking the thoughts of God before creation." Such thoughts remain at the level of the interrelated System of those concepts required for there to be the kind of beings, immanent within the Cosmos, where the Reason that structures the Cosmos can be fully manifest. Such a System is displayed in Hegel's *Encyclopaedia of the Philosophical Sciences*. Awareness of that systematic connectedness is "absolved awareness." Omniscience would involve the transparency of all the individuals and variations of species and contingent happenings, especially those rooted in free choice, that occur within that intelligible framework. That is just what absolute knowing is not. It remains a question whether, just as everything contingent is not known by knowing the System, there is thus place for a knowing that corresponds to the sum total of things as omniscience that Hegel brings up but does not develop in his Philosophy of Religion.

Reason for Hegel is "the unity of consciousness and self-consciousness." What is involved in consciousness is the subject–object relationship, where the object has priority; in self-consciousness awareness of the self as an individual comes to the fore. In universal self-consciousness the human other as such is recognized as a self, free and intelligent. Each person throws light on the others. Reason goes deeper, for Hegel also says that Reason is "the unity of Concept and Reality." Here the identity-in-difference realized in universal self-consciousness becomes the principle of all being. Fully developed, the Concept is the Idea appearing in Life, in Cognition, and in Absolute Awareness, absolved from all limits in its comprehension of the cosmic conditions for intelligibility. When this happens, the Cosmos has come to its telos at the speculative level. This does not stamp "finished" on the process of history, but only to the manifestation of the kind of systematic unity that makes possible further pursuit of the sciences and further human development in all directions.

Remember that for Hegel "truth" involves completion, a given essence becoming in truth, in actuality, what it was meant to be. That entails the completion of a dialectical series. Here, the mere awareness of others as in principle identical with oneself is still unarticulated, undeveloped in the diversity it entails. It finds its truth in the development of Reason as principle of the Whole. At this stage, in the first discovery of Reason, it is only *principle* of the Whole, of the Totality present to a subject in the plurality of individuals encountered outside the subject that must still be uncovered and arranged rationally. Reason has to work at concretely grasping the actual intelligible articulation of the Whole and at developing institutions corresponding to it.

Reason

§438. Reason as the truth existing in and for itself is the simple *identity* of the *subjectivity* of the Concept and its *objectivity* and universality. The universality of Reason thus has the meaning of the *object* that was merely given in consciousness as such, but that is now itself *universal*, penetrating and encompassing the I. Equally important, Reason also has the meaning of the pure *I*, the pure form overreaching the object and possessing it in itself.

The completion of Reason involves not only the working out of the logical categories (the "subjectivity" of the Concept) but their application in the realms of Nature and Spirit that exist "objectively" outside the Concept. In Reason the object standing over against the conscious I becomes the encompassing of the object and the I that is purified into a universal I overreaching all objectivity. I and object are one: there is a *cognitive identity* between mind and thing; "the intellect in act is the intelligible in act," as Aristotle put it.

In the *Zusatz* Hegel remarks, "In this context, "Reason" has the meaning only of the initially still abstract or formal unity of self-consciousness with its object. This unity establishes what must be called, in specific contrast to the true, the merely correct." It is at the end of the treatment of theoretical Spirit in the Psychology (§467) that Reason will appear in a more developed way.

The distinction between the correct and the true is crucial. Remember that the true is the teleologically complete, that which has moved from directed potentiality to actuality. This holds not only for individual living things, but also for Nature and History. Such a view overcomes the modern dichotomy between fact and value. The task of speculative thought is to find the actualization of the "true" in the "factual," that which has reached its completion from that which is merely "there" factually and scientifically observable. This harkens back to the categories of Essence, where the Existent is the realm of Appearance that refers back to a Ground of potentialities that are fully manifest only when those potentialities reach their full unfolding in Actuality. Things that fail to reach completion are factually "there" but are not yet "truly" what they were meant to be.

§439. Reason is thus self-consciousness as the certitude that its determinations are no less determinations of the essence of things than they are its own thoughts. As this identity, Reason is not only the absolute *substance* but *truth* as knowing (*Wissen*). For truth has here attained to its characteristic *determination*, the immanent form of the pure Concept existing for itself, the I, the certitude of itself as infinite universality. This truth aware [of itself] is *Spirit*.

When Reason is aware that its properly articulated concepts are the essences of things, it is aware of itself as the encompassing reality of all things arriving at their truth. The I itself is the pure Concept penetrating all things. Here we move from Spinozistic Substance to Hegelian Subject. This for Hegel is the meaning of Spirit. Here he has melded the Divine Spirit with the human Spirit, Creator and Sustainer of all with the human subject.

For Hegel the Christian revelation of the God-Man "lets the secret out," hidden throughout the history of Religion, that the divine and the human are, at ground, identical. This is the basis for the intrinsic dignity of each individual human being and for the community of confession and forgiveness as the presence of the Spirit in His community.

Hegel introduced his consideration of this community as the culmination of his treatment of Morality in the 1807 Phenomenology. It follows the phenomenon of the self-styled "beautiful soul" who refuses to besmirch its purity by entering into action that is laden with ambiguity. The way forward is to enter into discourse with others who occupy the same situation, confess one's mistakes when necessary, and become reconciled to the community through forgiveness. This is in fact the milieu of so-called Absolute Knowing, where what is absolute is knowing the general framework without the riot of contingencies appearing in the situation of action. But it is in this situation that the Spirit appears in His community. As Feuerbach would later put it, "Man by himself is only man; man with man, the unity of the I and the Thou, is the divine."

The central issue here came to the fore in Plotinus, who asked, in effect: Where are we, each with our private awareness and opinions, when we see, for example, a geometric demonstration? Outside our privacy and personal preferences and within a kind of public space, whose publicity extends in principle to *all* humans. It is this fact that led commentators on Aristotle to posit a World-Mind or Agent Intellect in which we share. Even Aquinas, who vigorously opposed the separate Agent Intellect of Averroes and insisted, by reason of the priority of individual existence, that each human has his own agent intellect, still observes the need here for an encompassment of the Whole by intellectual beings: "Intellect is a *kind of* participation of intellectual beings in the divine light." (See our comments to §430.) The certitude involved here has moved beyond the indubitable self-presence of the Cartesian *cogito* to the more comprehensive indubitability of the in-principle intelligibility of the Whole and the underlying unity of all rational beings.

But this is only the ground of humanness. Humans develop in and through mutual recognition in love, in family, in friendship, in work, in the rationally ordered state that protects their rights, in the religious community of confession and forgiveness that grounds them in the Absolute, and in the philosophic endeavour to arrive at the conceptual system adequate to the whole of our experience. What at the level of the Concept is the Idea as the unity of the Subjective and the Objective Concept, at the level of Spirit is the unity of each Subject with its objective Other in mutual recognition as rationally free subjects that is completed in a lived way at the religious level as the community of confession and forgiveness and in an adequate conceptual way in the philosophic system.

Psychology

If the field of awareness is rooted from below in the unconsciousness of organic life, it is suspended from above by a hierarchical set of operations required for the full emergence of actuated Rationality. At the logical level of underlying Essence, the Anthropology involved the body-informing power of Spirit or the Soul, related to the manifest body as inner essence to outer expression, while the Phenomenology constituted the level of Existence or Appearance expressing the spiritual essence. Now we approach the Psychology as the in-principle Actuality (*Wirklichkeit*) of Spirit manifest in its full functionality. As in Aristotle, each of the rational functions springs from Rationality itself, as do the sensory powers that provide the material for rational penetration, and the nutritive power that grows the instruments for sensory activation. In parallel with the distinction at the level of sensing between "objective" sensations that reveal aspects of environing objects and "subjective" sensations that reveal the correlative self-feeling, including the appetites of the sensing subject, culminating in the fully functional animal, Spirit proper is thus divided into *Theoretical* and *Practical Spirit*, which find their culmination in *Free Spirit* or Spirit freed onto its full rational functioning, theoretical as well as practical.

Human Reason begins its operation with the sensations that arise from the interaction between the organism and the environment already treated in the Anthropology section as Sensibility, as the being-affected of the self, and appearing within the Phenomenology as Sensation proper, that is, as manifesting what is other than the sensing self. In fact, Sensation appears at several levels of analysis. It appears first of all in the Philosophy of Nature in terms of the manifest features grounded in the bodies that appear in the environment: their colours, sounds, and so on. It appears in the Anthropology as grounded in the organic constitution of the sensing human being who is capable of having sensations. It appears in the Phenomenology section as the correlativity between the manifest body and the sensing individual organism. It appears, finally, in the Psychology section as the starting point for the differing acts of attending belonging to the human Spirit as rational agency.

Operation at this final level involves that habituation that is the culmination of the Anthropology whereby Spirit comes to penetrate Sensation and Desire, so that there is only one Reason, from Feeling – and, indeed, further down in unconscious biological functioning – all the way up to fully rational agency and comprehensive knowing. Reason proper begins by focusing attention upon the sensorily given. But developed Reason focuses in terms of having become habituated to a whole region, such that a trained scientist sees significantly more in what is sensorily present than one not so trained. The scientist becomes intuitive and is able to apprehend possibilities suggested by the immediate evidence not even dimly apprehended by one not so trained. This is true also at the level of moral action. As Aristotle noted, one can understand ethical thought only if one has been brought up well, has become habituated to the realm of moral action, or, as Aquinas put it, has become "co-natural" with that realm.

In order to reach that level, fleeting sensations have to be retained and "inwardized," transferred from exterior Space and Time to the interior

Space and Time of the Imagination and associated in many different ways with what appears in that interior. When a recollected image is associated with an Intuition, we have *Representation* (*Vorstellung*). But Imagination is also capable of becoming creative in function of Reason itself. This occurs in the arts that employ images as symbols. But it also occurs in a more fundamental manner at the level of the production of signs that grounds language. Here, contrary to the case of the symbol, the sign has no intrinsic relation to the signified. A lion, for example, can come to symbolize royalty or power because of certain features of its demeanour, but the word "lion" has no intrinsic signing relation to the animal to which it refers. The invention of words is the work of Intellect creatively laying down its own tracks, so to speak.

The rational Soul laid down its first tracks in forming the organic body so as to furnish the instruments for the activation of its sensory powers; but it lays down its specifically rational tracks in the creation of a system of linguistic signs by transforming sensibility. And it lays them down simultaneously in its own inner space and in the space of external intersubjective relationships. The word is an "inward externality" as a bit of the sound and sight world transferred into the Space of Subjectivity. But, as Hegel put it in the 1807 *Phenomenology of Spirit* (§171), Language is not simply subjective; it occupies the space formed by "an I that is a We and a We that is an I." Language takes us out of our private interiority into a public space, a space where I am incorporated into a We, whereby each of us is able to develop our "interiority" intellectually, to speak to one's self about one's privacy in a way that can in principle be understood by others.

In Hegel's technically narrow usage, Memory (*Gedächtnis*), as distinct from inwardization (*Erinnerung*), is the retention of *signs*, not simply of experience as such. Signs ground the operation of Intellect proper, but they also ground the merely rote memorization of words. Thinking proper (*Denken*) operates in terms of Analytical Understanding that sorts experienced objects into systems of sameness and difference, culminating in the ultimate categories. These it employs in its judgments about things. And such judgments it weaves together into reasoning processes. The formal structures involved in thinking were explored in the first part of the logic of the Concept, the so-called Subjective Concept, as the sets of Concepts, Judgments, and Syllogisms the human subject uses in thinking about things. In the current text, Hegel attends here to the operations involved in employing the formal structures. Such thinking, even in its crudest forms, is the basis for the operation of the Will, which is Reason determining its own Self, even in choosing to pursue things theoretically.

Practical Spirit moves from the representational generality of Theoretical Spirit to the side of Existence, the side of Essence coming out of its Ground and appearing relative to others coming out of their Grounds. As Reason determining itself, Will is at first identified with its own appetites. Then it steps forth as formal Will, as the ability to choose whatever I will, following, opposed to, or shaping its appetites. But its intrinsic aim is to become essential or substantial Will when what it chooses accords with Reason and thus frees the Will to be more fully itself as rational Will.

Again, as in the Phenomenology, we begin with immediate tendencies to act rooted in the Heart, the sedimented resultant of past actions. The tendencies may be immediate in the most elementary sense as feelings of pleasure and pain. But they may also be mediated immediately by representations, as in joy and fear. The latter states, like the former, occur now – that is, immediately, in the present – just like the pleasures and pains we experience when engaged in sensient functions like eating and drinking. But such states as joy or fear entail a presentation or representation of their objects and thus some understanding of those objects. And they may also be mediated immediately by the higher content of Right, Morality, Customary Life (*Sittlichkeit*), and Religion, as in shame or remorse. When one's whole self is poured immediately into a line of action there emerges passion, without which nothing great is achieved.

However, there are multiple tendencies to act, so that the question emerges as to how they can be brought into harmonious relation with one another. This is where the notion of Happiness comes in as the anticipation of comprehensive satisfaction. When the deeper tendencies are organized in accord with Reason's apprehension of the overall order of things, we have the fully *Free Spirit*. A human being is meaningfully free not simply when he opines and chooses and is able to carry out his intentions, but also when he judges in accordance with evidence and acts rationally. Whereas Theoretical Spirit operates at the level of underlying Essence, Practical Spirit steps into Existence, and Free Spirit is Spirit in principle reaching Actuality.

What Hegel has analysed in the current section is *Subjective Spirit* or the structure of being a human Subject, culminating in the notion of free Spirit. What he will then explore will be the institutional structures that can aid in bringing about Free Spirit, not simply in principle but in concrete Actuality. That is the realm of *Objective Spirit*. And it will be surmounted by the realm of *Absolute Spirit* in Art, Religion, and Philosophy as a return to the encompassing Ground of the Whole.

We turn now to the paragraphs of the Psychology in the *Philosophy of Spirit*.

Hegel's Psychology

§440. *Spirit* has determined itself as the Truth of Soul and Consciousness, the former a simple immediate Totality, the latter an awareness (*Wissen*) which now, as unconfined (*unendlich*) form, is not hemmed in by content, does not stand in relation to the content as Object, but is aware of the substantial Totality that is neither subjective nor objective. The Spirit thus begins only from its own Being and relates itself only to its own characteristics.

"Soul" is Spirit insofar as it is immersed in Nature, a realm determined by Matter as a principle of exteriority and thus dispersal. In a view going back to Plato and Aristotle, "Matter" plays in tandem with "Form" as the principle of the multiplication of the same form or type in different individuals occupying different times and places. [*Aristotle* followed his teacher, Plato, in the *Timaeus*, which claims that the body is the house of the soul; but Aristotle claimed further that the soul builds its own house through its nutritive power, providing the various organs as instruments for activating the sensory and rational powers. The soul is not a separate thing but an active principle of organic life. In the introduction to the Encyclopaedia Philosophy of Spirit, Hegel claimed that Aristotle's works on the soul are unsurpassed, and that he, Hegel, is only developing the line Aristotle laid down.] In knowers, linkage to Matter is a principle of lack of self-presence, of opaqueness, of the tendency of self-dispersal for ideally concentrated awareness.

Soul is not a substance set over against "Body" but a concrete universal, a one-over-many, a pervasive Totality that generates and unifies all its parts. This was the level treated in the *Anthropology*. Consciousness emerges out of this level as the other to all appearing others. It is a kind of light that sets over against itself what appears through the Body in Sensation and allows it to appear as an instance of the Universal. The level of Consciousness is the level of the Subject of awareness correlated with the manifest Object. It was treated in the *Phenomenology*.

For Hegel, "Truth" is that which brings together the splits that naturally occur in the process of development by reaching their teleological completion. The unifying Truth of the split between ensouled Body and Consciousness is healed by Spirit, which "returns to itself" from its dispersal in the outer world present through the Body in Sensation through transforming its Body into a fit instrument of the Soul. This return to itself is the level treated in what Hegel here calls *Psychology*. Spirit is Reason aware of itself as such. Spirit in principle, as the locus of the manifestation of the Whole, encompasses, in its own way, the unconscious "Body" and the conscious "Spirit" as well as the things it confronts. It "overreaches" the otherness of what it senses and comes to understand the systematic relation of the underlying universal structures, the awareness of which brings the Spirit to itself, to its own fuller actualization. As such, it has its own characteristics.

Spirit is finite, hemmed in, confined, restricted from its own completion when it has not yet come to understand that its completion lies in reaching beyond the externality and separateness of what is initially presented to it in sensation, whether outside itself through seeing, hearing, and the like, or inside itself as its immediate desires. When it rises to the level of grasping the underlying unity of everything, it is unconfined or "infinite." Through the notion of Being it encompasses both itself and what are its manifest objects.

Psychology thus treats the capacities or the universal modes of operation of Spirit as such: External Intuition (*Anschauen*), Representation (*Vorstellen*), Interiorization (*Erinnern*) and the like, as well as Instinctive Desires (*Begierden*) and the like. It treats the capacities in abstraction from the contents that appear in empirical Representation (*Vorstellung*) and in Thinking proper (*Denken*) as well as in desiring and willing. It also abstracts from the forms found in the Soul as a natural determination and in Consciousness itself as Object of Consciousness present for itself.

Spirit's encompassing all things passes through levels of development rooted in its necessary embodiment. In passing chronologically from the lower to the higher, Spirit retains the lower in the higher. In analysing these levels, Hegel gives examples of theoretical and practical activities. Psychology treats the capacities for these activities in abstraction from their contents and from the ways they are present at two levels: the level of Soul, in which they are natural determinations side by side with one another, and the level of Consciousness, in which the contents are objects of a conscious subject. Empirical re-presenting presents again in the space of interiority what sensory awareness presents immediately in the space of exteriority as separate from one another, while Thinking proper grasps the necessary interrelations in which everything stands as intelligible.

Yet this is not an arbitrary abstraction. According to its Concept, Spirit is itself that which transcends Nature and natural determinations as well as involvement with an external object, that is, it transcends the material realm in general. Its present task is only to realize this concept of its Freedom, to cancel, preserve, and elevate the *form* of Immediacy with which it again begins. The contents raised to External Intuition are *its own* sensations, as its intuitions are transformed into empirical representations and its representations immediately into thoughts, etc.

Both Spirit's power of ensouling Matter and the power of detaching itself from objects in order that they might appear are, according to Hegel, linked to Matter both as the principle of dispersal and as a necessary, grounding element in the development of humanness. The task of Spirit is initially to free itself from this dispersal into the interior space of comprehensive Analytical Understanding. At the level of its returning to itself from this dispersal, Spirit begins by attending to what is immediately and externally presented in sensation, interiorizing this in re-presentations, and transforming representations into thoughts. This is the progression Hegel traces in what follows.

Elsewhere Hegel himself gives examples of Representation such as "blue" and "man." They are isolated re-presentations, presenting again to itself what is available empirically, through sensory inspection. Understanding as "the power of the negative" is able to isolate any object and re-present it in separate form. This is expressed in words as stand-ins for concepts. Each word can readily be treated "in itself" without reference to other words. "Thoughts," by contrast, are the linkage of such "representations" through categories into systematic relations within the Whole to which Spirit is oriented by its essence.

§441. The Soul is *finite* insofar as it is immediately determined or determined by Nature. Consciousness is finite insofar as it has an Object. Spirit is finite insofar as it indeed no longer has an Object in its awareness (*Wissen*) but a mode, that is to say, through its Immediacy, and what is the same, through the fact that it is subjective or is as the Concept.

Once again, "Nature" is what is determined by Matter, what antecedes and grounds, at an earlier phase, the self-possession of Spirit. As we noted, Matter as principle of dispersal is a principle of lack of self-possession and thus of darkness. The nutritive processes of Soul go on in the dark, beneath the light of Consciousness. Consciousness as a sphere of self-possession allows other things to appear in its light. If the unconscious is limited by not being self-possessed, Consciousness is limited by being determined by objects. "Spirit" becomes explicitly manifest as the Ground of the whole process, not only in the case of the ontogenesis of an individual, but also in the case of the development of the cosmic Whole. Spirit becomes aware of itself, in Aristotle's terms, as, "in a way, all things." Again, it has the "light of Being," the notion that includes everything in its scope, that grounds this observation. The human Spirit is the existence of the Concept as openness to the Whole; it is the place of the self-manifestation of the Cosmos. But at the level currently being considered, Spirit has attained to this concept, but not yet to its concrete filling. In this case he speaks of "only the concept," something formal, not yet the actualization of the Concept. And though in logic the Concept is the completion of the *categorial* Whole, it is not the completion of *the* Whole. The Logic has to spill over into the conceptual regions of Nature and Spirit and finally into the individuals belonging to both spheres. So the self-awareness of Spirit has to develop into the comprehension of the intelligible lines of the Whole, and the production of a human world correspondent with that Whole.

To be "subjective" or "as the Concept" involves Spirit's opening out to all things but not yet in possession of the full range of its operation. The I is the Concept entering into existence, that is, making its appearance through the I within the world of concrete existence.

And it is indifferent what is determined as Spirit's Concept and what as its Reality. If simply infinite, objective *Reason* is taken to be its Concept and Spirit's Reality is *cognitive awareness* (*Wissen*) or *Intellect*; or if

cognitive awareness is taken as its Concept, its Reality is *Reason* and the realization of awareness consists in Spirit's appropriating Reason to itself. Thus, the finitude of Spirit consists in this, that awareness does not grasp the Being in-and-for-Itself [the full development] of its Reason or equally that Reason has not brought itself to full manifestation in awareness. Reason is at the same time unconfined (*unendlich*) only insofar as it is Freedom absolved from its limits (*absolut*), thus confines itself through *presupposing* itself for its awareness, and is the eternal movement to cancel, preserve, and elevate this Immediacy, to grasp itself, and to be the cognitive awareness proper to Reason.

We can look at the situation in two ways: mature Spirit is the realization of Reason, or Reason is the realization of Spirit. Spirit remains finite, not reaching the infinitude of its Concept, when it has not yet realized that it is essentially Reason and when Reason's concrete reach has not yet been realized through the historical development of Thought.

Remember, in the case of human existence, the expression "in-and-for-itself" takes over the earlier position of "for itself" as the completion of the triad Being-in-itself, Determinate Being, and Being-for-itself. The Determinate Being of distinctive humanness is the "for itself" of awareness.

For Hegel, the Concept (*Begriff* as distinct from *Vorstellung* – one might say, the "objective" as distinct from the "subjective" concept) is that which contains the goal of a process. Thus, each living thing seeks to realize its concept, its truth as teleologially complete. But each type of living thing is the expression of the Concept of Life that reaches *its* fulfilment in the emergence of cognitive agents aimed at the manifestation of the cosmic Whole. As the Concept, Reason is in all things and is manifest through Spirit as the self-presence of Reason.

But this Meaning of the Concept of things is in its full manifestation through the development of Reason by being contained within the character of the Whole. This realization takes place in human beings. It is for this reason that Hegel calls the human I *the* Concept entering into existence, that is, the existent locus of the grasping (*Begriff*) after the Whole.

The *Zusatz* claims that Spirit's infinity is "the likeness of God, the divinity of man." The finitude of Spirit is a contradiction – like wooden iron or a square circle – and the struggle to overcome it is the stamp of the divine.

§442. The progression of Spirit is *development* insofar as its existence, *cognitive awareness* in itself, has being determined in-and-for-itself, that is, the rational, for its content and aim. Thus, the activity of translation is only the formal transition into manifestation and therein return into itself. Insofar as awareness is subject to its initial determinateness and is at first *abstract* or *formal*, it is the goal of Spirit to *produce* objective fulfilment and thus at the same time the Freedom of its cognitive awareness.

"Existence" is Essence coming out of its Ground to take its place among other existents. The stage of "Existence" for Spirit itself is its awareness of itself as Reason having designs upon the intelligibility of the Whole. Its appearance is its initial taking possession of itself formally, aware that it is Reason. This is a late development in the history of humankind. This is the "form" of Reason that has to be filled with content. Its fulfilment lies in freeing its power as Reason by following out the manifestation of the intelligible lines of the Cosmos and its own place in it as both Theoretical and Practical Reason. It does so insofar as it constructs, in an ever more adequate way, its Understanding and its Life-world out of the materials provided through Sensation.

Here one should not think of the development of the Individual connected with the *Anthropological* level, according to which the capacities and powers are treated as arising successively and externalizing themselves in Existence.

Remember that the "Anthropological" level involves the treatment of the human being insofar as Spirit ensouls, and thus is affected by, Matter. What conditions have to be met for there to emerge a reflective adult, aware of itself as essentially oriented towards the Whole in knowing and willing?

Following Condillac's philosophy, for a long time great stress had been laid on coming to understand this development as if such supposedly *natural* development could establish and *explain* the *origin* of these powers. We do not deny that the aim of this mode of inquiry is to conceive

of the *manifold* activities of Spirit according to their *unity* and to show their necessary connections. But the categories employed in this effort are generally of an impoverished sort. Above all, the governing conception is that the sensible is to be considered – and justly considered – as the first, as initiating ground. But from this point of departure the further determinations appear to arise only in an *affirmative* manner, and the *negative* element in the activity of Spirit, through which that material is spiritualized, and as sensible is cancelled, preserved, and elevated, is misconceived and overlooked. In this function, the sensible is not simply empirically first, but should continue to be the genuinely substantial ground.

Hegel is contrasting his own view with that initiated by *Étienne Bonnot de Condillac* (1715–80), who reduced knowledge to combinations of sensations. This view misses the essentially *negative* character of Spirit, its infinite otherness in relation to sensation. This otherness, as "absolute negativity," is grounded in its empty reference to the Whole via the notion of Being ("absolute universality") that allows it to abstract from the sensed individual, to leave aside individuating features, in order to grasp the type. As Aristotle noted, sensing yields the individual and actual, Intellect the universal and potential. Intellect, "in a way, all things," abstracts from the confinement of the essence of each thing to the Here-and-Now in what is given through sensation. Intellect grasps the underlying *powers* as universal orientations towards the *kinds* of objects correlative to the powers. But the sensory powers are only activated by the individual instances of the correlative types. Intellect, as other than any given other, *negates* the confinement presented in sensation to the peculiarities involved in the individual instances. At the same time, precisely as infinitely other in relation to Sensation, Spirit is free to determine itself. In this process, Sensation is not simply the starting point but the continuing ground of rising above it to the level of intelligibility.

Similarly, if the activities of the Spirit are treated only as *expressions* (*Aüsserungen*), as forces generally, perhaps with the determination of *utility*, that is, as serving one or other interest of the Intellect or of the Heart, in that case no *ultimate end* is present. Such an end can only be the Concept itself, and the activity of the Concept can only have the

Concept as its end: to sublate the form of Immediacy or Subjectivity, to attain and grasp itself, to free itself *unto itself*. In this way the so-called powers of the Spirit are to be treated in their distinction only as stages in this emancipation. And this alone should be considered the *rational* way of treating Spirit and its diverse activities.

Hegel contrasts his position with another that holds that spiritual activities are expressions of underlying forces. More recent parallels are found in *Sigmund Freud* (1856–1939), who represents conscious phenomena as disguised unconscious pressures, or in contemporary views that represent awareness as an epiphenomenon generated by the nervous system, or in *David Hume*, who views cognitive phenomena only as instruments for the achievement of desire. [Hume (1711–77) was the British Empiricist who, beginning with isolated sense data, claimed there is no necessary connection between them.] In either case, there is no final end such as Kant proposed for the Cosmos as an arena for the development of human capacities under the moral law. For Hegel the end can only be "the Concept" as the self-manifestation of the Whole in human awareness in which the conditions for intelligibility work themselves out systematically, the basic claim of his Philosophy. The chronological development of the individual human being shows the stages that have to be assimilated and transcended in reaching that end. The immediate way in which things present themselves, as sensorily given, actual individuals, and the individual subjectivism of awareness have both to be sublated into a higher mode of presentation that, through finding the grounds of the individual presentations in concrete universals (powers) and in abstract universals (types as types), measures the opinions of the individual subject.

§443. Just as Consciousness has the previous level, that of the natural Soul, for its Object (§413), so Spirit has Consciousness as its Object, or rather makes it so. That is, in so far as Consciousness is the identity of the I with its other only *in itself* [implicitly], Spirit posits this *for itself* [actually], so that now it knows this identity as this *concrete* unity. According to the determination of Reason, its productions consist in the fact that their content is what *exists in itself* as well as what according to Freedom is *its* [Spirit's] *own*. Thus, in that it is *determined* in its inception, this determinateness is two-fold, as *Being* and as *its own*. According to the former, Spirit finds in itself something that *is*; according to the latter, it posits it only as *its own*.

Consciousness objectifies the sensations present in the Soul; Spirit transforms the contents of Consciousness by grasping their deep, underlying intelligibility as identical with itself as actualized Spirit. Mere *Being* is the least category that applies first to what appears outside, but Spirit recognizes it as its own. The latter is "according to Freedom" as the former measures the opinions of the human subject.

Spirit recognizes its internal and external sensations and drives, not as a foreign imposition, but as self-posited, insofar as their appropriation and satisfaction ultimately requires choice. To be rational, choice requires the establishment of an integrated life and thus the subjugation of some drives to others. Thus, Spirit's *Being* is *its own* because it is the self-appropriated impetus to arrive at an integrated Life within the Whole. This can only take place through Objective Spirit, in the traditions, beginning with Language, that make possible the concrete possibilities for individual human development. It is only in the context of *Sittlichkeit*, the way of life of a given people, but especially in the development, through the Prussian Reform Movement, of the increasingly rational organization of ways of acting and thinking, that full human Freedom is possible.

The path of Spirit is thus:

(a) **to be *theoretical*, to have to deal with the rational as its own immediate determination and to posit it now as its own; or to free cognitive awareness from presupposition and thus from its abstraction and to render the determination subjective. Insofar as cognitive awareness is determined *in itself* [potentially] to be in-and-for-itself [fully actualized] and the determination posited as *its own*, it is *free Intellect*.**

The theoretical moment involves assimilation of content taken from without into one's own Subjectivity. It frees its content from presupposition and abstraction by working out the categories that follow from the dialectic of Being, thus integrating isolated aspects into a consistent whole. Insofar as it is *explained*, the sensorily given individual is not simply *given*, its presuppositions have been established. It is not abstractly isolated but fitted into an explanatory system.

(b) **As free Intellect it is *Will*, *Practical Spirit*, which at first is likewise formal, has a content as *only its own*, wills immediately and now**

frees the determination of its volition from its subjectivity as a one-sided form of its content.

Willing projects its content into Reality, carrying forth one's own intentions into the outer world, making them present to others in the form of words, actions, habits, transformed objects, and institutions. The "formal" quality lies in subjectivity's free choice that has to be measured according to its Rationality. Is it merely *my* choice or is it a choice adoptable by a rational agent as such?

(c) It becomes itself as *free* Spirit in which that two-fold one-sidedness is cancelled, preserved, and elevated.

A free Spirit is one that not only assimilates the rational order into itself theoretically, but also produces the rational order out of itself practically. The double one-sidedness is mere Subjectivity (or my unmeasured theoretical or practical choice) or mere Objectivity (or what-is as not yet manifest to Subjectivity). Freedom of Spirit is acting freed from arbitrariness by producing the rational. For Hegel it is also knowing freed from dependency upon isolated objects by grasping their underlying intelligibility, that is, their interrelatedness within the world of cognitive meaning.

§444. Theoretical as well as Practical Spirit are still in the sphere of *Subjective* Spirit in general. They should not be distinguished as passive and active. Subjective Spirit is generative, but its productions are formal. *Aimed at the inside*, the production of the Theoretical Spirit is only its ideal world and the attainment of abstract self-determination in itself. The Practical Spirit has admittedly to do only with self-determinations, with its own material, but at the same time with material that is still also formal and thus with limited content, for which it attains the form of Universality. *Aimed at the outside*, in so far as the Subjective Spirit is the unity of Soul and Consciousness, thus also Reality that has *Being*, a Reality simultaneously Anthropological and correspondingly appropriate to Consciousness, its products in the theoretical realm are the *word* and in the practical realm *enjoyment* (not yet deed [*Tat*] and action [*Handlung*]).

In both the theoretical and practical regions, Spirit is active, producing both its words and concepts as well as its external actions, habits, arts, and institutions. The *formality* of its products lies in both regions having the *form* of being subject-produced and thus involving the universality of principles for choice. Spirit's first theoretical products create an ideal world of abstractions and a practical world of relatively arbitrary structures. Viewed from the outside, Spirit produces the word to express its opinions and in its overt actions seems only to be gratifying itself.

Hegel is working with a certain set of abstractions, considering theoretical and practical activity within the human Subject apart from both content and the conditions in institutions that make them concretely possible. Theoretical activity depends upon traditions of inquiry as does practical activity upon traditions of practice. Both what Hegel is calling "deed" (*Tat*) as a single act and "action" (*Handlung*) as a connected series of acts are both in fact tradition-dependent.

Psychology belongs, as does Logic, to those Sciences that in recent times have still profited least from the more universal formation of Spirit and from the deeper concept of Reason, and continues to find itself in an extremely poor condition. Through the turn taken by Kantian philosophy, a greater import has admittedly been attributed to Psychology, so much so that Psychology *in its empirical condition is expected to provide* the foundation for Metaphysics. This Science is taken to consist in nothing other than that the *facts* of human *Consciousness* are to be grasped empirically and articulated, and precisely as *facts*, as they are given. With the placing of Psychology in which it is mixed with forms belonging to [the levels of] Consciousness and Anthropology, nothing has changed for its condition itself. It has thereby only reached the point that, even for Metaphysics and Philosophy generally as well as for Spirit as such, thinkers have renounced knowledge of *the Necessity* of *that which is in-and-for-itself*, the *Concept* and *Truth*.

Hegel is contrasting an empirical with a speculative standpoint. According to the former, the task of Thought is simply to describe what is given both outside and inside, laying the data out anatomically, without showing the necessary interconnectedness involved. Hume attempted the grounding of the sciences in the features of human awareness, but considered as a bundle of discrete functions. The same approach characterized post-Kantian psychology. The speculative standpoint that Hegel represents attempts to present the necessary interrelatedness of the Whole to which Spirit is oriented by its essence.

Theoretical Spirit

§445. Intellect *finds* itself *determined*. This is its level of the initially apparent (*Schein*) from which it begins in its Immediacy. But as *cognitive awareness (Wissen)* it is its role to posit as its own what is found. Its activity has to do with the empty form of *finding* Reason. Its aim is that its Concept might be *for it*; that is, its aim is to be *for itself* Reason actualized, through which it has its *content* become for it simultaneously rational in act. This activity is *cognition (Erkennen)*. Since Reason is concrete, the formality of awareness (*Wissen*) in its state of mere certitude (*Gewißheit*) elevates itself to determinate and conceptual awareness. The path of this elevation is itself rational and a necessary transition, determined by the Concept, from one determination of intelligent activity (a so-called *faculty* of the Spirit) to another. The refutation of the initially apparent (*Schein*), that is, finding the rational, which is cognition, proceeds from certitude, that is, the belief of Intellect in its capacity to be rationally aware, to the possibility of its being able to appropriate Reason which, together with the content, Intellect is in itself [potentially].

What we encounter we spontaneously understand, at least sufficiently to adjust to it and get on with our lives. We might call such understanding "dashboard knowledge," a felicitous metaphor introduced by *Owen Barfield* [1898–1997, critic, poet, and philosopher]. We learn what to turn, push, or pull to get the required output; but we need not know anything of what lies under the hood. Furthermore, as tradition-bound, our understanding often depends upon shared misunderstandings, mythical concoctions, and superstitions. This is the situation Plato described in his allegory of the Cave. It is the condition of what Heidegger described as *das Man*, the anonymous One absorbed in what They say and expect what One should do. It is the realm of what I have translated as "the initially apparent" (*Schein*) or "what shows up," the first phase of manifestation in which Reason has not yet arrived at its own self-awareness. The innate drive of Reason is to find the grounds that enable us to sort out the opinions in terms of appropriate evidence and to establish a connected view of the Whole based upon that evidence. It can then link its practices to a purified and developing Rationality. But it has to begin with the certainty that what-is corresponds to its rational activity, that it can succeed in uncovering the underlying intelligible order of things with increasing success. As it proceeds, its successes fortify its initial certitude. In developing itself Reason goes through a rational process involving clearly distinguishable levels ("faculties") that are necessarily linked to one another.

The distinction between *Intellect* and *Will* is often misunderstood in that each is taken as having an existence fixed and separate from the other, so that there could be Will without Intellect or Intellect without Will. The possibility that, as they say, abstract, Analytical *Understanding* (*Verstand*) could be developed without the *Heart* and the *Heart* without *Understanding*, that there are hearts one-sidedly without Understanding and heartless understanding, indicates in any case only this, that there are bad existents, untrue in themselves. But Philosophy should not hold such false existents and ideas as true and take what is the bad for the nature of things. A mass of other claims are made about Intellect: that it receives *impressions* from without and *takes them up*, that ideas arise through the *effects* of external things as causes, etc. Such claims belong to a view of the categories that is not the standpoint of Spirit and of proper philosophical consideration.

Will and Intellect are two sides of the highest level of human awareness, namely, Reason. Each presupposes the other as both presuppose the operations that link them with Sensation and Embodiment. Interestingly enough, Hegel here equates *Will* with *the Heart* that he elsewhere identifies as the core of individual Subjectivity. The Heart is the repository of past experience that forms the felt proclivity to behave along certain preferred lines. It is the Will as second nature. It is the locus where one appropriates content so that it becomes "mine." Will is not only the capacity for choice; through the pattern of its choices it becomes habituated, spontaneously inclined to move in certain directions. That is what is meant by the work of the "Heart": the felt disposition to move spontaneously towards that which attracts it and away from that which repels it. It is the other pole to Intellect as the capacity to rise to the level of the universally communicable that we share with others. For Hegel "true" (or, in recent Existentialist terms, "authentic") existence for the human being lies in assimilating into the depth of

Subjectivity the Truth available by Reason as the capacity for the Universal. Without attempting to invoke it, Hegel is quite aware of, and has a central place for, that centrally important "passion and inwardness" of which Kierkegaard claimed "the objective thinker" was unaware. Kierkegaard must have been thinking of someone other than Hegel: some Hegelian or some all-too-typical Hegel critic.

Hegel here contrasts and unites *Analytical Understanding* (*Verstand*) with the Heart. The former is "the power of the negative" based on Spirit's "absolute negativity," its complete otherness to all via the notion of Being. It is the capacity to abstract and isolate and thus make explicit the various kinds of distinction given in experience. It is a necessary phase in the drive of Reason (*Vernunft*) to synthesize what has been made explicit into an evidentially tested view of the Whole. But for Hegel, Reason can do that only insofar as one already *dwells* "rationally," that is, has assimilated into one's Heart ways of thinking and acting that correspond to the immanent Rationality of the Whole. In fact, having one's Heart identified with loved ones, finding one's own identity by identifying with and supporting those close to one's Heart, is for Hegel the core of the rational exemplified as the Ground of all things in the divine Trinity as the primary instance of Love as "the identity of identity and non-identity." But for human beings such identification takes place within the larger framework of the communal Life-world that may be more or less rational.

The fact is that we do receive impressions from without as effects of external things. That is why Spirit is embodied. What is crucial is that we do not receive them into a blank container. In the human case, sensibility is the sensibility *of Spirit*. And at the level of Spirit nothing is external: Spirit "overreaches" everything external through the employment of the basic universal and systematically connected categories.

One popular view concerns the *powers* and *faculties* of *Soul*, Intellect, or Spirit. *Faculty*, like *power*, is the *fixed <u>determination</u> of a content* conceived of as reflection-into-itself. *Power* [or Force, *Kraft*] (§136) is admittedly an *unrestrictedness* of form, of the inside and the outside; but its essential *restriction* entails the *indifference* of the *content* to the form (cf. ibid., note). Herein lies the irrational that this viewpoint and the consideration of Spirit as a mass of *forces* introduces into Spirit as well as into Nature. What can be *distinguished* in this activity is held as an *independent determination*. In this way Spirit is made into an ossified, mechanical *aggregate*. Thus, it makes no difference at all whether,

instead of faculties and forces, the expression *"activities"* (*Tätigkeiten*) is used. In the same manner, the *isolation* of activities makes Spirit into a mere aggregate and treats their relation as external and contingent.

The proper representation of power or force is not one of complete isolation, but entails spilling over the boundaries of whatever has the power in its exercise. One has to view a power as essentially related to its content as the nutritional power is related to the kinds of things that can nourish. A power is oriented towards *all*, the indeterminate, "infinite" number of instances in the environment of the type that correspond to the power; but it is actualized, in the case of sub-rational powers, only by individuals of the type correlative to the Power, not by types as universal. The latter is the province of Intellect.

The expression "reflection into itself" signifies a whole being separated from others, as in the case of an organism or a human subject whose "reflection into itself" out of its relation to its environment is the primary instance of this feature. In organisms there is a proto-self that is *self*-forming, *self*-sustaining, *self*-repairing, and *self*-reproducing. Such a Self sets itself over against its environment. "Reflection into itself" has a further meaning in the completion of the process that begins with an integrated bundle of potentialities and, going out into its environment to assimilate its materials, attains to full maturity. In the human case it involves the ability of the I to view everything, even its own inner determinations, as Objects and to develop into a fully rational Subject.

When Analytical Understanding sets to work reflecting upon the operations of the Spirit, it is inclined to turn the distinctions it finds into separations or independent factors whose relations are thought of as purely external and contingent. Each power is, as it were, a separately conceived entity. But, like the organs of the body, the powers of Spirit form an organic unity where each factor requires the others. Indeed, the first phase of the realized Concept is Life that requires not only the systematicity of the organism but its systematic relation both to its environment and to its genetic line. And its higher realization lies in the explicit life of the Spirit in knowing and loving, each of which require systematic relations. Further, because Spirit is oriented towards the Totality, the life of the Spirit requires the manifest systematicity of the Whole. That is the origin of Religion and Philosophy.

The section number in parentheses above (§136) refers to the first part of the *Encyclopaedia*, the Logic. The numbered sections in the Logic run from §§1–244.

The act of Intellect as theoretical Spirit has been called *cognition* (*Erkennen*), not in the sense that, *among other things*, it also cognizes and in addition also externally intuits, represents, inwardizes itself, imagines, and so forth. First of all, such a position is connected with the isolating of spiritual activities that was just criticized; but it is also further connected with the great question of recent times whether true cognition, that is, the cognition of Truth, is possible. So, since we [thinkers of today] view Truth as impossible, we have given up the attempt to achieve it. The multiple aspects, grounds, and categories with which an external reflection expands the scope of this question find their solution elsewhere. The more externally Analytical Understanding operates in this process, the more diffuse a simple object becomes for it. Here is the place of the simple concept of cognition which the generally accepted point of view on this question encounters, namely, the view which places in question the *possibility* of true cognition as such and passes off as a possibility and a matter of arbitrary choice whether to pursue cognition or abstain from it. The concept of cognition has turned out to be Intellect itself, the certitude of Reason. The actuality of Intellect *is* now cognition itself. It follows from this that it is absurd to speak of Intellect and still at the same time of the possibility or arbitrary choice of cognition. Cognition, however, is truthful insofar as it realizes it, that is, posits the Concept of that same cognition *for itself*. This formal determination has its concrete sense in the same sense in which cognition has it. The factors of its realizing agency are External Intuition, Representation, Interiorizing, etc. The activities have no other immanent sense. Their sole aim is the concept of cognition (§442). Only when they are isolated, it is imagined, on the one hand, that they are useful for something other than cognition, and, on the other hand, that they secure the satisfaction of that cognition for themselves, praising the pleasant nature of External Intuition, Interiorization, fantasizing, etc. Doubtless, as isolated, that is, as spiritless, External Intuition, fantasizing etc. can have their satisfactions. Arbitrary choice might partly achieve in Intellect what in physical nature is the basic determination, being outside itself, namely, conceiving of the factors of immanent Reason outside one another. That might also happen to Reason insofar as it is itself merely natural and unformed. However, one admits that *true satisfaction* would only be provided by an External Intuition penetrated with Analytical Understanding and Spirit, by rational representing, by productions of fantasy permeated with Reason and illustrative of Ideas, etc., that is, by External Intuition, Representation, and the like that become *cognitive*. The *Truth* ascribed to such satisfaction lies in this, that External Intuition or Representation etc. is not present as isolated but only as a factor in the Totality, that is, in cognition itself.

It is possible to gain some measure of satisfaction in the employment of the different capacities that human awareness has. One can simply look or imagine or remember. Either by arbitrary choice or because of lack of proper intellectual development, one might theoretically focus upon each capacity as if it were a separate function. But for knowing what is true, each of the capacities has to find its place in the overall functioning of the Spirit under the guidance of Reason. Each is involved in the collection and organization of evidence into a systematic view of the Whole. Considering each capacity as serving some practical need is secondary to considering practice itself within a responsible view of the Whole. A "spiritual" view is one that considers Identity-in-Difference and not simply the abstract identities of distinguishable functions.

1. External Intuition (Anschauung)

§446. (1) Spirit, which is determined *naturally* as *Soul*, which as *Consciousness* stands in relation to this determination as if to an *exterior* object, and which as Intellect *finds itself* thus determined, is this uncoordinated intermingling (*dumpfes Weben*) in itself, wherein it is *Matter-like* (*stoffartig*) to itself and possesses the entire *material* of its awareness. For the sake of the Immediacy in which it at first exists, Spirit therein is a mere *individual* and *common-subjective* Spirit. It thus appears as *Feeling (Gefühl).*

If previously (§399 ff.) *Feeling* appeared as a mode of existence of the Soul, so *finding* or Immediacy has there essentially the determination of natural being or bodiliness. But here it is to be taken only *abstractly* in the general sense of Immediacy.

In an individual, Spirit is first an unconscious activity, the ensouling of Matter, the formation of an organic body able to be affected by the outer world in the form of sensations. This being-affected is objectified when Consciousness emerges as an other to any other, even its own Body, sensations, and desires. The latter are the psychic materials that, as Reason, Spirit has to penetrate and organize in terms of its own immanent categories. The categories are the inner essence of both things and itself; they are what lies behind the curtain of sensory manifestation. In its first appearance, Spirit is Feeling, the peculiar subjective state of the Individual. As an element in Spirit's cognition, it is the element of Immediacy.

In German *Gefühl* is a generic term that covers both what originates through the external sense organs and what arises from within in the form of Feeling. "Sensation" in English carries the same connotation but is more limited than "Feeling" because the latter can cover such inner states as religious Feeling, while "Sensation" is more restricted and would be inappropriate for religious Feeling. We have rendered the German, alternatively or together, as "Feeling" and "Sensation," depending upon the context.

§447. The *formal feature* of Feeling or Sensation lies in that, while it is a *determinate* affection, this *determination* is nevertheless simple. Thus, a Feeling or a Sensation, though its content be the worthiest and truest, has the form of contingent particularity, in addition to the fact that its content can just as well be even the most impoverished and untrue.
It is a very common assumption that Spirit has the *material* of its representations in its Feeling or Sensation, but more usually in a sense opposite to what is claimed here. Over against the simplicity of Feeling, it is usually the *Judgment* as such, the distinction of Consciousness into a Subject and an Object, that is taken as the most basic. So then the determination of Feeling or Sensation is derived from an *independent* external or internal *Object*. When we arrive at the Truth of Spirit as the Idealism of Consciousness, the standpoint of Consciousness opposite to this collapses and the material of Feeling or Sensation is rather posited as already immanent in Spirit.

Truth or falsity is not found in Feeling or Sensation as such but in the content it takes on – for example, the red of a red bird – which is certified at a level beyond mere Feeling. A common position is that the judgment, the *Ur-teil* or primordial partition of Subject and Object, whereby the Subject is determined by an independent Object, is the final locus of Truth. But the Truth of Spirit for Hegel lies in the "Idealism" of Consciousness, in the view that the materials of knowledge lie within Spirit itself. Ultimately everything external is produced by the divine Spirit, as in the theistic tradition generally. And human Reason participates in divine Reason, as in Thomas Aquinas. To understand is to sublate the exteriority of things, to take them up into an interconnected rational view through an apprehension of their grounds.

As concerns the content, it is commonly assumed that *there is more in Feeling than in Thinking.* This position is held especially in relation to moral and religious feelings. The material which Spirit itself is as Feeling has also turned out here as the being of Spirit determined in-and-for itself. Thus, all rational and more precisely all spiritual content enters into Feeling. But the form of selfish Singularity that Spirit has in Feeling is the lowest and worst, in which it does not exist as free, unrestricted Universality, but rather its worth and content (*Gehalt und Inhalt*) are contingent, subjective, and particular. *Mature,* true Sensation (*Empfindung*) is the Sensation of a mature Spirit that has itself acquired Consciousness of determinate distinctions, essential relations, true determinations, and so forth. And in such a Spirit it is this material already reconfigured that enters into its Feeling, that is, attains this form. Feeling is the immediate and, as it were, the most present form in which the Subject relates itself to a given content. At first it reacts against the content with its particular self-Feeling, which can indeed be more worthy and encompassing than a one-sided standpoint of Analytical Understanding, but it can also be limited and poor. In any case, Feeling is the form of the Particular and Subjective. If a person *makes a judgment* about something, not on the basis of the nature and the concept of the thing or at least on the basis of reasonable grounds involving the Universality afforded by Analytical Understanding, but has recourse to his own *Feeling,* there is nothing else to do but to leave him alone, since he has thereby repudiated the rational community and closed himself in his isolated Subjectivity and *Particularity.*

The appeal to Feeling is understandable, since it is the mode closest to the individual cluster of proclivities to behave. Thus, when asked for one's opinion, one often says "I *feel* that X." This is the expression of the Heart. Such appeal has a certain legitimacy, but only insofar as Feeling has been properly developed by rational practice. For Hegel, as for Aristotle, that does not entail explicit rational reflection but living in accordance with those traditional practices that are themselves rational, that is, that fit the general and particular requirements of the situations in which one is regularly called upon to act. Such Feeling may be more rational than Analytical Understanding, which always operates with isolated abstractions – but it also may not be. Again, the criterion does not lie in the Feeling but in the Rationality, that is, in the appropriateness of the thought or action to the context.

Note that Hegel alternates between Feeling (*Gefühl*) and Sensation (*Empfindung*). As we noted, in English we distinguish the former as subjective and the latter as objective. Hegel considers both under the form of Immediacy: what is simply found in experience, not integrated into judgments.

§448. **(2) In the departure from this immediate mode of encountering, one factor is *Attention*. In the case of Feeling or Sensation, as in all its other features, Attention is the abstract focus of Spirit in the *same* direction, without which there is nothing for it [to work with]. Attention is active *Interiorization*, making its object *its own*, but as the still *formal* self-determination of Intelligence.**

This (2) is part of a list of three, where the third will immediately follow. One has to go back to §446 for (1). The three are: being determined in sensory Feeling, the fixing of Attention, and the unity of the two.

What is immediately present in Sensation is an encompassing, flowing stream of shapes, movements, colours, sounds, smells, bodily feelings, urges, imaginings, remembrances, and the like. Spirit begins to appropriate them into its systematic life or coherent living by isolating one object from that encompassing stream and focusing sustained attention upon it. Hegel calls this "formal." In a *formal* determination, one has located an essence without yet articulating it. And full articulation entails its concrete relations to the whole from which one has abstracted the focal object.

The term *Intelligenz* is used for the theoretical activity of Reason, for whose practical activity Hegel uses the term *Wille*.

The other factor is that attention posits against its own inwardness the determination of Feeling or Sensation as *Being*, but as *negative*, [that is,] as abstract being other than itself. In this way Intelligence determines the content of Feeling or Sensation as *being outside itself*, projects it *into Space and Time*, which are the forms wherein it immediately views things. According to Consciousness, the material is only its own object, a relative other: but by Spirit it receives rational determination as the *other of itself* (§§247, 254).

Hegel is employing the earliest categories of his Logic. "Being" is the least one can say about what one encounters immediately. But a being is always determinate (*Daseyn*) as an other to any other. In attention this being is set over against the Self as its other. The sensorily present is located in Space and Time as the first forms in which material beings present themselves. Every sensorily appearing other appears in a Here-and-Now within a Space and Time given as indeterminately exceeding and encompassing the Here-and-Now. Space and Time are not, as exceeding, derived from sensation but brought to it by Reason related to the Whole. Beyond Kant, both Space and Time as forms of intuition and the a priori categories through which our experience is sorted out belong as well to the "thing-in-itself." The interlocking set of categories presented in the Logic is the ground of both external things and the Spirit that comes to know those things.

There are two levels: the relative one of Consciousness and the final one of Spirit. As Consciousness one is a Subject related to externally given objects. As Spirit one rises above the privacy and Individuality of the I to stand at the level of the encompassing Universal in order to view things *sub specie aeternitatis*, from the perspective of eternity. The intention of the Whole includes the Subjectivity of the viewer and the Objectivity of the viewed. But it finds its practical achievement in the identity-in-difference of the self and the human other mediated by rational institutions, especially in the religious community of confession and forgiveness.

§449. (3) As this concrete unity of both factors, Intelligence is *External Intuition*. These two factors are, on the one hand, being immediately interiorized into itself in this material that is external and, on the other hand, in its interiorization into itself, being immersed in being-outside-itself.

We begin by being caught up in our sensations and desires. Through Attention one is absorbed again in what is present outside one's self, but in an active and focused manner. One can only be so absorbed insofar as one is self-directed from the distance of Intellect, not simply passively being carried by whatever sensation flows through one's consciousness. So, greater interiorization is greater exteriorization – that is, the deeper the level from which one attends to what is exterior, the deeper one is capable of penetrating what is exterior. As Hegel says elsewhere, for one who looks at the world rationally, the world looks back rationally. Kierkegaard, speaking of his own work, quotes Lichtenberg, who said, "Such books are mirrors: when an ape gawks in, no apostle gazes out."

§450. Just as essentially, Intelligence directs its attention at and against this, its own Being-outside-Itself. It awakens to itself in its Immediacy, its *interiorizing in itself* in the same Immediacy. Thus, External Intuition becomes the concretion of material with [Intelligence] itself, making it *its own* so that it no longer needs this Immediacy and no longer needs to find the content [outside itself].

In the same act whereby one fixes attention on the object, the object is "interiorized," transferred into an interior space and retained, allowing re-collection when the same object or similar objects are encountered later, but also permitting a recollection in the absence of the object.

2. *Representation* (Vorstellung)

§451. Representation as interiorization of Intuition is the mean between *Intelligence*'s finding itself immediately determined and Intelligence's attaining to its Freedom, that is, to Thought proper [*Denken*, for which see below, §465]. Representation *belongs* to Intelligence, but is still burdened with one-sided Subjectivity in that what it possesses is still, due to the Immediacy, not in itself *Being*. The path of Intelligence in the case of representations is as much to interiorize the Immediacy, to posit *itself as immediately intuitive in itself*, as it is to cancel, preserve, and elevate the Subjectivity of inwardness, to divest itself of it in itself, and *to be in itself in its own Externality*. But in so far as representing begins with External Intuition and its *found* material, this activity is still affected by this difference and its concrete productions in External Intuition are still *synthetic productions* (Synthesen), which only acquire the concrete immanence of the Concept in Thought proper.

A Representation (*Vorstellung*) is an isolated re-presentation, whether it be an individual image or an isolated universal. Intellect is free when it understands and does not merely look at what is given in re-presentation. While choice is involved in the attempt to understand, one is free to understand any given thing when one has a developed understanding of things in general. Notice the use of the term "Freedom" here, where free choice involves the freeing of our capacity to understand.

"To be in itself its own Externality" refers to the fact that what one thinks after having experienced something is now an object in mind's own Interiority. Language itself is an internal exteriority, a sensory configuration in internalized words that bears meaning only for an intellectual being because they stand in for the apprehension of universals.

Thought proper (*Denken*) involves the interpretation of what is encountered by fitting it into the categorial system. Materials are merely found at hand in the field of awareness and put together. What Hegel means here by "synthetic" is "artificial," "merely juxtaposed" as distinct from being displayed conceptually through the necessary synthesis of the factors involved. The use of the term *Synthesen* (the plural of *Synthesis*) here can be misleading, since it usually refers to what has been brought together conceptually and not merely externally, as is the case here.

(A) INTERIORIZATION (*ERINNERUNG*)

§452. Intelligence, in so far as it initially interiorizes the External Intuition, places the *content of Feeling or Sensation* in its [Intelligence's own] interior, in *its own Space* and *its own Time*. Thus, on the one hand, the content becomes (1) an *image* freed from its first Immediacy and abstract Singularity in isolation from others and taken up into the Universality of the I as such. The image no longer has the complete determination that External Intuition has and is arbitrary or contingent, on the whole isolated from the external place, time, and immediate context in which it stood.

From being an external presentation in the Time and Space and contextual relation of externally given things, the Sensation becomes an interior image located within the encompassing reality (concrete Universality) of the I. It has only a residue of its original clarity and can pop up on its own without apparent rhyme or reason or be called up within Imagination for whatever reason, shorn of its external connections.

Erinnerung is usually translated as "Memory," for which there is another term, *Gedächtnis*. We have translated the former, according to its etymology, as "Inwardization." The latter we will translate as "Memory." Hegel uses this latter term in a technically narrow sense for the retention of signs, as when we "memorize" a poem. He does not treat of Memory as one might immediately think of it: as the recognition of the past *as past*.

In terms of contemporary concerns, a computer does not have a Memory, except in a metaphorical sense. It contains the *effects* of the past in its current *non-conscious* spatial storage. Memory involves current *manifestation* and thus the *self-presence* of the one who remembers; but *as Memory* it involves the possible manifestation of the past *as past*. Aristotle makes a set of related observations. One who thinks that seeing is a matter of an inner physical mirroring of external *sensa* does not account for why, as he said, mirrors cannot see. Again, there is distinction between a picture and a portrait. The picture, like the portrait, is currently manifest, but the recognition of the subject of the portrait requires a different mental operation.

§453. (2) For itself [in actuality] the image is transitory, and in attending to it Intelligence itself furnishes this image's time and likewise its space, its when and where. But Intelligence is not only Consciousness and Determinate Being (*Daseyn*); it is, as such, Subject, the in-itself [potentiality] of its own determinations. *Interiorized* in it, the image is *preserved*, no longer existing [outside], but *unconsciously* within.

The meaning is clear: the interiorized image appears and disappears. In paying attention, Intellect determines the time and place of its appearance. But Intellect is not only the scene of awareness together with its objects; it stores the images in its own unconscious.

To grasp Intelligence as this nocturnal pit, in which a world of limitlessly many images and representations is preserved without being in Consciousness, involves (a), on the one hand, the universal demand to apprehend the Concept as concrete, when, for example, we apprehend the seed that contains *affirmatively*, in *virtual* possibility, all the *determinations* that only enter into actual *existence* in the course of the development of the tree. It is the inability to apprehend this type of universal that is concrete [or articulated] in itself while still remaining *simple* that has occasioned [the view] that particular representations are contained in special *brain-fibres* and *locations*. According to this view, the diversity of images is said in essence to have each only an individuated spatial existence. But it is only in an other, that is, in the seed of the fruit, that the seed [from which the plant grew] eventually *returns* to its simplicity once again from its existing articulations, [that is,] to the existence of Being-in-Itself [potentially]. But Intelligence is as such the free *existence* of *Being-in-Itself* interiorizing itself into itself in its development. (b) On the other hand, Intelligence is to be grasped as this *unconscious* pit, as the *existing* Universal, in which the diversity is still not posited as discrete. And in fact this *in itself* is the first form of Universality that offers itself in representing.

Here is a crucial determination of what the Concept is as in-principle developed. It is what Hegel calls "the Idea," "*the absolute unity of Concept and Objectivity*" (Logic §213) found in Life, Cognition, and Absolved Cognitive Awareness (*absolutes Wissen*), but most concretely in the mutual recognition of rationally free beings that culminates in the community of confession and forgiveness as stages in the development of Subjectivity. In Life, there is a "concrete universal," the Soul articulating, sustaining, and pervading the Body as an organized whole. In individual instances, Life begins as a set of potentialities in the seed and develops its powers through the articulation of the living organism. Aristotle claimed that, if the eye were an organism and not an organ within an organ-system, its soul would be the power of seeing (to which its nutritive power is subordinate) and its full actualization would be the act of seeing. In the Soul, the powers are not side-by-side, outside each other as in the case of the organs of the Body; hence, the expression of the activity in the organs involves an internal relation between the observable organs.

When one views all relations as external relations, one is easily tempted to consider the unconscious contents of Spirit as stored, one for one, in particular cerebral locations. But Hegel observes that Intellect is like the plant: its powers do not stand outside one another but are inner articulations of the Soul. However, whereas the plant returns to its state of potentiality in the seed that endures external to the parent plant, the contents of Spirit return to a state of potentiality *within* the Spirit's own unconscious. This potentiality can be taken up again at will and thus freely. As the Soul is the concrete universal, the one-over-many producing and gathering the organs into one self-enclosed entity, so the Spirit is the concrete universal holding the diversity of assimilated representations within itself unconsciously and capable of drawing them up consciously.

§454. (3) Such an abstractly preserved image requires an External Intuition to give it Determinate Being (*Daseyn*). Interiorization (*Erinnerung*), properly so-called, is the reference of an image to an External Intuition. That is to say, it is the *subsumption* of the immediate, individual, External Intuition under the form of Universality, under *Representation*, while preserving the same content. So Intelligence in the determinate sensation and its intuition operates internally and *recognizes this sensation as already its own*. At the same time, *though* it was at first aware of it only as an inner image, now it knows it also as something immediate for External Intuition, as something *proven* in such Intuition. The image, which was only its property (*Eigenthum*) buried in the pit of Intellect, is, through the determination of Externality, now also its possession (*Besitz*) [that is, something that can be made use of]. It is thus posited at the same time as distinguishable from External Intuition and separable from the simple night in which it is initially hidden. Intelligence is thus the power to externalize its property, no longer requiring External Intuition for its existence. This synthesis of inner image with interiorized Determinate Being is *Representation proper* in that what is internal image now has determination in it, can be *posited* for Intelligence, and have Determinate Being in Intelligence.

Determinate Being (*Daseyn*) is the category that follows the first three in the Logic: Being, Non-being, Becoming. Being makes sense only in Becoming, and Becoming makes sense only in something determinate, a being (*Sein*) that is *there* (*Da*), as something other than others in the process of becoming continually other than its past. Drawing up the stored images and relating them to a recollected external thing allows Intellect to carry on an inward process of proof. From past experience, one comes to see that something is the case, although one is not now directly intuiting the external object. Things enter the mode of Objectivity in the knowledge one has of them. They have a new determinate mode of being, a new *Determinate Being* (*Daseyn*) in the Spirit.

(B) IMAGINATION (*EINBILDUNGSKRAFT*)

§455. (1) Intelligence as engaged in this act of taking possession is *Reproductive Imagination*. It is the *emerging* of images from the I's own interior as the power now controlling them. The proximate *reference* of the images is to the immediate, external space and time which are co-contained. But it is only in the subject where it is contained that the image has its individuality in which the determinations of its content are bound together. The immediate, initially merely spatial and temporal concretion which it has as a *single thing* in External Intuition is, however, dissolved. The reproduced content, belonging to the self-identical unity of Intelligence and brought forth from out of the universal pit, has a *universal* Representation to provide the *associative relation* of images that are more abstract or more concrete representations, depending on the peculiarities of circumstances.

The space of Intellect in its conscious and unconscious phases encompasses all the images that have been internalized in it. One is reminded of Socrates's image of the Spirit as an aviary in the *Theaetetus*. One owns all the birds and has all of them in one's possession, but it is another thing to reach in and take them out. In Intellectual operations, one does so in function of the ends one seeks. Thus images, removed from their original connections outside the Spirit, are brought into relation to one another in service of those ends.

The so-called *laws for the association of ideas* have attracted much interest, especially in the blossoming of empirical Psychology contemporaneous with the decline of Philosophy. For one thing, it is not *Ideas* [properly so-called] that are associated. For another thing, these modes of relation are not *laws*, obviously because there are so *many* laws covering the same facts. Due to this, the very opposite of law occurs, namely, arbitrariness and contingency. It is purely contingent whether the associating element is something imagistic or a category of the Analytical Understanding, such as Similarity and Dissimilarity, Ground and Consequent, etc. When the Imagination is acting associatively, the succession of images and Representations is the play of a spiritless representing, where the determination of Intelligence is still formal Universality as such, but the content is given in images.

An "Idea" in Hegel's technical usage is a synthesis of subjective and objective that is found in Life, in Cognition, and in Absolved Cognitive Awareness. The "ideas" that are supposed to be associated according to laws (cf. Hume) are not Ideas but images, and have such diverse relations and are subjected to such idiosyncratic combinations that there really are no such laws. Categories too might come to be associated arbitrarily, as in a random list we might make according to no principle of ordering. But like the cognitive faculties, the categories stand in the necessary relations to one another explored in the Logic.

Image and Representation, disregarding the more exact determination of form previously mentioned, are distinguished according to content insofar as an image is a more sensible-concrete Representation. The general nature of a Representation according to its content has the character of something given and immediate, though it is indeed something belonging to Intelligence, whether the content be something imagistic or a Concept and an Idea. *Being*, Intelligence's *finding itself determined*, is still attached to Representation, and the Universality which the material receives through representing is still abstract. Representation is the middle term in the conclusion [of the syllogism involved] in the elevation of Intelligence. It is the connection of *both meanings of relation-to-self*, namely, *Being* and *Universality*, determined in Consciousness as Object and Subject. Intelligence complements what is merely *found* by supplying universal Meaning, and it complements its own, the inward, through the meaning of the being that is, however, posited by Intelligence itself. (On the distinction between Representations and thoughts proper cf. the note in Intro. [to the Encyclopaedia in the Logic], §20.)

A representation might be an image or it might be a concept or an Idea. The key is that it has the categorial mode of *Being*, which means something immediate, separate from what is necessarily connected with it. According to the Logic, the distinguishing character of a Representation lies in its isolation (§20).

Hegel implies here the function of the syllogism as what most would call a figurative term – though Hegel considers it more technically. Intelligence reaches its "conclusion" by passing through the "middle term" or mediation of Representation that connects the "premises" of external

Being and internal Universality. Hegel considers the Syllogism, like the Concept, ontologically and not simply formally or figuratively.

The abstraction that takes place in representational activity through which *universal representations* are produced (the representations as such having already the form of Universality in them) is often explained as a *coincidence* of many *similar* images, which is supposed to render the matter intelligible. In order that this *coincidence* might not be entirely *contingent* and unintelligible, a *power* of *attraction* of like images or something similar might be assumed. At the same time, this would be the negative power that still erases what remains different. This power is indeed Intelligence itself, the I that is identical with itself. Through its interiorizing it immediately bestows Universality on the images and *subsumes* the individual External Intuition under the already interiorized image (§453).

Kant establishes "the Ideal of Beauty" in the coincidence of an indeterminate number of shapes of the human body to give a kind of average shape. Some might think that any universalization of the sensible is arrived at in this way. Hegel's claim is that Intelligence is the power that negates difference in the multiplicity of images in order to apprehend the identity in the images that correlates with Intelligence.

§456. The association of representations as well is thus to be conceived as the subsumption of individual representations under a universal representation that connects them. However, in this matter Intelligence is not only the universal [encompassing] form; its inwardness is a concrete Subjectivity, determinate in itself, with its own content derived from some interest, some Concept or some Idea existing in it insofar as one can speak of such content by way of anticipation. Intelligence wields power over its own stock of images and representations. It thus (2) freely connects and subsumes this stock under the characteristic content. [(1) is §455 on *reproductive Imagination*.] Hence, in this stock it is interiorized as *determinate* in itself, informing (*einbildend*) it with its own content: it is *Creative Imagination* (*Einbildungskraft* or power of forming images), Imagination *symbolizing*, *allegorizing*, or *poetizing*. These more or less concrete individualized sets of images (*Gebilde*) are still artificially conjoined insofar as the material in which the subjective content

(*Gehalt*) gives the determinate existence of Representation arises from that which is found in External Intuition.

Hegel here distinguishes from the first function of Imagination (§455), the reproductive, a second, the creative function. Creative Imagination is the capacity to conjoin images so that they refer to what Intelligence intends rather than to that to which they naturally refer: it creates metaphors. Even though formed according to some principle, determined, for example, by a poet, there is a certain artificiality in the conjunction that is created rather than found. So to refer to someone as "a bull in a china shop" does not entail attributing to him the shape and all the behavioural features of the animal, but referring only to what, in that situation, would be a certain unintentional, clumsy destructiveness. Aristotle said that genius is the ability to see samenesses where everyone else only sees differences. That is the work of Creative Imagination.

§457. In Creative Imagination (*Phantasie*), Intelligence is so perfected as to reach an immediate Intuition of itself (*Selbstanschauung*) to the extent that the content derived from itself acquires imagistic existence. This set of images in which it immediately views itself is subjective and lacks the factor of *Being* [as something outside mere Subjectivity]. But in the unity, found in this set, of inner content and material, Intelligence has equally returned to identical relation to itself as to Immediacy *in itself* [implicitly]. Just as Intelligence understood as Reason begins by appropriating the immediate found in itself, that is, determining it as *universal* (§445; cf. note to §438), so its activity exists as Reason (§438) from that point onward where it determines as *Being* what has attained to completion as to become concrete self-Intuition, that is, from the point where it makes itself into *Being* and into being a *Thing*. Active in this determination, it is self-*externalizing*, producing *External Intuition*. It is (3) *sign-making Creative Imagination*.

What is crucial is that Reason comes through Imagination, working at the transformation of the sensory, to establish a sensible representation of itself – eventually one that abstracts from all associations except that which Reason gives itself in its conceptual activity. However, the present point of view is indifferent to two different types of sign: those in which the sensible object's Meaning is associated with what Reason intends through Imagination, as in the case of metaphor, and those in which Reason constructs signs in a purely arbitrary manner, with no connection to its thought except what Reason itself intends. This is the case with linguistic signs generally.

Creative Imagination is the centre in which the Universal and [external] Being, one's own and what is found, the inner and the outer, are made perfectly one. The previous syntheses, accomplished in External Intuition or Inwardization and the like, are unifications of the same factors. But they are artificial. It is only in Creative Imagination that Intelligence is not the indeterminate pit and the [concretely encompassing] Universal; it is Individuality, concrete Subjectivity. Its relation to itself is determined equally towards external Being and towards Universality. The sets of images of Creative Imagination are recognized everywhere as such combinations of Spirit's very own inward possession with *External Intuition*. The further determination of their content belongs to other regions of inquiry. Here Imagination's inner workshop is to be grasped only in terms of those abstract factors. As the activity of this unification, Creative Imagination is Reason, but *formal* Reason only, insofar as the *content* of Creative Imagination is as such indifferent, but Reason as such also requires the *content* to be *the Truth*.

One must still underscore in particular that when Creative Imagination makes the inner content into image and External Intuition and when this is expressed as Imagination's determining this content to be a[n external] *Being*, then the expression that Intelligence makes itself into such a *Being*, makes itself into a *Thing*, should also not seem surprising. For its is Intelligence itself and so is the determination the content has been given by Intelligence. The image produced by Creative Imagination is only subjectively intuitable. It is in *signs* that Intelligence affords the image real intuitability. In *mechanical* Memory (*Gedächtnis*) it completes this form of [external] *Being* in it.

In the creation of signs, Reason shows itself as Identity-in-Difference, synthesizing its own Universality with the Externality of the sensory carrier of meaning, and doing so in such a way as to announce the peculiar Individuality of the one expressing himself or herself through the creation and employment of signs. In expressing itself, Reason moves out of the interior space, where it views images, and takes on external being. In doing so, it enters into its own self-possession. In this corporealization of Spirit, Spirit and Body are one, an Identity-in-Difference, through the transformation of the sensory into a carrier of meaning. At the same time, the individual exercising Reason moves into a communal space of meaning constituted by previous generations as a linguistic tradition. What Hegel said earlier in relation to sociality also applies here: language is "a We that is an I and an I that is a We."

Creative Imagination, considered by itself and expressing its Subjectivity, can produce anything; whether it corresponds to anything outside itself or not is irrelevant. That is not the case with Reason, for that demands Truth in its external expressions.

§458. In this unity, proceeding from Intelligence, of *independent Representation* and an *External Intuition*, the material of the latter is at first admittedly something assumed, something immediate or given (for example, the colour of a cockade and the like). However, in this identity *Intuition* is said to be positive and representative, not of itself but of *something other*. It is an image that has received into itself an *independent* Representation of Intelligence as Soul, as *Meaning*. This Intuition is the *Sign*. A *Sign* is a kind of immediate Intuition that represents a completely different content than that which it has for itself. It is a *pyramid* in which a foreign Soul is transferred and conserved. The *Sign* is distinguished from the *Symbol*. The latter is an Intuition whose *own* determinateness, according to its own essence and concept, is more or less the content it expresses as Symbol. On the contrary, in the case of the Sign as such there is no relationship between its own content given in Intuition and the content which it signifies. By employing Intuition, Intelligence exhibits a freer choice and control in *signifying* than in symbolizing.

Hegel distinguishes a generic and a specific sense of Sign. Generically, a Sign is a sensory given that stands for a meaning furnished by Intelligence. Specifically, a Sign is distinguished from a Symbol in that the meaning the latter has apart from its signifying use is partially preserved in that use, whereas in the former, the linkage between sensory presentation and meaning is solely that provided by the Spirit, that is, by choice. A metaphor is a Symbol; a word is a Sign. Words can be used to refer to metaphors, but words in different languages can refer to the same metaphor. Both are free creations of the Spirit. Interestingly, Hegel uses a Symbol, the pyramid, to illuminate the nature of a Sign. The point of the pyramid is to contain the body of a dead king. The point of a Sign is to contain the dead meaning that has to be activated by the Soul of a live speaker, writer, or reader.

In Psychology or also in Logic, *Language* and *Sign* are usually inserted into an *appendix* without being thought through in their necessary interconnection within the systematic activity of Intelligence. The true place of the Sign is that which we have indicated. Intelligence as intuiting *generates* the forms of Time and Space, but appears to take up the sensory content and to form representations from this material for itself. From itself it now provides for its independent representations a Determinate Being (*Daseyn*), filled space and time; it *uses Intuition as its own*, cancels its immediate and peculiar content, and gives it a different content as its Meaning and Soul. This Sign-creating activity can be called *Productive* Memory (*Gedächtnis*, the at first abstract *Mnemosyne*) primarily insofar as Memory – which in common Life is often confused and used synonymously with recollective interiorizing (*Erinnerung*) and also with Representation (*Vorstellung*) and Imagination [or Image-forming Power (*Einbildungs-kraft*)] – has generally to do only with Signs.

As we noted previously, in German *Gedächtnis* and *Erinnerung* are used interchangeably for Memory. In English we would probably use "Retention" for *Erinnerung* and "Memory" for the recollection of the past as past. But we would not take the retention of Signs as Memory proper, only as one form of Memory. In German *Gedächtnis* is related to *Gedanke* or Thought as the capacity for conceptualization. Since we conceptualize in Signs, Hegel sees their retention as proper to Memory and the retention of images as proper to *Erinnerung* or the transfer of what is received from without and in the form of Sensation into the space of our interior life.

§459. Insofar as it is used in relation to a sign, Intuition as immediate is at first something given and spatial, has the essential feature of something that is cancelled, preserved, and elevated. Intelligence is its negativity. Thus, the truer form of Intuition as a sign is to be a determinate existent in *time*, to be *sound*, the filled exteriorization of a self-manifesting interiority. Such sound is a vanishing of Determinate Existence in that it is *posited* by Intelligence from its own (anthropological) naturalness and according to its further external psychical determinateness. Sound, further articulating itself for determinate representations in *Speech*, and in *Language* as its system, provides to sensations, intuitions, and representations a second Determinate Existence superior to their immediate one and, as such, one that has validity in the *realm of representing*.

The external appearance of the sign in sensory Intuition has already been cancelled as purely sensory, retained as necessary carrier of meaning, and elevated by the activity of Spirit negating the identification of the sound with its external intuitability by ensouling it with Meaning. In speech, this appearance is sound that passes away as it is uttered; but it functions to hold the outer display of psychic inwardness. The production of sound is made possible by Spirit's existing in Nature, that is, in a Body articulated to produce sound. The patterning of such sound is not only a matter of the individual Spirit expressing itself through its functioning in a bodily manner as in a cry; it is also a matter of that mode of expression having more than subjective meaning through the antecedent existence of a linguistic system. Such a system is the work of generations into which the individual is introduced and without which the individual cannot come to understand itself or the world around it. To come to possess one's self requires being introduced into a set of public meanings.

Language is treated here only according to its characteristic feature as a product of Intelligence fashioned to display its representations in an external medium. If one were to consider Language in a more concrete manner, for its *material* or lexical part, one would have to have recourse to the anthropological, more precisely to the psychic-physiological, standpoint (§401); for the *formal* or grammatical part one would anticipate the standpoint of Analytical Understanding.

In Hegel's peculiar usage, the "lexical" (from Greek *lexis*, meaning, in Plato, "mode of speaking") does not refer to what is contained in the lexicon, but is the material that will vary according to sound relations and the way in which different linguistic groups articulate the sound, depending upon their anthropological sensibilities. The syntactical, or what Husserl would call "the categorial" in the strict sense, is provided by the logical operations brought to bear upon the sensible.

On the one hand, the *elementary material* of Language has lost the notion (*Vorstellung*) of mere contingency; on the other hand, the onomatopoeic principle has shrunken to the narrow compass of sounding objects. Yet one can still hear the German language praised for its richness because of many peculiar expressions which it possesses for peculiar sounds – *Rauschen* (rushing), *Sausen* (whistling), *Knarren* (creaking), etc. – of which perhaps more than a hundred have been collected, while the mood of the moment arbitrarily creates new expressions. Such an abundance in the sensory and meaningless should not be considered as comprising the richness of a developed language. The properly elementary material itself rests not so much upon a symbolism that refers to external objects as upon an inner symbolism, namely, anthropological articulation, a *gesture*, as it were (*gleichsam*), of embodied speech-utterances (*Aüsserrungen*). Thus, some have tried to find the particular Meaning for each vowel and consonant as well as for the more abstract elements (positioning of the lips, palate, and tongue) and then for their combinations. But through such further external matters as the requirements of education, these dull unconscious beginnings become unnoticed and meaningless. This is rooted essentially in the fact that, as sensory intuitions, they are themselves reduced to signs through which their own original Meaning becomes obscured and lost.

The sensuousness of language consists in the sounds we make as determined by the positioning of the various aspects of the oral cavity. Some attempts have been made to root language in imitation of sounds in the outer world, but there are only a limited number of words that can be traced to that origin. In English we have such terms as the mooing of cows, the chirping of birds, the neighing of horses, and the like. The sounds of language have their origin within the speaker and whatever symbolic value they might have lies in their exhibiting the gestural style of the individual speaker. However, these relations are submerged in the habituality of the Sign manufactured or appropriated by Intelligence.

However, the *formal aspect* of Language is the work of Analytical Understanding that forms this material with its categories; this logical instinct
produces grammar. The study of languages that have remained primitive, which have come to be known thoroughly only in recent times, has
shown that they contain a grammar very well developed in particulars
and express distinctions lacking or blurred in the language of more
cultivated people. It appears that the language of the most highly cultivated peoples has a less perfect grammar, while the same language
at a more uncultivated stage of its people has a more perfect grammar
than in the more cultivated stage. (Cf. W. v. Humboldt, *Über den Dualis*,
I.10.11.)

Subsuming the lexical is the grammatical as a distinctive intellectual
product. Hegel refers to the surprisingly more sophisticated grammar
found in primitive people as compared with more cultivated people.
He refers to that fact about primitive grammar without explaining it or
drawing any conclusion from it.

Wilhelm von Humboldt (1767–1835) was a student of languages but
also the minister of education in Prussia and the founding father, in
1810, of the University of Berlin, now known as the Wilhelm von Humboldt University. It was as a colleague of von Humboldt's at the University of Berlin that Hegel spent the last thirteen years of his life.

As in the case of spoken language as original language, so also with
written language; however, we can only mention it here in passing. Writing is simply a further development in the *special* region of Language
that takes an external practical activity as an aid. Written language
moves onto the field of immediate spatial Intuition in which it takes up
and brings forth signs (§454). Looking more closely, *hieroglyphic writing* signifies *representations* by spatial figures, while *alphabetical writing*
signifies representations in *sounds* that are themselves already signs.
The latter thus consists of signs of signs, and in such a manner that it
dissolves the concrete signs of spoken language, the words, into their
simple elements and signifies these elements.

Hegel contrasts hieroglyphic and alphabetical writing, both of which
involve a transfer from temporal speech patterns to spatial, visible

patterns. (We might note that this reverses the direction of the reception of sensations and words that "inscribe" the temporality of what is received into the spatiality of the brain.) Just as there is a purely conventional relation between sound and Meaning in spoken language, so there is a conventional relation between sound patterns and the visual patterns that translate them. Hieroglyphics refer directly to their objects, while alphabetical writing refers indirectly through the mediation of sounds. There is a sense in which the latter is not entirely conventional, since it is based upon an analysis of the sounds of spoken language into units for which a written equivalent is invented. Vowels are formed through the ways in which the open oral cavity is shaped, while consonants "sound with" (*sonare con*) the vowels by clipping them in various ways. Writing refers to speech which refers to things.

Leibnitz has let himself be led astray by his Analytical Understanding [to think] that a complete written language formed in a hieroglyphic manner (which partially occurs also in alphabetical writing as in our signs for numbers, the planets, chemical materials, etc.) would be something quite valuable as a universal written language for the intercourse of peoples and in particular for scholars. But one might hold that it is rather the intercourse of peoples that led to the desire for alphabetical writing and its genesis. This was perhaps the case in Phoenicia and currently in Canton – cf. McCartney's _Staunton's Journey_.

Hegel does not explain *how* the intercourse of nations was the origin of alphabetical writing. Several East Asian peoples use the same hieroglyphic characters to stand for the same objects signified by different spoken words. Alphabetical writing is not, as in hieroglyphic writing, linked directly to the objects, but signifies directly the sounds and only indirectly the things signified. One could then learn to speak the language from the writing – something not possible through the use of hieroglyphs.

Gottfried Wilhelm Leibniz (1646–1716) was a polymath: philosopher, mathematician, and inventor who attempted to bring together the Moderns and the Ancients, Catholics and Protestants, East and West. One of his projects was to develop a *mathesis universalis*, a universal logical language for which hieroglyphics was the basic form. Each one could read such hieroglyphics in their own native languages.

Staunton was secretary for the 1793 British trade mission to the Chinese emperor headed by Lord McCartney and was commissioned to write an account of the expedition. Hegel might have the names switched.

At any rate, one should not think of any comprehensive hieroglyphic language that is *complete*. Sensory objects are indeed capable of functioning as permanent signs; but for the signs of Spiritual matters, the progress of thought and progressive logical development leads to a transformation of views into their inner relations and thus into their nature. This would also require a different hieroglyphic determination. It is already the case with regard to sensory objects that their signs in spoken language, their names, are frequently changed, as for example in the case of chemical and mineralogical objects.

A completely static language involved in hieroglyphics is impossible because of the broadening and deepening Understanding involved in the progress of thought for which appropriate words have to be invented. Hence, it is not entirely clear why hieroglyphic writing could not accommodate new symbols. What is clear is that a single character would have to hold place for all the spoken discourse that would pertain to its objects. One of the problems is finding hieroglyphs for non-pictureable considerations.

Since it has been forgotten what names are as such, namely, *externalities* that are *meaningless* in themselves, but which have meaning only as *signs*, and since, instead of proper names, one requires the expression of a kind of definition, which again is even often formed arbitrarily and accidentally, the denomination changes (that is, only the formation out of signs of their generic character or of other properties supposed to be characteristic) in accordance with the diverse views one has of the genus or at least of a characteristic supposed to be specific.

Proper names refer to one thing. But when one says something about any one thing, language provides signs for universal notions. The signs are the outside for which universal meanings provide the inside.

Definitions depend upon how the definer views a given genus to be defined or what property is characteristic of it, and that view can change in the course of time. This is the case, for example, in the attempts to develop a taxonomy of the animal kingdom.

Hieroglyphic literary language is suitable only for the fixed (*statarisch*) intellectual culture of the Chinese. This mode of literary language can only be the preserve of a narrow segment of a people, a segment that has exclusive possession of intellectual culture. At the same time, the formation of spoken language is correlated in the most exact manner with the habit of alphabetical writing through which alone spoken language attains the determinateness and purity of its articulation. The imperfection of the spoken Chinese language is well known. Many of its words have several completely different meanings, as many as ten and indeed even twenty, so that in speech the difference is made clear only through accent, intensity, speaking more softly or more loudly. When Europeans begin to speak Chinese before they have familiarized themselves with these absurd refinements of emphasis they fall victim to the most ludicrous misunderstandings. Here speaking stands perfectly in opposition to the *parler sans accent* which in Europe is rightly required for educated speech. Because of hieroglyphic writing, the Chinese spoken language lacks the objective determinateness attained in articulation through alphabetical writing.

Why a literary culture based on hieroglyphics has to be static is not clear. Hegel himself had just referred to Leibniz's proposal of a universal hieroglyphic language and, at the same time, to the addition of new symbols for new scientific discoveries. But, since a given hieroglyph could be the locus of an indeterminate number of other hieroglyphs that interpret it, and since a given hieroglyph has a panoply of meanings, a highly sophisticated scholarly class would be required to unpack them properly through contextualization.

Hegel links hieroglyphics and the role of accentuation in determining Meaning. In alphabetical writing, based as it is on phonology, there is a one-for-one correspondence between the sound and the words. In hieroglyphics one could have different sounds for the same words, and thus different languages could use the same symbols. That Chinese spoken language relies heavily upon intonation means that such a language does not lend itself to alphabetical representation.

It was a significant feat of Intelligence to have isolated the relatively small numbers of sounds that constitute a given language. Philosopher *Paul Weiss* [(1901–2002), founder of the Metaphysical Society of America and the *Review of Metaphysics*, of whom Mortimer Adler said that he was the wisest man in America] said that his first philosophical experience involved the recognition that *anything* which could be said could be said by the combination of a mere twenty-six units of sound. That, he said in his own emphatic way, was astonishing!

Alphabetical writing is more intelligent in-and-for-itself [potentially and actually]. In it the *word*, the characteristic and worthiest mode whereby the Intelligence externalizes its Representations, is brought to Consciousness and made an object of reflection. In Intellect's dealing with it the word is analysed. That is to say, this sign making is reduced to its few simple elements (the primary gestures of articulation [*die Urgebährden als Articulierens*]). They are the sensible aspects of speech brought to the form of Universality, which in this elementary manner at the same time attain complete determination and purity.

The vowels and consonants represented by the ABCs are the culturally formed universals isolated by the analytical work of Intelligence. Aristotle viewed them as elements (*stoikeia*) ensouled by Meaning the way the physical elements are ensouled in a living being. The former seems to be the origin of the latter conception.

Alphabetical writing thus also retains the advantage of spoken language in that, in it as in the latter, representations have proper (*eigentliche*) names. The name is the simple sign for the genuine, that is, *simple* representation that has not been dissolved into its determinations and composed out of them. Hieroglyphics does not arise from the immediate analysis of sensory signs as does alphabetical writing, but from the antecedent analysis of representations. From this one can easily understand the view that all representations can be reduced to their elements, to simple logical features. So, hieroglyphics would be formed from the conjunction of the elementary signs selected to stand for these features (as with the Chinese *Koua*, the simple stroke and the stroke broken into two parts). This fact that in hieroglyphic writing representations are signified analytically misled *Leibnitz* into preferring it to alphabetical

writing. But it is rather what contradicts the basic requirement of Language as such, the name, the requirement to have a simple immediate sign for the immediate Representation, which, as rich as its content might be in itself [implicitly], is in name simple for the Spirit.

What Hegel seems to mean is that there is not a one-for-one correspondence between a hieroglyphic character and the variety of sounds that are linked to it. What is a "proper" name is not so clear.

A Representation is like Hegel's view of the Soul: it is a single whole. Before developing itself through the articulation of an organism, the Soul is simple, with parts only implicit within it. So the Representation can be grasped as a single whole without articulation into its parts. Indeed, that is the basic characteristic Hegel assigns to the Representation. Definition goes further and fits it into an interlocking hierarchy of meanings. Hieroglyphics presupposes the isolation of features of Reality that can be represented by a single sign. Hence, it presupposes separation of those features from the multiplicity present in the environment.

This simple immediate Sign as a Being offers for itself nothing to Thought and has only the purpose of signifying the simple Representation as such and representing it sensuously. It requires the name also in order to have a simple immediate Sign which as a Being [an immediately given object] does not present itself to Thought for itself but only functions as signifying and sensibly representing the simple Representation as such. It is not only representational Intelligence that does this: tarrying by the simplicity of representations and also synthesizing these again from the more abstract aspects into which they were analysed; Thinking proper [*Speculative Thinking*] also takes up the concrete content into the form of a simple thought from the analysis in which the content has become a conjunction of the multiplicity of features. Both [representational Intelligence and Speculative Thinking] also require having signs, simple in their meaning, consisting of multiple letters or syllables and which, even if they are articulated into these, still do not constitute a conjunction of multiple representations.

The name is a single whole whose elements remain subsidiary and not focal in our attending to it. In speaking or writing, we do not attend to the audile or visual elements as such; we attend through them to the

Meaning they convey, as I attend through my glasses to the visual ambiance clarified through the lenses. Of course, just as we can make the glasses the theme of our attention, so also with the words that can then be subjected to a phonological or visual analysis.

The distinction between representational intelligence and speculative thinking is not made clear here. The former breaks things into analytical units that suggest external conjoining; the latter establishes an internal relation, like the ensouling of an organism, holding together from the inside the multiplicity of features involved in a given thing.

What we have said furnishes the basic principle for judging the value of these written languages. It then follows that in hieroglyphic writing the relations of concrete intellectual representations must necessarily be complicated and confused and it seems possible to analyse them in the most manifold and divergent ways. The proximate results of such analysis are in turn to be analysed again. Every divergence in analysis would bring about another formation of the written name, as, according to the observation made before regarding the sensory region, in recent times muriatic acid has undergone many name changes. Hieroglyphic writing requires a philosophy just as fixed (*statarisch*) as Chinese culture generally.

Again, hieroglyphics, it is claimed, cannot deal with changes in how we analyse a given representation, presumably because a single sign is capable of being interpreted in a wide variety of different ways. It is not clear how it requires a static philosophy.

It follows from what has been said that learning to read and write alphabetical script should be considered as an insufficiently appreciated, ongoing (*unendliches*) means of education insofar as it brings the Spirit, from attending to the concrete sensory, to something more formal: the sounding word and its abstract elements. It contributes essentially to creating and purifying the soil of inwardness in the Subject.

In order to learn to read alphabetical writing one has to develop the habit of abstract analysis, moving from a given spoken whole word to its phonological elements. Early Greek writing further imitated speech as a continuous flow by not separating the words and sentences. Later conventions separated words by spaces and commas and sentences by periods or question marks, making the analysis easier.

Habit once attained also later removes that characteristic of alphabetical writing whereby it appears, in the interest of seeing, as a detour by way of hearing to representations. It transforms it for us into hieroglyphic writing so that in using it we no longer need to have the mediation of sound before us in Consciousness. On the contrary, people who have a little developed habit of reading pronounce what is read out loud in order to understand it in its sounding. Apart from the fact that, in this ability to transform alphabetical writing into hieroglyphics, the capacity for abstraction attained through that first practice remains, still, hieroglyphic reading is a deaf reading and a dumb writing. Indeed, the audible or temporal and the visible or spatial each have their own basis, one of equal value to the other. With alphabetical writing, however, there is only *one* basis. The correct relation of writing to speech is that language as seen relates itself to what is heard only as its sign. Intelligence externalizes itself immediately and unconditionally through speech. The mediation of representations through the less sensible medium of sound shows itself further in its peculiar essentiality for the following transition from Representation to Thought proper, namely, Memory (*Gedächtnis*).

Learning to read alphabetical script makes us attend reflectively to the sound and its elements because it is based upon phonological analysis. We initially learn to read by sounding out. But reading eventually involves forgetting the sound and directly relating the written word to the meaning. Eventually the script turns into a new hieroglyphics in a direct relation between Sign and Object as we discount the phonological elements that function only subsidiarily in attending to the meaning they represent. We even learn to recognize whole phrases and sentences in a single Gestalt.

Speaking about "deaf reading and dumb writing" focuses upon the abstraction from sound in relation to the hieroglyph both in writing it and in reading it. Unlike the case of alphabetization, the hieroglyph is disconnected from the sound and thus can be used by different languages using different sounds. Alphabetization involves an analysis of the sounds peculiar to a given language, so, as we said, one can learn to "sound out" the word from its written presentation. But hieroglyphic writing does not afford such sounding out since its phonemes have not been articulated; hence, it is dumb writing (it does not permit sounding out) and deaf reading (since the reader cannot hear the sound units through the writing).

While speaking is the immediate expression of Spirit, writing is only mediate. (What about sign language?)

In what sense does writing have only one basis? It seems to have two: the visual pattern of the word, itself rooted in the audile patterns of the voice. But since alphabetic writing is based on phonological analysis, the single basis would seem to lie in sound.

§460. The name as synthesis of the Intuition produced by Intelligence with its Meaning is at first a *single*, transient product and the conjunction of the Representation, as something inward, with Intuition, as something outward, is itself *external*. The interiorizing of this exteriority is *Memory*.

The transience evidently refers to the spoken word that externalizes the apprehended meaning as it is simultaneously transferred into and thus preserved in the interior space of Intelligence.

(C) MEMORY (*GEDÄCHTNIS*)

§461. In relation to the Intuition of the word, Intelligence as Memory runs through the same activities of interiorizing (*des Erinnerns*) as does Representation in general in relation to the first immediate, Intuition (§451 ff.).

The activities involved are (1) attention to the sensorily given, (2) retention as initial "interiorizing," (3) recognition of Meaning, followed by (4) deeper interiorizing. How is this linked to the recognition of words? We see a colour as a feature of a thing. We identify the thing and the colour because we have learned language as a set of sounds standing for the abstract Meaning instantiated for human intelligence in the signs for "thing" and "colour."

(1) Intelligence, appropriating the synthesis (*Verknüpfung*) that is the Sign, elevates the *individual* synthesis to a *universal* enduring synthesis

in which name and Meaning are objectively linked for Intelligence itself. It makes the Intuition, which the name is at first, into a *Representation*. Hence, the content (the Meaning) and the Sign are identified and form *one* Representation. The representing is concrete in its inwardness, the content as its *Determinate Being (Daseyn)*, [the product of] the Memory that *retains* names.

In order to speak one must have first noticed the connection of name and thing and retained that. There is further activity involved in recognizing, beyond proper names, the common name that is not confined to an individual but applies to a class. This involves a capacity for abstraction. Beyond use in a given situation, signs have a general function. Memory retains the names together with their Meaning.

§462. Thus, the *name* is the *thing* as present and having validity in *the realm of Representation*. (2) The *reproductive* Memory possesses and recognizes the thing in the name, and with the thing [it possesses and recognizes] the name without Intuition and image. The name as the *Existence* of the content in the Intelligence is the *Externality* of Intelligence itself in it and the *Interiorization* of the name as the Intuition brought forth from Intelligence is at the same time an Exteriorization in which Intelligence posits itself within itself. The association of particular names lies in the Meaning of the determinations of sensing, representing, or speculatively thinking Intelligence, from which, as sensing, representing, or speculatively thinking, it runs through the series of sensing, etc. in itself.

[(1) was retentive Memory; (2) is reproductive Memory.] Memory retains names, but it also reproduces them in appropriate connections representing the facts to which they refer. Names are associated fundamentally through their linkage with a set of logically related meanings. Memory places the conjunction of names in sentences within the inward cavern in which Intelligence has developed an inwardly existent externalization of itself. One can recall the memorized sequences without attending to their Meaning or their referents. One can also recognize the Truth of the statement memorized without attending to an inward image.

In the case of the name "lion" we require neither the Intuition of such an animal nor even its image. Rather, insofar as we *understand* the name, it is the simple, imageless Representation. It is in the name that we *think speculatively.*

The *mnemonic* of the ancients has for some time now been rehashed and deservedly forgotten again. It consists in transforming names into images and thus degrading Memory again into Imagination. The place of the *power* of Memory is replaced by a tableau of a series of images permanently fixed in the Imagination. The essay to be learned by heart [*auswendig*] and the sequence of its representations is then joined to these series of images. Given the heterogeneity between the content of the representations and those permanent images and also because of the quickness in which the linkage has to happen, it cannot occur other than through shallow, silly, and completely arbitrary connections. Not only is Spirit put to the torture of bothering itself with insane material, but what is learned by heart in this manner is even for that reason quickly forgotten again. This is because the same tableau is used for learning by rote every other series of representations and thus what previously was linked to it again vanishes. What is mnemonically impressed is not, like what is retained in Memory, brought forth and so recited *by heart*, [in the sense of] authentically *from within*, from the deep cavern of the I and uttered in this manner. It is, so to speak, read off from the tableau of the Imagination.

The ancient tradition goes back to Simonides, but the first extant record of the techniques was *Rhetorica ad Herrenium,* written in the first century BC. Plato complained that writing, as an "external memory," would lead to the atrophy of memory proper. Before the invention of printing, books were rare, so that a scholar learned to memorize entire books which he might only be able to examine once. Hegel was too quick to reject these practices that have been revised and developed until incredible memory feats are displayed at national and world competitions, while the rest of us rely more and more upon our "external memories." Hegel would be astonished at the memory feats exhibited at the memory competitions: for example, memorizing the order of the cards in two decks within a limited time frame.

Mnemonic is connected with the common prejudices one has of Memory in relationship to Imagination, as though Imagination is a higher spiritual activity than Memory. Instead, Memory has no longer to do with the *image* taken from the immediate, non-spiritual determination of Intelligence, from Intuition. Rather, it has to do with an *Determinate Being (Daseyn)* that is the product of Intelligence itself – it has to do with such an *Externality [Auswendigen]* that remains enclosed within the Internality of Intelligence and inside Intelligence is only Intelligence's external [*auswendige*], existing side.

Because Memory is not directly related to the external images that initiated all our thinking processes, Hegel takes it to be superior to Imagination. Creation of signs proper is higher than creation of symbols that bear the marks of their relation to this sensory origin. Symbols have to be analysed so as to sort out what applies and what does not apply to what they symbolize. Thus, a lion as a symbol of strength, courage, and regality is not literally transferred over to Richard the Lion-Hearted, who does not run on all fours, have claws, a tail, and thick hair covering all his body. Signs, as distinct from symbols, have no such first sensory referent. In retaining signs, Intelligence establishes an Exteriority within its own Interiority, the Exteriority being the sensible character of the sign, the Interiority being supplied by Memory itself.

§463. (3) Insofar as the connection between names lies in the Meaning, the linkage of Meaning with external Being [*Sein*] as name is still something artificial. In this form of its Externality Intelligence is not simply turned back into itself. But Intelligence is the universal, the simple Truth of its particular externalizations. Intelligence's completely developed appropriation is the sublation of that distinction of Meaning and name. This highest Interiorization of representing is its highest Externalization in which [the Interiorization] posits itself as *Being* [external interiority], as the universal space of names merely as names, that is, meaning less words. At the same time, the I, which is this abstract [interiorized external] Being, is, as Subjectivity, the Power dominating the multiplicity of names, the empty *bond* that fixes in itself the series of words and holds them in stable order. Insofar as they only *are* [internally exterior] and Intelligence in itself is their Being, Intelligence is this power as the *completely abstract Subjectivity* of Memory. Memory is then called *mechanical* because of the utter Externality in which the members of such series stand to one another. Memory itself is this Externality, albeit subjective (§195).

[(1) dealt with retentive, and (2) with reproductive Memory; (3) deals with mechanical Memory.] Remember that when Hegel uses the term "Being" (*Sein*) technically, it refers to the least, most external, immediate, merely potential (*in sich*) aspect of a thing for awareness. Hegel is claiming such a Representation for inwardness as well as for empirical Externality. It is rote or mechanical Memory, an "outside," within Subjectivity itself, for its deeper Interiority, something it has not only to attend to but to penetrate conceptually, just as it must do with something sensorily given outside it.

It is commonly known that a piece is only really known by heart when one is no longer aware of the Meaning of the words. The utterance of what is thus known by heart becomes therefore of itself accentless. Bringing in the correct accent here involves the Meaning. The Meaning, the Representation that is invoked, disturbs the mechanical connection and thus simply confuses the act of reciting. The ability to be able to retain by heart a series of words whose connection is not understood or which are already meaningless in themselves (for example, a series of proper names) is thus so completely astonishing because, though Spirit is essentially Being *with itself* (*bei sich selbst*), here it is exteriorized *in itself* and it is its activity as mechanical. Spirit is only *with itself* as unity of *Subjectivity* and *Objectivity*. At first, after Spirit has been so externalized in Intuition that it *finds* determinations and through Representation interiorizes *what is found*, making it into its own, as Memory it turns itself into something external inside itself, so that what is its own appears as something found. One of the aspects of thought proper, *Objectivity*, is here posited in it as the quality of Intelligence itself. It is reasonable to conceive Memory as mechanical, as an activity of the meaningless, whereby it is justified only through its utility, perhaps its indispensability for other ends and activities of Spirit. However, in this way the proper Meaning that it has in Spirit is overlooked.

Spirit comes into possession of itself through the union of Objectivity and Subjectivity. This means that what is given "over against" (*ob* means "over against," *jectum* means "thrown") is assimilated into one's awareness as *understood*. When it operates by rote, Memory becomes like an impersonal mechanism. But that is not the only way Memory operates. Memory of the logical connections between the meanings represented by the words is guided by Understanding and thus does not fade the way in which rote memorization might.

§464. External Existence as *name* requires *something else* in order to become a Thing and have true Objectivity: the *Meaning* provided by representing Intelligence. Intelligence as mechanical Memory is at one and the same time that external Objectivity itself and its *Meaning*. It is thus *posited* as the *Existence* of this identity. It is here active *for itself* [actualized] as such identity which as Reason it is *in itself* [potentially]. In this way *Memory* is the transition to the activity of *Thought* that no longer has *Meaning*, in the sense that Subjectivity is no longer something separate from this Objectivity, just as this Inwardness is in itself [external] Being.

What is the significance of substituting "Existence" for "Being"? "Being" is a categorial set that includes itself, "*Daseyn*," and "Being-for-itself," all in the mode of External Existence (categories that apply in the first instance to the sensory surface). Being as *Daseyn* is something as distinguished from other things as well as from its previous phase of Becoming. "Existence" is being conceived of as emergent from its Ground, having a reason, and thus being not only "there" but also expressive and being mutually conditioned by other existents that have their own Grounds. "Existence" adds a certain inwardness of Essence in relation to external display. So here, Meaning as connectedness of concepts is added to the merely external "Being" of what is learned by rote.

German language even assigns *Gedächtniß* [or *Memory*], about which it is customary to speak contemptuously, the higher place of immediate kinship with *Gedanken* [or thought].

Hegel throws in this remark about the etymological affinity between Memory and Thought in German, a hint that their affinity was early recognized. The contempt may be directed at merely rote memory.

It is not accidental that youth has a better Memory than old age, and its Memory is not only exercised for the sake of utility. It has a good Memory since it does not yet act in a reflective manner, and Memory is thus exercised, deliberately or not, in order to prepare the Ground of its inwardness for pure Being, for pure Space. In this Being or Space the thing, the content that merely has Being, may prove and unfold itself without opposition to a subjective inwardness. In youth basic talent usually goes hand in hand with a good Memory.

Why would reflection hamper Memory? Memory levels everything to inner Externality, without discrimination of import, as in the case of students memorizing answers without Understanding. Hegel apparently sees this as allowing for assimilation of everything without the prejudice involved in evaluation.

The really interesting expression is "to prepare the Ground of its inwardness for pure Being, for pure Space." In his Philosophy of Nature, Space is the externalization of the notion of Being from the Logic. It is existent emptiness as the possible location for those Determinate Beings that have parts outside parts, that is, for material things. The exteriority within Spirit is the interior Space of memorization into which an indeterminate amount of content can be placed in a fashion merely juxtaposed. It is as though early memorization expanded that inward Space in preparation for the reception of Meaningful content.

Memorization requires special attention, repeating what is to be memorized several times until it is fixed in Memory. But good Memory in one really gifted automatically retains what it reads without having to repeat it. Some even have a photographic Memory. Nonetheless, by reason of special training in associating odd images with what is to be memorized, persons with only average native memory can win world competitions.

But such empirical claims do not aid in recognizing (*erkennen*) what Memory in itself is. It is that point in the doctrine of Spirit that is thus far entirely neglected and indeed the most difficult: to grasp the place and significance of Memory and its organic connection with Thought proper in the systematizing work of Intelligence. Memory as such is itself the merely external manner or the one-sided aspect of *Existence* for Thought proper. For us Memory is transition to, or in itself [potentially]

the identity of, Reason with this mode called "Existence." Such identity brings it about that Reason now exists in a subject as its activity. Thus, it is *Thought proper.*

Assimilation into Memory is the basis for the penetration of all experience by speculative thought. Thinking proper involves the retention of insight into the interconnection of the categories embedded in signs. Memory is the exteriority within the interiority of Spirit, the place of *Existence* for thought as the place where Thought appears to one whose Memory it is.

3. *Thought Proper* (Denken)

§465. Intelligence is *re-cognitive.* It *cognizes* a sensory Intuition insofar as it has already appropriated it. Further, it cognizes the Thing in the name (§462). But now for Intelligence the Thing is Intelligence's *own* Universal in a twofold sense of the term: the Universal as such and the Universal as immediate or as Being, thus as the true Universal, the encompassing unity of itself with its other or Being.

We have the fact, the name, the sensory Intuition, and the Intellectual apprehension. "The universal as such" is the Intelligence as the concrete universal encompassing in principle all being. Developed theoretical Intelligence not only understands the Object as an instance of the Universal; it also understands, as Aristotle put it, that "the intelligible in act is the Intelligence in act." Behind the empirical surface it finds itself identical with the intelligible depth of things. "Being" turns out to be the Identity of Thought with itself, announced in the beginning of the speculative tradition by Parmenides and at the beginning of the *Science of Logic* by Hegel.

Thus, Intelligence is, *for itself* and *in itself*, cognitive: *in itself* it is the *universal*; its product, *thought* (*Gedanke*), is the Thing (*Sache*), the simple identity of the subjective and the objective. It is aware that what is *Thought is* and that what *is* only *is* insofar as it is Thought (cf. §5. 21). *For itself* [actualized], the thinking of Intelligence is to have thoughts; they are its content and object.

At the level of Life and Cognition, Being-in-itself is the potentiality, while for Determinate Being Hegel substitutes Being-for-Itself as development, and Being-in-and-for-Itself is completed Actuality. Here he says *"für sich an ihr selbst"* (for itself in its self). Does he mean something different? Substituting *"ihr selbst"* for the usual *"sich"* underscores that, with Life and Cognition, there are genuine selves, self-forming, self-sustaining, self-repairing, and self-reproducing. Here the potency is for universal encompassment. Again as in Aristotle: "The Soul is, in a way, all things." By reason of its own concrete Universality, Reason is able to reach cognitive Identity with an object by Understanding it, subsuming it under the object's proper universal network.

§466. However, thinking cognition is at first still *formal*: the Universality and its Being constitute the simple Subjectivity of Intelligence. Thus, thoughts are not determinate as in-and-for-themselves and the representations interiorized for Thought are in that regard still a given content.

What is it to be "formal"? It is to operate in terms of the thought-forms involved in conception, judgment, and reasoning. What does "the Universality and its Being" mean? The coincidence of orientation towards the Whole and the singular existence of an intelligent being as required for the *form* of Thought proper. At first Thought simply receives its content in and through the names assigned to things. As developed through linkage within its proper intellectual system, the content is assimilated and cognitive identity is reached.

§467. Regarding this content, (1) formally identical *Analytical Understanding* processes the interiorized representations into species, genera, laws, and forces – that is to say, generally speaking, into categories such that the material has the Truth of its being only in these Thought-forms. (2) Thought as in itself infinite negativity is essentially *diremption* or *judgment*, which, however, no longer dissolves the concept into the previous opposition of Universality and Being, but divides it according to the characteristic interconnections of the Concept.

At first we have Individuality and Universality in thinking something *as* an instance of something universal presented through the name. But thinking about that involves articulating the concept into its parts, defining it within a classificatory hierarchy of samenesses and differences. To take an example we have used before, let's say *human being* is the representation applied to you as reader. Let's say we define it, in Aristotelian fashion, as *rational animal*, and animal as *sentient organism*, and organism as *living body*, and body as *material* substance. We thus unpack the definition of the concept of the human species as a less extensive universal class located under progressively more universal genera, distinguishing each division from the others in its line by generic differences. Such articulation is followed by dividing the subject from the predicate in the judgment as "primordial partitioning" (*Ur-teilen*), an expression of recognition of the distinction of, and fit between, subject and predicate. Such thinking is accomplished by Thought as "infinite negativity," as totally other than all others by reason of its being referred to the Whole. It has no limits in that it is referred to *all*. Being infinite negativity, it can dissolve any content upon which it focuses, abstracting, isolating, and analysing it.

(3) [Still regarding the content] thinking cancels, preserves, and elevates the formal determination and at the same time posits the Identity of what has been distinguished: thus, it is *formal Reason, inferential Understanding*. Intelligence *cognizes* when it thinks; that is to say, (a) as Analytical Understanding it *explains* (*erklärt*) the individual in terms of its universal aspects (the categories) and thus is called self-*conceptualizing*. (b) It *declares* (*erklärt*) the same individual *to be* a universal (genus, species) in the judgment; in these forms the *content* appears as given. (c) But in the *inference* it *determines* the *content* from itself in that it cancels, preserves, and elevates that distinction of form. In insight into Necessity the final Immediacy which still adheres to formal thinking has disappeared.

Concept, judgment, and inferential reasoning are three analytically distinguishable moments in intellectual activity. They are the organizing principles of traditional formal logic. Concepts articulate meanings, judgments apply them, and inferences express insight into causes that necessitate the conclusion by linking the major premise with the minor premise by reason of the middle term. The middle term is so-called because it functions as "middle man," it *mediates* between the subject and the predicate of the final judgment. The distinctions of form involved here are concepts and judgments that are assimilated into higher unity in the syllogism. In the hackneyed favourite – All men are mortal; Socrates is a man; thus, Socrates is mortal – the middle or mediating term is "man" (universal in the first premise, individual in the second as subsumed under the first). What is being expressed is that his being mortal is not contingent but is a Necessity *caused* by or grounded in the human essence of Socrates as a member of the human species.

In *logic*, thinking is how it first is *in itself* [potential], and thinking is how Reason develops in this non-contradictory element. Thinking occurs at the same time as a stage of *Consciousness* (see note in §437). Here Reason is the Truth of the opposition, as it had determined itself within Spirit itself. Thinking ever again arises in these different parts of Science, since these parts are distinguished only through the element and form of opposition. But thinking is the one and identical centre, in which the opposites return as into their Truth.

Logic, governed by the principle of non-contradiction, is the "element" in which Thinking proper develops. In Phenomenology the stage of Reason is initiated by Consciousness discovering that "it is, in a way, all things" and can come to understand what it merely confronts. At this stage Reason recognizes that what appear to be contradictions, opposites – such as Universal and Individual, Self and Other – are held together by the very nature of Spirit as Identity-in-Difference.

§468. Intelligence, which, as theoretical, appropriates the immediate determination, is now, after completely *taking possession*, in *its proper domain*. Through the final negation of Immediacy, the fact that *for Intelligence* the content is determined through Intelligence is posited in itself [potentially]. Thinking, as the free Concept, is now also free according to *content*. Intelligence is *Will* when it knows itself as determining the content that is as much its own as it is determined as merely Being.

When Intelligence discovers its own Identity with the Object through its Intellectual activity of universalizing, articulating, and inferring, it learns that it determines its content and is thus Will. What does this mean? Certainly not that whatever it chooses is true. It means that Will as perfected identifies itself with the intelligible order of things. Before that, however, it begins identified with the instinctive life of the human being who wills what it desires. When it breaks with that identity, it is able to form itself, but does so arbitrarily and faultily until it discovers its own identity with the underlying order of things. It then learns to think and act rationally.

The expression "thinking, as the free Concept" involves Hegel's peculiar usage of the term "Concept" (*Begriff*) here, which it would be useful to repeat. The *Begriff* is the "grasp" after the Whole via the all-encompassing but empty notion of Being. One who *is* the *Begriff* entering Existence – that is, the human being – discovering its disentanglement from all by its reference to the Whole, is thus free to determine itself. But such Freedom is realized in fact when it allows itself to be measured, both theoretically and practically, by the concepts/essences of things, thus freeing itself from mere arbitrariness in judgment and in action.

Practical Spirit

§469. Spirit as Will is aware of itself as determining itself within itself, giving itself its own content. This Determinate Being *for itself* or *Individuality* constitutes the side of Existence or *Reality* of the *Idea* of Spirit. As Will, Spirit enters into Actuality; as cognitive awareness (*Wissen*), it is in the Ground of the Universality of the Concept. As providing itself content, Will is *self-possessed* (*bei sich*), *free* as such. This is its characteristic concept.

Spirit can only exist explicitly in individuals that develop through their own choices. There are two regions here: the Theoretical and the Practical. Both come into Existence by human choice, but that choice is measured in both cases by the Universality of its content. However, in the case of the Practical, the essence of humanness as Freedom operates creatively and individually within a wide range consonant with the Universality that obtains within the Practical. Characteristic of the modern world is the opening up of that range through Freedom under Law. Hegel elsewhere notes that the ability to say "I" sets each individual human apart from everything and forces it to take responsibility for how it develops itself from the resources provided by its context. Not until it makes its own choices is the Will formally free. Jean-Paul Sartre's *pour soi*, as Hegel's *für sich* involving personal Freedom, has its historical origin here; but its real origin lies in the phenomena as such.

Theoretical awareness is the side of *Ideality*; practical awareness steps into *Reality* or Existence. Remember that "Existence" adds to *Daseyn* (as something contrasted with what is other) coming out of the Ground of Essence and standing in relation to what is other coming out of its Ground. The two, Ideality and Reality, join in rational action to [constitute] the truly Free Spirit.

Its finitude consists in the *formalism* of that Concept: the fact that it is being filled through itself, the merely *abstract* determination that is *its own* as such, is not identified with developed *Reason*.

The *"negative Freedom,"* spirit's being other than every other, or the "formalism" of the Will – its form – is the capacity for choice. It can be filled only through its own choice. Will is limited insofar as it is not identified with Reason and is the origin of arbitrariness. We might suggest again that it is by reason of the notion of Being – that is, the initially empty orientation towards the Whole – that we have both intellectual and volitional capacities. That means both that we can come to have Science and that we must make choices, including the choice to pursue Science. Referred to the Whole, we are each "I," inwardly free from the "parts," even those parts that belong to us as our own desires and capacities. We are thus "condemned to choose" how to relate to the parts. The identical grounding of the Theoretical and Practical calls for their ultimate identity in Free Spirit, choosing the rational.

The vocation (*Bestimmung*) of the Will *in itself* [as a potentiality] is to bring Freedom in the formal Will into Existence and thus its aim is to fill itself with its Concept, that is, to make Freedom its characteristic, its content, and aim as well as its External Existence (*Daseyn*). Only as thinking does this concept, Freedom, have being essentially.

"Existence," once again, involves coming out of its essential ground and standing in relation to others coming out of theirs, each expressing its underlying essence in its sensory surface. Through choice as the act of "formal Will" the I steps forth into the world of other selves. The Concept of anything is what it was meant to be. In Hegel this is Essence (*Wesen*): *Wesen ist was gewesen ist* – Essence is what it was; this is a variation on Aristotle's *to ti en einai*, or "to be what was," to become in Actuality what it already was in Potentiality. In Hegel that "what" is expressed by the Concept. But by reason of the identical origin of Theoretical and Practical Spirit in reference to the Whole, Practical Spirit completes itself by becoming rational, by its alignment with Thought proper. In this way *formal* or *negative Freedom* becomes *essential* or *substantial Freedom*.

The way of the Will to make itself into *Objective* Spirit is to elevate itself into thinking Will, giving itself the content which it can only have as something self-thinking. *True* Freedom lies in the way of life of a people [*Sittlichkeit*] that consists in the Will having universal content as its goal, not something subjective and egoistic. However, such content exists only in and through thinking. It is no less than absurd to want to exclude Thinking from *Sittlichkeit*, religiosity, lawfulness, and the like.

Hegel takes a significant step here. The step out of interior Subjectivity through choice is something other than an empty gesture insofar as it is linked to the prior choices of other subjectivities long dead. Such choices have come to be recognized by others as the grounds for their own identities. They are the institutions and practices that sustain us and provide the real possibilities for our choices. They are the objectifications of Subjectivity enduring beyond the deaths of those individuals who initiated, sustained, and transformed what became typical ways of thinking and acting. They are the traditions of a people, their customary ways that Hegel accordingly calls *Sittlichkeit*, usually translated as "ethical life," which literally means customariness or tradition or even community as the linkage of subjectivities throughout generations. Institutions in their togetherness constitute *Objective Spirit*, the locus of objectifications enduring beyond the subjectivities that produced them. They are Rationality in action: establishing identities in the different subjectivities. They define the content of such articulations of our belonging together within the whole as community and, within community, as institutions of Economy, Law, Religion, and the like. But in all this Hegel distinguishes between the actual practice of a community and the *Rationality* of its practice. Someone like Socrates stands as a critic of the limited Rationality of the practices of his community.

§470. Practical Spirit, as formal or immediate Will, at first contains a double *Ought*. It contains this Ought (1) in the opposition between the determination posited from itself over against the *immediate* determinateness that again enters with it, that is, its *Determinate Being* (*Daseyn*) and *condition*, which determinateness also at the same time develops in Consciousness in its relations with external objects. (2) That initial self-determination, as itself immediate, is at first not elevated into the Universality of Thinking. This Universality thus does not only constitute *in itself* [potentially] the *Ought* over against self-determination according to form, but also is able to constitute it according to content: an opposition that at first is only for us [as observers].

The double Ought is, first of all, for the Self to be self-determining in relation to its own desires and its cultural context, as well as its own past choices. But second, those determinations have to be measured by their Rationality. We might put the first point this way: every I is I only in relation to a Me that furnishes it the artist's material for whose ultimate shape it is responsible. The Me at any given moment is three-fold: there is the genetically developed Me, the culturally shaped Me, and the Me of my past choices based upon my limited understanding of what possibilities the first two determinisms afforded. Any I is not responsible for its initial genetic stamp or for its initial cultural shaping. It is responsible for the choices it has made from the possibilities afforded by that material once it was able, in its growth towards maturity, to make rational choices. But its past choices are also a form of determinism that limits its current possibilities. It cannot change its past choices, and their effects set limits to what is immediately possible. Furthermore, the choices it makes and the cultural context within which it possesses the possibilities from which it chooses might not correspond to the Universality of Thought. To repeat: the form of Will lies in *choice*; its fulfilled content only in *rational* choice.

1. Felt Proclivity (Das praktische Gefühl)

§471. At first practical Spirit has its self-determination within it in an immediate and thus *formal* manner, so that it *finds itself* as *Individuality*

determined in *its own* inner *nature*. In this way it is *felt proclivity*. Since practical Spirit is *in itself* [potentially] Subjectivity simply identical with Reason, it admittedly possesses in such Feeling the content of Reason, but as *immediately individual*, therefore *natural, arbitrary*, and *subjective*. It thus determines itself from the particularity of need, mere opinion, and the like and from Subjectivity positing itself for itself [actualizing itself] against the Universal; but it might also be measured as in itself [potentially] rational.

We become first aware of ourselves as identical with the drives that emanate from our bodily nature as well as from our early and continuing cultural shaping; they express themselves in Consciousness as Feelings. At first we are potentially rational, but far from so actually. What is given as individual nature differs from person to person, even though given as a variation on the general theme of humanness. In relation to human nature as such, Feeling is contingent and is the ground of the arbitrariness of much that we choose. That, however, is an aspect of a larger Rationality whereby the satisfaction of feelings contributes to the well-being of the organism, and individual differences, under law and felt identity with a community, contribute to the enrichment of the community.

There is often an appeal made to the *Feeling* that man has in himself for Right, Morality, and Religion, appeal to benevolent inclinations etc., to the *Heart* actually, to the Subject, insofar as in it all the various felt proclivities are united. This appeal is legitimate (1) insofar as these determinations are its *own immanent* determinations, and (2) insofar as Feeling is opposed to *Analytical Understanding*, so that it *may be* the *Totality* over against the one-sided abstractions of such Understanding. But just as much, Feeling itself may be *one-sided*, unessential, and just bad. The *rational*, which has the form of Rationality as thought, has the same content which the *good* felt tendency to behave has, but in its Universality and Necessity, in its Objectivity and Truth.

When asked about moral or religious questions, people often claim that they "feel" that such is the case. The conscience whereby we guide our actions is often experienced as a kind of feeling. *Blaise Pascal* [(1623–62), mathematician, philosopher, and a religious Jansenist – rigorous French

Catholic – writer] famously said in this regard, that "The Heart has its 'reasons' of which 'Reason' knows nothing." Aristotle claimed that one cannot understand ethics unless one is "brought up rightly" and thereby experiences proclivities to act in certain ways. "Being brought up rightly" implies that the community in which one is brought up is itself "right." Further for Aristotle, one is habitually virtuous when one feels rightly regarding good and bad.

Hegel would understand that to imply several things. Minimally, it involves acting in accordance with the communal practices that allow that community to survive. Maximally, it involves the sort of community that fosters maximum Rationality among its members, allowing for unfettered inquiry and a maximal range of individual choices compatible with the cohesion of the community and all that this implies. Abstract Understanding holds second place to the felt proclivities in the members of such community.

However, the community and the individual might be so constituted that their feelings are mal-oriented by reason of choices that are less than rational – that do not foster either individual or community development. Acting in accordance with feeling is thus not the measure. It is rather the case that feeling must itself be measured by the explicit development of rational reflection.

Because of this, on the one hand it is *foolish* to think that content and excellence are diminished in the transition from Feeling to Right and Duty. It is this transition alone that brings Feeling to its Truth. It is equally foolish to hold that Intelligence is superfluous and indeed harmful to Feeling, Heart, and Will. The Truth and, what is the same thing, the realized Rationality of the Heart and Will can occur only in the *Universality* of Intelligence, not in the Singularity of Feeling as such. If the feelings are of the true sort, they are so through their determination, that is, through their content, which is true only insofar as it is in itself [potentially] universal, that is, has thinking Spirit as its source. The difficulty for Analytical Understanding consists in freeing itself from the division which it has arbitrarily introduced between the powers of the Soul – Feeling and the Thinking Spirit – and arriving at the notion that in the human being there is only *one* Reason, in Feeling, Willing, and Thought.

"Right" and "duty" are, for Hegel, correlative representations. What is a right for one involves a duty for others. Parents' right to order their children involves the correlative duty to obey, as the child's right to life involves the parents' duty to sustain it. Rights and duties involve articulations of reflection met initially by Subjectivity "from the outside" and thus appearing "imposed." When an individual's spontaneous proclivities stand opposed to what is taken as right and duty, Subjectivity, insofar as it still operates out of an identity with its spontaneous inclinations, feels violated. But, as Kant noted, it is precisely the imposition of duties that awakens the animal-like child to its ability to act against inclinations and thus to begin to be in a position to shape its own spontaneities rather than being their slave. In this sense, duty awakens the child to distinctively human Freedom. And that Freedom is fulfilled in a progressively "rational" shaping.

The distinctions involved are not arbitrary, and when we analyse we are right to make them. But what is arbitrary is to turn analytical abstractions into separations. Now there is even a certain justification for doing so when Feeling resists Rationality or one-sided abstraction opposes the wholeness of Feeling in those rightly brought up. However, this occurs *within* the unitary structure of the human being, whose overarching principle is Rationality. Bodily functions are rational insofar as they produce the health of the organism. Indeed, organic functioning is both the model of Rationality as overall coherence in operation and the initial Ground of explicit Reason in the realm of Nature. And the felt proclivities that arise out of Nature and are shaped by culture are themselves implicitly rational insofar as they serve the overall coherent functioning of individuals in community. Explicit Rationality involves articulating the standards for improving the overall Rationality of communal organization working in tandem with scientific inquiry into the true underlying order of things. There is thus *one* Reason in the human Totality. As in Aristotle, Reason here is the telos of embryogenesis and of the developmental psychology of the individual, but Rationality is fully itself only for the political animal, one who participates in the inclusive community.

Connected with this is the difficulty that notions that belong properly to thinking Spirit – God, Right, and *Sittlichkeit* – can also be *felt*. However, Feeling is nothing but the form of the immediate, peculiar Singularity of the Subject, in which the content of Ideas can be posited just as any other objective content to which Consciousness also ascribes Objectivity.

The list – Feeling, Heart, and Will – calls for distinctions. Will is the basic capacity for choice, while Heart is the ground of its immediate proclivity, and Feeling is the felt instance of such proclivity. But they are all facets of one Reason.

On the other hand, it is *suspicious*, and very much more than suspicious, when one clings to Feeling and the Heart against the thoughtful Rationality of Right, Duty, and Law, since what the former contains *more* than the latter is only peculiar Subjectivity, vain and arbitrary. For the same reason, in the scientific treatment of Feelings it is inept to consider anything more than their *form* and to treat their content, since, as thought about, this content constitutes the self-determinations of Spirit in their Universality and Necessity (rights and duties). If we were to focus upon such felt proclivities just as inclinations, there would remain only the egoistic, bad, and evil ones, for only they belong to the Singularity that holds firm against the Universal. Their content is the opposite over against the content of Rights and Duties; however, precisely in this way they obtain their more exact determination only in this opposition to Rights and Duties.

Hegel distinguishes between Feeling considered abstractly as Feeling and Feeling considered concretely as penetrated by the higher faculties. Abstracted from the Universality that arises from the development of the higher faculties, Feeling is what belongs to the individual as individual. Insofar as this is the case, the individual set apart from the Universal is, for Hegel, evil. Indeed, for him evil is precisely the choice of the individual and arbitrary over against the Universal and Necessary. It is important to qualify that: the exercise of rational Freedom allows for a wide range of individual choices within the framework of Rationality – not simply choosing what to eat or what to wear or where to go or with whom to associate, but engaging in higher creative activity like technological invention, creative entrepreneurship, scientific exploration, and artistic creativity. In any case, authentic existence for Hegel is existence unified through the assimilation of the rational into one's Heart, into the centre of one's Subjectivity. And Religion itself is the rising of the Heart out of the everyday to the Eternal and Encompassing that calls for Conceptual comprehension.

§472. A felt proclivity contains the *Ought*, i.e., its self-determination as being *in itself* [potential] *related* to its *existing* (*seyende*) Singularity that

would validly exist only in being appropriate to that self-determination. Since in this Immediacy both still lack objective determination, this relation of *need* to Determinate Being (*Daseyn*) is the entirely subjective and superficial *feeling* of *that which is pleasant* or *unpleasant*.

We find ourselves as individuals with certain needs that can be properly realized as distinctively *human* needs only in relation to free choice. "Objective determination" would involve rational choice in fulfilling needs which would only be otherwise governed by pleasure and pain.

Such Feelings as pleasure, joy, pain, and the like, and shame, regret, contentment, and the like are partly only modifications of formal felt proclivity as such, but they are partly distinguished through their content, which constitutes the determinateness of the Ought.

Particular states of Feeling are distinguished as felt proclivities through their respective objects that determine towards what kinds of fulfilment they are respectively oriented. Pleasure and pain are clearly distinguished from shame or regret in that the latter involve, not immediate appetitive reactions, but a recognition of standards of judgment. Joy is distinguished from pleasure in its association with a higher state of mind and in its serendipitous character – one can pursue pleasure but not joy. Contentment could involve accepting one's lot, but also not aspiring further than one has reached in life.

From this standpoint of the formally practical there arises *the famous question about the origin of evil* in the world, at least insofar as by "evil" one first understands only the disagreeable and the *painful*. Evil is nothing other than the fact that *Being* does not measure up to the *Ought*. This "Ought" has many meanings; and, since the arbitrary aims also have the form of the Ought, infinitely many meanings.

Note the restriction of evil at this level to suffering that follows from the frustration of desire. Natural desires clearly are such that they *ought* to be realized in order to complete or sustain the nature. It is more difficult to see how mere whims contain an *Ought*, but also why – as Hegel will claim immediately – their fulfilment is actually evil.

In view of these arbitrary aims, evil is only the right that is brought to bear upon the vanity and nothingness of their delusion. They are themselves already evil. The finitude of Life and Spirit falls under their *judgment* in which at the same time they have in themselves their opposite separated from them as their negative. Thus, they exist as the contradiction that is called "evil." In the dead there is no evil or pain, since in inorganic nature the Concept does not appear over against its *Determinate Being (Daseyn)* and does not at the same time remain its subject in that distinction.

The finitude of Life and its fulfilment expressed in pleasure lie in the necessary relation to death and suffering; the finitude of Spirit is its not rising to the level of the Encompassing. The Concept being against its *Determinate Being (Daseyn)* refers to innate potencies not actualized. But evil lies in being opposed in actualization to the good that lies here in the proper fulfilment of organic drives. The Concept further refers to the species, as the concrete universal, continuing after the death of the individual through the individual's own reproductive activity. The Concept remaining in distinction refers first of all to Soul as the individual concrete universal over against the particularity of its organs and its function. It refers secondly to awareness, whether animal or human, that is other than its simple being-there.

In Life already and still more in Spirit this immanent distinction obtains, and with it there enters an *Ought*. And this negativity, Subjectivity, I, Freedom are the principles of evil and pain. Jacob *Böhme* has conceived *I-ness* as *pain* and torment and as the *Source* of Nature and Spirit.

As we have said many times, at the level of explicit Spirit, what makes an I an I is its reference, via the notion of Being, to the Whole. This makes it other than any finite other, a negativity involved in the ability to abstract from everything, a "universal negativity." It is this reference through which we are "condemned to Freedom" (Sartre), forced to make choices. For *Augustine* [(354–430), bishop of Hippo in Africa and the leading Western theologian who assimilated Neoplatonism to Christianity] this creates "the restless Heart." For Martin Heidegger [associated with the Existentialists, he focused on "authentic" relations to Being and Time], reference to Being, which refers us to the Totality, produces a fundamental anxiety, one's being aware, at least implicitly, of the inability of anything finite to fill it completely. The distinction of the principle of Life at all levels from its embodied articulation is the foundation of all forms of suffering and death.

In his *Lectures on the History of Philosophy*, Hegel devoted almost as much space to *Jacob Böhme* as he did to Descartes and Spinoza, an emphasis that has not been repeated in subsequent histories of philosophy. Böhme (1575–1624) is noted as a mystic but also as the *Philosophus Teutonicus* who gave a peculiar stamp to German Philosophy. Hegel found him a marvellous speculative thinker, but one stuck in images – much like Scripture – and thus lacking in proper method for comprehension, which Hegel claims to provide.

2. Drives (Triebe) and Choice

§473. The practical *Ought* is a *real* judgment.

Remember that for Hegel judgment is literally *Ur-teil* or "primordial partition," separating subject and predicate. As distinct from a judgment that *we* make, in consciously living things there is a natural separation of appetite from its objects that initiates the drive to union with them. Appetite is for Hegel a "contradiction," the existence of nonbeing or lack within a being that, like any contradiction, demands its overcoming.

The *immediate*, merely *given* appropriateness for need of a determination that *merely is* is a negation for the *self*-determination of the Will and inappropriate for that self-determination.

Natural appetite is directed towards certain features found in the environment. Merely acting on its impulse is the negation of the self-determination of Will that can and should choose whether and how to satisfy the impulse in relation to the possible unity of the life goals of a person and the well-being of others.

In order that the Will, that is, the [potential] unity *in itself* of Universality and determination, may satisfy itself, i.e., be *for itself* [actual], the *appropriateness* of its inner determination and Determinate Being (*Daseyn*) *should* be posited by the Will.

The Universality involved here is the concrete Universality of the I's all-encompassing reference to the Whole. The "inner determination" is *self*-determination that is not carried by appetite but governs it and gives it a chosen shape. However, choice can itself be afflicted with arbitrariness unless it instantiates universal principles that encompass others. Hegel sees marriage as an instance wherein natural drive is united with a vow according to the stipulations of a tradition and in a ceremony before the public. Will has to create external forms commensurate with it, forms that it itself has chosen according to rational principles.

According to the form of its content, the Will is at first still *natural* Will, immediately identical with its prior determination, with *drive* (*Triebe*) and *inclination* (*Neigung*).

The first form in which the Will finds itself – that is, in which the I thinks of itself – is in a state in which it is one with its appetites. This is the state of the child governed completely by its appetites insofar as it is not constrained and directed by its caregivers. It is not clear what distinction there is between drives and inclinations. The former seem more insistent, the latter less: being *driven* to something is stronger than merely being *inclined* to it.

Insofar as the Totality of practical Spirit throws itself into one individual determination among *many limited* determinations posited with opposition as such, it is *passion*.

In traditional ethical thought passion is considered something negative, something that takes over one's freedom. But for Hegel, passion is Spirit insofar as it is completely absorbed in one project. As he will shortly observe, nothing great is achieved without passion.

§474. As their content, the inclinations (*Neigungen*) and passions have the same determinations as the felt proclivities.

What is the distinction between felt proclivities (*die praktischen Gefühlen*), drives (*Trieben*), and inclinations (*Neigungen*)? The first, which Hegel treated first, seems to encompass all felt proclivities, those given by nature and those developed through culture and choice. My suggestion is to consider drives as well as inclinations as the result of choice; the former are more insistent than the latter. Passion is a felt proclivity following choice that absorbs one totally.

In the *Zusatz* Hegel distinguishes appetites (*Begierden*) and drives (*Trieben*). The former are oriented towards singular and immediate gratification; the latter, rooted in the choices we make, encompass all the acts that follow from the drive. This follows from the universal orientation of the Will as the practical side of Reason: we choose according to a principle. But if that principle is not rational, we are governed by our drives and not completely free.

On the one hand, they have at the same time the rational nature of Spirit as their basis; on the other hand, they are affected by arbitrariness in so far as they still belong to the subjective individual Will. They appear to behave as particulars external both to the individual and to one another. Hence, they appear to behave according to unfree Necessity.

The reason why there are such feelings is to serve as the basis for Spirit's practical activities. They are Spirit in the mode of being-outside-itself in order to be with-itself. As in Aristotle, Spirit lays down its tracks in an organic body in order to allow for the sensations and desires to emerge as the materials for rational shaping. Such materials are subject to the necessities of Nature but open to co-determination by human choice. The sedimented history of such choices shapes the felt proclivities of those born into a given culture.

It belongs to the basic character of *passion* that it is confined to one *particular* determination of the Will in which the entire Subjectivity of the individual buries itself, the import of that determination otherwise being what it may. Because of this formality, however, passion is neither good nor evil. This form only expresses the fact that a subject has placed the entire living interest of its Spirit, talent, character, and enjoyment in one content. Nothing great was accomplished nor can be accomplished without passion. It is only a dead, indeed too often hypocritical morality that inveighs against the form of passion as such.

Passion may be good or evil, depending upon its content; but it is a prerequisite of greatness. Hegel resists the Stoic denigration of the passions (though there may be equivocation on the term). His own work is the result of his passionate commitment to the pursuit of speculative Truth. He is scarcely lacking in that passion and inwardness Kierkegaard thought Hegel – or at least "the objective thinker" – lacked. Hegel not only *had* it; he was also able to describe and *locate* it within the Totality of human experience.

But one might immediately raise this question concerning inclinations: which are *good* and which *bad*, and similarly to what extent the good remains good? Further, since they are particulars in relation to one another, and since there are many of them, given the fact that, after all, they exist in *one* subject, and according to experience can hardly all be satisfied, what is the minimum restriction of each in relation to the others?

The human being is not like animal being in that human natural inclinations do not operate safely independent of human choice. By reason of our orientation to the Whole, natural drives are not coordinated as they are in the animal but are themselves open to being shaped by choice. Ontological openness blows the lid off the smooth operation of natural drives. To these are added cultural proclivities following from human choice that shapes and orders the natural drives. Each can be given more value than it has in the overall order of things human and can seriously skew human behaviour.

First of all, there is the same case of the relation between these many drives and inclinations as between the powers of the Soul of which theoretical Spirit is supposed to be the gathering – a gathering that now is

further increased with the *mass* of drives. The *formal* Rationality of drive (*des Triebes*) and inclination (*der Neigung*) consists only in their universal impulse (*Triebe*) not to be subjective but to sublate Subjectivity through the action of the subject itself – that is, to be realized.

Just as Theoretical Reason gathers together Sensing, Interiorization, Memory, and Thought, so Practical Reason has to gather together multiple Felt Proclivities. "Being subjective" here only means existing within the subject as its desire. Subjectivity in this sense is sublated through the action that secures the object of appetite.

If one only reflects upon them *externally*, presupposing *independent* natural determinations and *immediate* drives without their unitary principle and final goal, their true Rationality cannot present itself.

"External reflection" is that of Analytical Understanding, which treats every joining of plurality mechanically, that is to say, as a matter of external conjoining. It thus misses what is essential to Life, namely, the generation and integration from within of the plurality of living parts. The same is true, a fortiori, in reflection upon Spirit.

But it is the immanent reflection of Spirit itself to proceed beyond the *particularity* of drives and their natural *Immediacy* and give Rationality and Objectivity to their content wherein they exist as *necessary* relationships, as *Rights* and *Duties*. It is then this objectivizing that demonstrates both their import and their modes of mutual relation as well as, actually, their Truth.

There are two fundamental modes of objectivation. One involves the movement from Subjectivity as inwardness – whether of a natural power or of a conscious desire or deliberate choice – to outer Reality through action. The other involves the correspondence of such objectivation to Rationality as such. In the human case, rational objectivation involves the inclusion of others as equal subjects in considering the principles for choice. This is the origin of rights and duties rendered concrete through the formations that arise through tradition. And such formations, in turn, are to be judged in terms of how they fulfil or fail to fulfil the essential possibilities of human existence for inquiry and choice. Such fulfilment is authentic humanness.

As *Plato* indicated, only in the *objective* form of Justice, namely, in the construction of the *State* as Ethical (*sittlichen*) Life, could *Justice* in the true sense be shown in and for itself [as fully realized]. He indicated this also insofar as he understood the entire nature of Spirit under the *Right of Spirit*.

The fundamental right of the Spirit is to advance to those institutional forms wherein it can be most fully realized: in the rational State, an encompassing mode of Life in which individual rational subjectivities can find their due places through the linkage of generations. This, as we have said, is the realm of "Objective Spirit" or the locus of those forms of Life originating in individual subjectivities but passed on to future generations after the death of their originators. They endure in Objectivity, even though the subjectivities that produced, mediated, sustained, and altered them have long since passed away. States are constructed through a centuries-long process. It is only through them that subjectivities can more fully realize their immanent potentialities.

Thus, the question what the *good*, rational inclinations and their rank-ordering might be transforms itself into the description of which relations Spirit produces in so far as it develops as *Objective* Spirit, a development in which the *content* of self-determination sheds its contingency or arbitrariness. The treatment of drives, inclinations, and passions according to their true import is thus essentially the *doctrine* of legal, moral, and ethical (*sittlichen*) duties.

The institutions that allow a community to hold together over the centuries give concrete focus to the multiple possibilities lying in what today we would call the human gene pool. What my concrete possibilities are depends upon the community in which I have been brought up and continue to function. They allow me not only to make choices but, through anticipating the regular behaviour of others, to realize them over extended periods of time. The three adjectives legal, moral, and *sittlich* correspond to the three phases of Objective Spirit treated in the second major part of the Philosophy of Spirit: the abstract exteriority of right in the laws governing property, the interiority of Conscience as the core of Morality, and the union of the two in *Sittlichkeit* or "customariness," that is, in the forms of life characteristic of a given community. The basic structures of such life are the life of the Family, Civil Society, and State. (See my summary of this in the section following the Psychology.)

§475. The *Subject* is the *activity* realizing the satisfaction of drives; it is the activity of formal Rationality, that is to say, of the translation of content out of Subjectivity, which in this regard *is* intention (*Zweck*), into Objectivity in which the Subject fuses itself with itself.

Note the identification of the rational Subject with its activity. The human being is the kind of being that forms itself through choice. Becoming one with itself involves being in actuality (for itself) what it was in potentiality (in itself). One has to view this both in terms of individuals and, especially, in terms of the human essence itself, which develops only in relation to the accumulated result of the labour of many hundreds of generations. The possibility of rational human existence increases over time in a properly developing State.

Insofar as the content of the drive is distinguished as a thing from its activity, the fact that a thing which has come to be contains the moment of subjective Individuality and its activity – this fact is called *interest*. Thus, nothing comes to be without interest.

An action (*Handlung*) is an intention of the Subject and it is also the Subject's activity (*Tätigkeit*) that carries out the intention. There is action at all only through the fact that the Subject is engaged through its interest, [even] in the most unselfish action. On the one hand, the drives and passions are contrasted with the stale fantasy of a natural happiness through which needs are supposed to find their satisfaction without the activity of the Subject, as that activity to bring about the suitability of immediate existence and its inner determinations. On the other hand, the drives and passions are contrasted quite absolutely with Duty for the sake of Duty, that is to say, with Morality. But drive and passion are

nothing else than the Life of the Subject, according to which it itself exists in its intention and its execution.

Drives and passions have been viewed as the source of evil since duty involves not always acting them out and thus resisting them. One might fantasize about a passion-free existence, perhaps as an original state, with desire the result of a primordial fall. *John Cassian* (360–433), the father of Western monasticism, attempted to develop "spiritual exercises" for the extirpation of sexual desire. By contrast, Hegel sees drives and passions as essential to human existence, precisely part of the material that has to be integrated into a fully rational existence. Such drives are rational in their essence because they fulfil a function within the Totality: they sustain an organism, allow for the propagation of the species, and contribute to an ecosystem. Drives are irrational only in the human case, and in our case *only* insofar as they are not integrated within a rational way of Life. Hegel views monasticism, following from Cassian and others, as a kind of abdication from life.

The distinction between action (*Handlung*) and activity (*Tätigkeit*) is that between the full action that involves the conjoining of intention and the external activity that follows from it. External activity here could be considered apart from the intention which informs it, as Hegel does at the level of Objective Spirit, treating the Right to Property abstractly at the beginning of his *Philosophy of Right*.

What is ethical (*sittlich*) concerns the content that as such is the Universal, something inactive that is rendered active through the Subject. Interest consists in the content's being immanent in the Subject. As laying claim to the entire active Subjectivity, it is passion. The Rationality involved in *Sittlichkeit* gives content to Subjectivity, but only insofar as Subjectivity actualizes that Rationality through its own free choice. It must take an interest and might even rise to passionate dedication.

§476. The Will as thinking and free in itself [potentially] distinguishes itself from the *particularity* of drives, and places itself over their manifold content as the simple Subjectivity of thinking; thus, it is *reflective* Will.

Reflective Will is a stage above its initial identity with its natural impulses. The I reflects back from being immersed in its appetites and is able to shape them according to its choices, to determine if, when, and how to indulge them. This is a stage on the way to essentially free Will that not only is able to choose and act, but also has its choices informed by Rationality, having freed itself, from the dominance of impulse and opinion, unto its Rationality.

§477. In this way such particularity of drive is no longer immediate but only belongs to the reflective Will in that it [Will] unites itself with that particularity and in this way gives itself determinate Individuality and Actuality. It is in the position of *electing* [*zu wählen*] among inclinations and is *choice* [*Willkür*].

"Immediacy" is sheer givenness, the being-there of drive without the mediation of Will. Reflective Will, stepping back, must choose which among its inclinations it will actualize and thus give it the stamp of its own selfhood. *Willkür* here is what Hegel elsewhere calls "formal or negative freedom."

§478. Will as choice is free *for itself* [self-actualizing] in that it is reflected into itself as the negation of its merely immediate self-determining.

"Merely immediate self-determining" refers to the situation where one can "do what I damned well please." Will that is developing as rationally free Will denies that Immediacy and measures its choices by Rationality.

Still, in so far as the content in which this formal Universality *resolves* (*beschliesst*) itself into Actuality is still nothing other than the content of drives and inclinations, it is actual only as *subjective* and *arbitrary* Will.

One chooses among drives rather than acting out every impulse. One thus includes the chosen within the encompassing concrete Universality of the I as its way of being in the world. But the question at this point is the nature of the principle of selection. Insofar as one has not yet found measure outside of inclination and choice, one acts arbitrarily.

This Will is the contradiction that is involved in realizing itself in a particularity which is at the same time a nullity for it, and in having a satisfaction in it, from which it has at the same time emerged. As such, it is at first the process of dispersal and sublation of an inclination or enjoyment through another and of the satisfaction which is equally not this [satisfaction] through another, and that to infinity. But the Truth of *particular* satisfactions is the *universal* Truth that the Thinking Will makes its intention as *Happiness*.

Being projected towards the Whole and yet condemned to choose particular goals, Will is always beyond any particular which is empty by itself. Desire satisfied arises again or leads one to other desires that are subjected to the same fate: Socrates's "leaky vessel" that requires constant refilling.

"Truth" here, once again, means not factuality but teleological completion, as in the expression "a true man." "Universality" here, once again, does not refer to an abstract principle but to an encompassing whole or concrete universal. The Universality sought in all choices is the unification of all legitimate satisfactions as the realization of happiness.

3. Happiness

§479. In this representation, produced by reflective thinking, of a universal satisfaction, the drives are posited as *negative* in function of their particularity. In part they should be sacrificed one to another, in part sacrificed completely or partially for the benefit of Happiness as the goal. On the one hand, their mutual limitation is a mixture of qualitative and quantitative determination. On the other hand, since happiness has *affirmative* content only in the drives, the decision lies in them and it is subjective Feeling and preference which must determine whereof Happiness consists.

Drives are both negative and positive. They are negative because they cannot fill the whole scope of the Spirit's native orientation. They are positive in that it is the individual with its own drives who has to be satisfied. The task is to learn to cut and trim them in order to make a unified whole. Each person's decision in this regard depends upon the peculiar constellation of drives and how he or she comes to view their integration.

§480. Happiness is the merely representational, abstract *Universality* of content that is only *meant* to be. But the *particular* determination, that so much *is* as it is *preserved, cancelled, and elevated*, and the *abstract Singularity*, that is to say, choice that gives itself an end in Happiness so much as not, both find their Truth in the *universal* determination of the Will in itself, that is, in its very self-determination, *Freedom*. In this manner, choice is the Will only as pure Subjectivity, which is at the same time pure and concrete through the fact that it has as its content and aim only that infinite determination which is Freedom itself. In the Truth of its self-determination, wherein Concept and Object are identical, the Will is *actually Free Will*.

Natural Will becomes reflective Will through choosing among inclinations. Reflective Will becomes actually Free Will through choosing rationally. Its abstract aim is happiness that has to become concretized in particular choices that satisfy particular inclinations. Abstract Universality (happiness) joins abstract Singularity (choice) through particular determinations (realization of aims) that form the actual concrete singular person. The particular determinations are assimilated into the comprehensive human project by an *Aufhebung*, which negates their Immediacy, preserves their content, and elevates them to compatibility with others. But the truly Free Will is one where the principles of choice are themselves universal by including all human beings as autonomous subjects.

Free Spirit

§481. The actual Free Will is the unity of Theoretical and Practical Spirit.

Will is correlative to Intelligence: it is, indeed, Reason developing into Actuality. Both facets together are rooted in our founding reference to the Totality via the all-encompassing notion of Being. Theoretical Spirit is free when it is able to follow the actual facts and laws and principles of Nature and History and not remain locked in its own arbitrary opinions. Practical Spirit is free when it follows from an Understanding of the character of the Whole and organizes its Life so as to correspond to it. This involves its participation in a rational community whose basic principles are articulated in Hegel's treatment of Objective Spirit worked out in his *Philosophy of Right* (1821).

Free will exists *as free will for itself* [actualized], in that the formalism, contingency, and finitude of the practical content up to this point have come to be preserved, cancelled, and elevated.

The "formalism" consists in the factual form of choice and thus responsibility without consideration of content. The contingency lies in the arbitrary character of what is chosen. The practical content is finite in that it has not yet been developed to correspond to the complete orientation of the human Spirit. It becomes "infinite," no longer limited to arbitrariness, when it has become theoretically and practically rational. All these factors are taken up and receive their proper shape through being included in the fully rational project. But remember that the rationality of choices establishes a wide range for individual choices and a variety of types of choices.

By sublating the mediation that was contained in that content, the actual Free Will is the *Individuality immediately* posited through itself, but purified so as to reach to its *Universality*, Freedom itself.

The mediation consists in all the factors chosen being taken up as means into the unified whole of one's life. Individual choice or "formal Freedom" is purified from its arbitrariness by identifying with what is rational.

The Will has this *universal* determination as its Object and end only in that it *thinks* itself, is aware of its Concept, and is *Will* as free *Intelligence.*

Being aware of its Concept involves recognizing that it is fulfilled in identifying with the rational, both theoretically and practically. Unthinking activity is the exhibition of merely "natural Will," Will that is identified with one's individual proclivities without having achieved the reflective distance that allows one to shape his proclivities into a rational whole. "Freedom itself" is individual reason arrived at its rational maturity in a rational State.

§482. Spirit that is aware of itself as free and wills itself as its own object, that is, has its essence for its determination and end, is at first rational Will *in general*, or the Idea *in itself* [potentially], and is thus only the *Concept* of Absolute Spirit.

When the human Spirit breaks from its immersion in appetites and arbitrary choices and recognizes its Concept, it still has to pursue the way in which that Concept is to be concretely achieved. "The Idea" is "the absolute unity of Concept and Objectivity" (§213). Truth is achieved when what we think "inside" corresponds to what exists "outside." It is "absolute" when we ourselves are included in and include the overarching order of the Whole as the interrelated set of Concepts required for a world in which rational existence, both theoretical and practical, is the telos. At this stage that is only potential and thus abstract – or rather, since Hegel has already traversed the Logic and the Philosophy of Nature and is about to conclude the treatment of the structure of Subjective Spirit, Freedom is found in the process of concretion. In this section, Subjective Spirit is being treated as it reaches this abstract Idea.

Hegel's usage of the notion of the Concept here is somewhat unusual, since identification with its Concept is the actualization of an entity. But here, being "*only* in Concept" means it has not yet reached its actuality in Idea.

As *abstract* Idea, it is again existent only in the *immediate* Will; it is the side of the *Determinate Being (Daseyn)* of Reason; it is the *single* Will aware of the determination that constitutes its content and end and whose merely formal activity it is.

The individual human being is distinguished from other types by being the carrier of Reason. But when one is aware of this, Reason takes the first step out of its mere potentiality in the human essence. The Idea enters into Existence in an individual.

The Idea thus only appears in the finite Will whose *activity (Thätigkeit)* is to develop the Idea and to posit its self-unfolding content as externally

existent, which, as the *Determinate Being* (*Daseyn*) of the Idea, is *Actuality*: such is *Objective Spirit*.

"Actuality" is the identity of Essence and Existence when an instance of a given essence not only exists but develops its full potential. A plant or an animal reaches such a stage when its organic structure is fully articulated and thus it is able to reproduce its kind. Human beings become *actual* as rational agents and not merely contingently operating only when they are aware of themselves as rational and have developed the sciences and institutions that support rational Freedom. This can only occur over the centuries as inquiry and practices are passed on and develop. Knowledge and concrete praxis are developed in individuals who die but pass on their knowledge and practice to others who, in their turn, resting on the past, are able to go further. This passing on is the objectification of Spirit, progressively fuller than the contributions of individual subjects as the centuries pass.

No Idea is so universally recognized as indeterminate, ambiguous, and capable of the greatest misunderstandings and, for this very reason, is subject to them, as the Idea of *Freedom* – and no Idea is so much in common usage with so little awareness of its real meaning. In that the free Spirit is *actual* Spirit, misinterpretations concerning it have the most monstrous practical consequences; so much so that nothing else has this indomitable power, once individuals and nations have grasped representationally (*in ihren Vorstellung*) the abstract Concept (*Begriff*) of the actualization of Freedom (*der für sich seyenden Freyheit*), precisely because it is the proper essence of Spirit and indeed its very actualization.

People confuse the Freedom that is most praiseworthy with the free flow of impulse or with the ability to carry out, unhindered, one's arbitrary choices, and do not link it up with Rationality. Unbridled Freedom of the former two sorts destroys traditions and individuals. Restraint is viewed as a violation of Freedom, Law as an imposition. Hegel links such a view of Freedom to the Terror following the French Revolution. In this view, "Freedom" has to be sacrificed to mutual advantage (Hobbes). But entering into long-term relations with others is the condition for freeing potentialities lying fallow in the gene pool. By restraining our impulses and concentrating our attention in submitting to the discipline of a given tradition, we free the potentiality for intelligent participation. Generalizing that, one who thinks merely of Freedom of choice fails to see that Freedom is realized in the rational freeing of our potentialities that is possible only through participation in the development of tradition.

Entire parts of the globe – Africa and the Orient – have never had this Idea and still do not have it. The Greeks and Romans, Plato and Aristotle, even the Stoics, did not have it. On the contrary, they were aware only that a person is free in actuality by birth (as citizens of Athens, Sparta, and the like) or by strong character, or by formation through Philosophy (the wise man is free even as a slave and in chains).

Hegel moves here among the several stages in Spirit's relation to Freedom: in *Vorstellung*, *Begriff*, and *Idee*. The basic feature of *Vorstellung* is the isolation of an object, whether an image or a Concept; the *Begriff* is the apprehension of the Essence of that object; the *Idee* is the union of the Concept with Actuality in living forms and in the development of human beings.

The fact that the Idea of rational Freedom arrived very late in human history means that the human essence itself matures only through millennia, even though there is a relative maturity available to each individual through the development over time of the human community to which he/she belongs. Indeed, the deepest potentiality for relation to the Eternal and Encompassing is possible any time in human history through Religion, though that itself matures through time. The translation of this into the development of the fundamental possibilities of rational existence is millennia long. One is free for certain possibilities only if there are the developed institutions that allow one to be so free. One is free to travel with some dispatch across and between large cities today because there are the developed laws of the road and the technological production of roads and cars with safety features. One is free to pursue a career as a concert pianist only because there are the centuries-long development of the technology that produced and developed the piano, the creativity that introduced musical genres and the musical repertoire, and the discipline of the conservatory that teaches the techniques of playing. Without submitting one's self to that tradition one is only free to *try* to play, but freedom of execution would be extremely limited.

Every tradition operates in this way; but what Hegel is focusing upon is the specific complex of freedoms that constitutes the modern State. These are specified in the rights of individuals, which it is one of the functions of the larger society to preserve and promote. The modern State, particularly through the development of the market economy, has established a region of free-entry associations that unleashed the full panoply of human creativity.

This Idea has come into this world through Christianity according to which the individual *as such* has an *infinite* worth in that it is the object and aim of God's Love. It is oriented towards having an absolute relation to God as Spirit and having this Spirit dwelling within it. That means that a human being *in itself* [potentially] is oriented to the highest Freedom. When, in Religion as such, a person is aware of the relation to Absolute Spirit as his or her essence, such a one, moreover, has the divine Spirit also present as entering the sphere of *worldly Existence*, as the substance of the State, of Family, and so forth. These relations are formed through the Spirit and constituted in a way adequate to It, just as much as the individual internalizes through such existence the ethos of ethical behaviour *(Sittlichkeit)* and then is *free in Actuality* in this sphere of particular existence, of present sensing and willing.

For Hegel Christianity reveals the inner mystery of the Cosmos: God becomes Man to send His Spirit to bind the community in Love. Such community gives absolute value to each human being. According to the structure of humanness, each individual is oriented towards the Whole. According to Hegelian Philosophy, God is the inward Ground of the Whole, and Creation is His outward display, at one level in Nature, but at the deepest level in human History. The human essence develops only in and through relation to others, past, present, and to come. The divine Spirit guides the development of History so that institutions come into being that progressively correspond to the essence of humanness as that itself comes to progressive articulation in History. The divine Spirit dwells in the community through its institutions, and the individual's sense of dwelling in them is the Spirit's indwelling in him or her.

Notice that Hegel speaks here of "the highest Freedom" as relation to the divine. It is always possible, at any stage of human development, to elevate one's Heart to the Eternal and Encompassing as the essence of Religion. That is the highest Freedom available in any age. However, religion historically tied and in many places continues to tie people to narrowness, superstition, and fanaticism that stand in the way of the rational pursuit of understanding of our place in the cosmos and the rational organization of society based upon freedom and rights properly understood. Through the development of our concrete understanding of what is involved in Christianity – the revelation of the identity of God with a human being in Christ and thus with all those who follow in His way, and the working out historically of all that is involved in that revelation – "the highest Freedom" comes to an understanding of itself, and thus becomes higher still than at the early stages of historical development.

If awareness of the Idea is speculative, that is, the awareness of the knowledge of human beings that their essence, aim, and object is Freedom, then this Idea itself as such is the actualization of human beings, not something they thus *have* but something they *are*.

The Speculative for Hegel is not, as in our ordinary usage, a matter of guesswork, for example, in speculating on the stock market. It is, according to its older usage, a matter of becoming a mirror (Latin *speculum*) of what is the case. However, Hegel avoids the implication of one's being a *mirror* of the rational order of things, because he maintains that in cognition we have more than a *representation* of things; we have *the things themselves*. But what is thus seen must permeate all of human existence. It can do this only insofar as it is developed into institutions and permeates practice.

In its adherents Christianity has made this awareness into their actuality [by admonishing them,] for example, not to be slaves. If they were made into slaves, if the decision regarding their property were made in an arbitrary manner and not through laws and courts of justice, they would find the substance of their *Determinate Being (Daseyn)* violated. This willing of Freedom is no longer a drive that requires its satisfaction, but a matter of character, spiritual Consciousness having become *being* without [mere] drive [for it].

There is a difference between being aware that rational Freedom constitutes the essence of being human and having rational Freedom as the settled disposition of a person. Once again, this is typically found only on the basis of rationally developed institutions. If a Socrates can exhibit a high degree of personal Rationality in thought and behaviour, that is only because of the prior institution of the Greek language and Greek customs, the tradition of Greek literature, and particularly the tradition of philosophic inquiry, even though he stood out as its severest critic.

The notion of "being without drive" focuses the unfulfilled character of drive as drive. But once that settles into concrete habit, it is not simply drive but current actuality. That does not mean that we no longer experience drives, but that the drives themselves are not merely naturally given but have taken on a rational form.

But this Freedom, which possesses the content and aim of Freedom, is itself at first only Concept, principle of Spirit and Heart, and destined to develop into Objectivity, into legal, ethical (*sittlich*), religious, and scientific Actuality.

Whenever humans reflectively grasped the notion of Freedom, that notion had still to work its way into institutions that would unfold the notion in Actuality. This is the work of centuries, preparing for the day when one could see progressive Rationality more clearly established in human relations. Hence, we move to the level of Objective Spirit. Human beings, having the structure of Subjective Spirit, objectify their actions, at a fundamental level through the development of Language as primary institution. And having objectified their actions, they pass away, leaving their objectifications to those who follow, providing over time a richer matrix for the discovery and freeing of human potentialities. Nature is the tree; Subjective Spirit is the bud; Objective Spirit is the flower; Absolute Spirit is the fruit.

PART IV

Overview of the Concluding Sections of "Philosophy of Spirit"

Chapter Eight

Objective Spirit

1. Abstract Right
   a. Property
   b. Contract
   c. Right and Wrong
2. Morality
   a. Intention
   b. Purpose and Well-Being
   c. The Good and the Bad
3. *Sittlichkeit*
   a. Family
   b. Civil Society
      i.   System of Needs
      ii. Administration of Justice
      iii. Police and Corporation
   c. State
      i.   Constitution
      ii. International Law
      iii. World History

Hegel's analysis of Subjective Spirit gives us the general structure of a human subject. As we noted, it culminates in the representation of Free Spirit as the union of Theoretical and Practical Spirit. That does not simply involve a biologically mature individual, but an individual having assimilated and having been assimilated to a tradition of comprehensive inquiry and practice aware of itself as such. The latter is the phase of Objective Spirit, wherein individual humans, long dead, have brought into being by their own personal habits a realm of regular practices that still endures in having passed them on to their epigones through language and example. They have objectified their own subjectivity by taking possession of their own bodies, by shaping the external environment, and by engaging in various forms of interchange between their peers. It is into such a matrix that each of us is born.

Hegel's analysis of Objective Spirit presupposes the recognition of the essential rationality of each human being, a process developed in the Phenomenology and Psychology sections of Subjective Spirit. Such recognition is anticipated in the emergence of language, "an I that is a We, and a We that is an I" (1807 *Phenomenology of Spirit*). Language had its origin in the relation between individual humans moved by their natural appetites and mediated by their manifest environment. The stability of natural needs anchors the common understanding involved in all languages. Language, as the basic medium of interpersonal relations, is the fundamental institution into which every subsequent generation is initiated. Hegel's analysis of Objective Spirit presupposes both the institution of Language and the overcoming of the Master–Slave relation through the recognition of our common rationality and hence our fundamental rights.

Objective Spirit is the Appearance, the *Erscheinung* of the human essence in Existence for which the Actuality, the *Wirklichkeit*, is the sphere of Absolute Spirit, the level of Art, Religion, and Philosophy. Objective Spirit is the Absolute Idea "on the plane of finitude," which, projected out of Spirit, has not fully returned to itself as Absolute Spirit. The plane of finitude is the political level in the broader Aristotelian sense that includes the social and economic aspects along with overarching political authority. The materials upon which Spirit works are personal needs, external nature, and relations between individual choosers. Its work settles into common practices. Authority and obedience are the external manifestation of the inner principles developed and organized around the principles of Freedom, that is, the principles involved in the free exercise of the *Rational* Subject.

Law is the union of the single will with the rational Will, a deliberate formation of what previously existed in the form of custom. Law spells out the interrelation of rights and duties. To a right on someone's part corresponds a duty on that of others, and vice versa. Father's rights over their children involve the duty to care for and educate them to responsible adulthood. Taxes and military service are duties tied to the right to property and life that put property and life on the line for the sake of the survival of a tradition dedicated to their preservation.

Hegel divides his treatment into his customary three parts, governed this time by the overall scheme of his Logic: outer Being, inner Essence, and the Concept as union of the two. This schema is instantiated in Law or Abstract Right (*Recht*), the Morality of Conscience (*Moralität*), and Customary Life (*Sittlichkeit*), respectively.

In the introduction to his *Elements of the Philosophy of Right*, Hegel begins with a treatment of the Will, prepared for at the end of the section on Subjective Spirit, where the notion of Free Spirit synthesizes Theoretical and Practical Reason. The development of Free Spirit through the articulation of the operation of the Will begins with the most immediately given external level, the level of Property, and moves to its teleological ground in *Sittlichkeit* rationally ordered. This parallels the treatment of Subjective Spirit that began with its most external features, its being affected by embodiment, and moved through the level of the field of experience itself, eventually to the ground of its operations in the various levels of its "psychological" character, the goal of which is the fully Free Spirit. At the level of Objective Spirit, each individual Spirit first takes possession of its own body as the basis for its coming into possession of things in the external environment by which it anchors itself in relation to others.

Governing the procedure here is the distinction between Freedom of choice, which he calls *Formal* or *Negative Freedom*, and *Essential* or *Substantial* or *Rational Freedom*, which is involved most fully in what he calls *Customary Life* (*Sittlichkeit*). Formal Freedom is fulfilled in Substantial Freedom, choice in choosing rationally. One possesses Rational Freedom when one is identified with others on the basis of the universality found in the institutional practices of one's community, including the practices of inquiry. Rational Freedom presupposes that the institutional practices have been articulated in a fully rational way.

Both Abstract Right and the Morality of Conscience are modern developments historically rooted in Christianity's proclamation of the infinite dignity of the human individual. At the level of Customary Life, they become the key principles of what Hegel calls *Civil Society* (*bürgerliche Gesellschaft*). His general aim is to create a region for the operation of the principles of human rights and conscience, developed in modernity, between the two poles of Aristotle's political analysis: the Family and the comprehensive life of the polis. Such insertion, however, modifies the character of both ends of the Aristotelian frame.

In Civil Society there is a very wide sphere for the exercise of individual rights, beginning with property rights, free enterprise, religious choice, choice of marriage partner and occupation, freedom of assembly, freedom of inquiry and publicity, and the right to a jury trial. Hegel sees these rights as based upon the dignity of the individual, whose free choice must be respected in as wide a range of activities as possible consonant with the overall unity and rationality of the sociopolitical whole and the stabilization of the Family. It is only in the modern world, actually carrying forward Christianity's announcement of the infinite worth of the individual human being, that the focus upon individual rights takes centre stage.

Hegel's analysis of this interpersonal sphere begins with exteriority, with the individual will taking possession, first of its own body through the development of skills and, in and through that, of the things in the environment. Through one's choice and holding oneself to long-term courses of action, one lays hold of, marks, and shapes mere things that thus become extensions of the person. In considering what is occurring at this stage of the analysis, one has to keep in mind the achievement at the level of the Phenomenology of mutual recognition by the members of a given community as rational agents. Recognition has advanced to the stage, beyond the Master–Slave relation, of Law governing the disposition of Property.

The term "Person" here has a technical limitation, rooted in its etymology, *per-sonare* or to "sound through" the mask worn by the actor who has assumed a role. Here the role is that of appearing before others as a property owner. The representation of Property extends from land and crops and housing to the books and paintings one might produce as well as one's labour itself. Now, one can choose or not choose to possess any of these things, so that once one does so choose, one is also free to dispose of what one possesses. One can "put one's will into" the piece of property and just as well "take it out of" it. Hence, if the first phase of the analysis focuses upon Property, the next phase is upon *Contract* or the mutual agreement to dispose of Property. One must underscore that the property here is also what one has in one's own person, so that one can contract for labour as well as for external property. In this context, the question of value arises and thus also money as a way of measuring equivalencies and fixing standard prices.

What emerges from this is conflict over Property, whether in civil suits involving disputed claims or in criminal suits involving fraud or outright theft, hence, legal *Right and Wrong*. Law settles the principles for determining the Right involved in Property, investing judgment and finally coercive power in legal authority. The individual will, correlative to Reason, finds its own substance in the universality of the principles of legal order. The consideration of individual rights leads on to the institutional matrix that fosters them. But that is more fully treated in Hegel's consideration of Civil Society.

The term *Moralität* in Hegel has the restricted meaning of an appeal to Conscience as the inner depths of the individual subject, to what he or she takes to be absolutely binding upon him/herself, that is, as morally universal over against his/her own individuality as an arbitrary subject. Conscience is something not imposed from without but justified from within in terms of inner sentiment. Here Hegel distinguishes the moral *Subject* from the legal *Person* insofar as the latter is shown through Property and the external relations with others which that entails, while the former attends to its own inwardness – hence the distinction between Legality and Morality. The Subject only allows what it does as well as its consequences to be attributable insofar as he or she has deliberately chosen them. Hence, contrary to both early Hebrew and Greek views, deed is distinguished from external action, the former alone being the sphere of responsibility wherein action is determined by how the agent intends what is achieved. The right of subjective freedom, the right to the satisfaction of particularity, both at the level of inner conviction and at the level of personal fulfilment, is the basic difference between Antiquity and Modernity. Hence again, note Hegel's positioning of Civil Society, based upon Property and Conscience, between the Aristotelian poles of Family and State (*polis*), a positioning, we said, that affects both poles.

Hegel's treatment of Conscience begins with *Purpose* (*Vorsatz*), which involves an individual claiming an action as "mine." The appeal to Conscience also involves *Intention* (*Absicht*) or the reason I think the action good. Its content is *Welfare* (*Wohl*) as the absolute end of the Will in opposition to mere "subjective universality," or what an individual happens to think as universally binding. The Good is the Idea as the unity of the Concept of the Will with the particular Will. Contained within it are Abstract Right, Welfare, subjectivity of knowing, and the contingency of external fact. Freedom is realized in the Good which is the ultimate goal of the cosmos. So conceived, the Good has absolute

Right compared with Property and the particular aims of Welfare. But note well that Freedom is not fully realized unless there is a freeing of our relation to the Absolute Spirit in Religion and its adequate comprehension in Philosophy.

But what is the content of Good and the duty to pursue it? At this point, only to do what is right and to strive after welfare in one's own case and in the case of others universally. This basically involves Kant's representation of so-called perfect and imperfect duties, or better *completable (vollendete)* and *(unvollendete) incompletable* duties. Respecting humanity, one's own and that of any other, is "perfect," that is, always demanded and always achievable; working for the well-being of others and developing one's talents are "imperfect" in the sense of never being capable of complete fulfilment. Neither imperative tells one what to do in particular. By itself, this way of thinking is an empty formalism of duty for duty's sake. Kant appeals to non-contradiction as the basis for judging the principles one feels to be binding, but non-contradiction can be no criterion by itself because it involves prior contradiction of *something*, of some content. At this point subjective Will stands as means in relation to the Good as an Ought. In Hegel's reading, this leads to a never-ending Ought-to-be.

Hegel claims that, as the unity of subjective knowing and the absolute, conscience is sacred, and its violation a sacrilege. But Conscience is subject to the judgment of its truth or falsity. It is "a piece of monstrous conceit" to set my Conscience against Law that claims authority from God or the State, having tens of centuries during which it gave coherence and substance to the common life of human beings. So Hegel moves from the inward Morality of private Conscience to the unity of inner and outer in the actual Customary Life (*Sittlichkeit*) of a State.

Customary Life has two anchors: the immediacy of the Family and the encompassing mediation of what he calls "the State." As we said, in between lie the modern structures of Civil Society based on contract and individual interests. Note once again that State (*Staat*) is a term having broader application than simply government. Like Aristotle's *polis*, it is the encompassing life of a people, only in modern times having significantly greater geographical extension and greater institutional complexity than that of the relatively small ancient Greek *polis*.

The *Family* is rooted in giving spiritual significance to the natural sexual relation, establishing a permanent relation of the couple, sanctioned in Law, by directing attention to the procreation and rearing of children. The dispositions of love and trust root Spirit in the heart and its feelings, shaped by institutionalized commitment.

Contrary to the case of the Family, which is a kind of encompassing substance securing the individuals, *Civil Society* is "the system of atomistic" individuals. That is, its principle is the individual as unit, guided by its needs into external, contractual relations with others. These relations develop naturally into a division of labour and, further, into natural "Estates" fulfilling essential functions: Agriculture, Business, and Civil Service. In such an articulated society, Law emerges as the explicitly chosen set of means governing the external relations between individuals. Hegel distinguishes the form of publicity and authority necessary to regulate these relations from the specific content of the law, which may be reasonable or unreasonable. Hence, he follows the traditional distinction between positive law and the deeper principles, based upon what is essential to humanness, which could measure positive law. Slavery, for example, is an eternal affront to the dignity of human beings, though some state of subjection to command that involves acting contrary to one's immediate desires is essential to civilized development. Crucial to truly rational principles is the inherent dignity and Freedom of the rational individual. But Hegel also underscores the basic demand of Reason for a codification of laws into a coherent system. And, with Aquinas, he notes the different ways in which the most fundamental principles can be applied in different cultural contexts. Hegel restricts legislation to external relations of Right and, because of the basis of the dignity of the human subject in its infinite inner orientation, he sets the inner realm of moral and religious will apart from the law.

The point of Civil Society is the satisfaction of want. But the contingencies of the market system lead to many undesirable consequences, requiring the function of the "*Polizei*" – a function much broader than our police and better translated as "public administration." *Polizei* is etymologically derived from *polis*. Through its "policies" it "polices" not only the inner safety of the community, but also the working of the market, both in order to provide infrastructure, to stabilize the market so as to keep it from wild swings, and to provide for those adversely affected by such swings. Today we think of government establishing a "safety net" for those whose welfare cannot for many reasons be met by the current system of production and exchange. Hegel anticipated these governmental functions.

There is another institutional set that emerges in Civil Society, what Hegel calls the *Korporation*. The term covers not only business enterprises but also "incorporated" areas such as municipalities as well as free-entry associations such as churches, learned societies, fine arts

societies, fraternal orders, and the like. A business corporation in this
sense embraces both owners and workers and is aimed at the common
good of its own community. In them the individual finds himself em-
braced by a wider set of supportive relations aimed at specific ends.
Family and "corporation" root the bourgeois "atoms of self-interest" in
these embracing institutions; but State embraces them all.

State is the all-encompassing society for a given people. It is the family principle applied to the whole people. To familial love corresponds
patriotism, both dispositions involving a willingness to sacrifice individual interests to the good of the whole. But both also involve enduring dispositions to follow the typical ways of behaving that allow
people to coordinate their actions. However, the whole involves no to-
talitarian submergence of the individual; rather, it involves the constitutionally protected grounding of the individual. Here Hegel affirms
what Catholic social teaching has called "the principle of subsidiarity,"
which likely had its ground in the German tradition stemming from
Hegel. Negatively stated, it reads: "Do not do at a more encompassing level of organization what can be done at a lower and ultimately
individual level." Of course, its correlative positive articulation would
be: "Do at a more encompassing level of organization what cannot be
done at a lower level." Against the immediate aftermath of the French
Revolution that destroyed mediating institutions in favour of the newly
emergent central government, Hegel calls for a constitutional articulation of different institutional layers buffering the individual and the local from the arbitrary exercise of power from above or from the centre.
The State protects the Family and the rights of individuals, promotes
general welfare, and brings self-interested individuals back to a view
of their own belonging to the substantial whole. Hence, the State can
call upon individuals, in situations of national emergency, to sacrifice
the very things that the State was called into being to protect and foster,
namely, Life and Property.

Hegel carefully defines Liberty and Equality, the watchwords of
modern Civil Society. Equality is based on the right to Property, which
eventuates in the establishment of differences based on natural – and
functional – Inequality. It is essentially equality before Law. Liberty is
given its proper scope through rational laws that respect Conscience
and allow the greatest latitude for individual choice consonant with
the stability of the overarching whole. That stability is secured through
multilevelled organization, where each level has its constitutionally defined sphere of operation.

The constitution of a State cannot be abstractly imposed on a people, but must grow from within its own history as its innermost Spirit. It is deeply tied to a people's religion, which spells out what is most substantial in that people's existence, its "ultimate concern." Hegel sees Protestantism, with its emphasis upon the inner "witness of the Spirit," as the ground of the modern State. He sees Catholicism as a stabilizing force only in States where individual liberty cannot thrive because of the general externalist authoritarianism of the Catholic mentality. For the former he cites the United States, for the latter the states of Latin America.

In Hegel's view, the rationally articulated State requires a hereditary Monarchy, basically as the symbol of unity, but constitutionally restricted by legislative, judicial, and administrative functions open to the talent of qualified civil servants. The legislative assembly draws from the Estates of Civil Society (Agriculture, Business, and Civil Service), who operate in assembly together with the Monarch.

Voting on the part of the public is only meaningful at the local level. Here it involves selecting local officials and corporate representatives to the national legislative assembly. Applied to broader levels, voting on the part of the public will lead to relative indifference and hence to control by special interests. (Note that, in America, given that only about half the eligible voters vote, often only one quarter or fewer of eligible voters elects the president and Congress – hardly providing a mandate.) However, public opinion is crucial in maintaining the feeling of identity with the social whole. But public opinion is of mixed value. The publicity of the legislative assembly mediated through the free press ideally presents the public with instances of rational argumentation so as to aid in the rational shaping of public opinion and thus the free adhesion to the laws and practices of one's country (a consummation devoutly to be wished for in today's Congress).

States exist amid other States, relations among which are established by treaties and by international law. But there is not and, in Hegel's view, ought not to be any international power that can override the will of the sovereign State. There ought only to be cooperative alliances between States that leave final judgment to each individual State. The potential threat that each State bears to others keeps its citizens from falling back exclusively into merely private pursuits, forgetting their rational substance as identified with the overarching but still particular and thus limited whole that is their State.

States begin with the establishment of settled institutions of marriage along with agricultural production and distribution that appear together with the development of writing. The history of States has passed through several developmental stages, from oriental despotism where only the emperor is free, through Greek and Roman citizenship where some – citizens and not slaves – are free, to the modern State where all are in principle free. The latter was introduced by Christianity with its emphasis upon the infinite value of the individual; but it took many centuries for that to find its place among the common practices and laws of a given country. In Hegel's reading, the State that exhibits the highest instantiation of the fully free [mind] Spirit has absolute right in World History. It carries forward the advancement of the Spirit.

History is guided by "the cunning of Reason," which operates, like Adam Smith's "invisible hand," as Divine Providence, beneath or behind the consciousness of individuals. Hegel appropriates Rousseau's General Will and Montesqieu's Spirit of the Laws in his notion of *Sittlichkeit*, or Customary Life. People dwell in the spirit of their country that undergoes shifts in the development of its history. What Hegel calls "world-historical individuals" sense what is ready to burst forth in the "general will" and rally the people to their standards. Hegel cites such figures as Alexander the Great, who broke through the limits of the *polis* to establish empire; Julius Caesar, who brought into the Roman republic the lands of the North and laid the ground for the establishment of the Empire by his adopted son Octavius/Augustus; and Napoleon, who spread the French Revolution's dissolution of the *ancien régime* and developed it into the order of Freedom, reached through the opening of careers to talent, the abolition of serfdom, codified law, and, in general, most of the political institutions that characterize the nineteenth and twentieth centuries. Such figures are not necessarily or even usually men outstanding for their personal morality; but they fulfil their role in world history and, at times, like Caesar and Napoleon, are cast aside.

The age following Napoleon allows the fundamental features of a free, rational State to be discerned underneath the contingencies that accompany it. According to Hegel's famous but too often scarcely understood dictum, "The rational is the actual and the actual is the rational." The rational is the operative core of any long-term society. But what is actual in it is only the rational that reaches its culmination in the operation of the principles of a rationally free society. Reason is historically actualized in and through and against the contingencies that accompany it. The post-Revolutionary world is the locus of the development of the fundamental principles of the fully rational State. Now, the coming into being of the proximate possibility of the fully rational state provides the matrix for rising above it, in it, and through it, to the Eternal and Encompassing in Art, Religion, and Philosophy. Our consideration of Objective Spirit leads to Absolute Spirit as the culmination of the System.

Chapter Nine

Absolute Spirit

1. Art
2. Religion
3. Philosophy

Subjective Spirit is the Being-in-itself or the Essence underlying the sensory presence of the human being. Objective Spirit is the Determinate Being (*Daseyn*) or the Existence of the human subject, the Appearance of Spirit as one comprehensively organized community set over against others. But each human subject is human by reason of being referred to Being as a whole; each is directed beyond its culture to the encompassing Whole. In Religion this relation is the For-Itself, the Actuality of the human Essence. Religion is articulated by inspired individuals in images and isolated proclamations. It is lived through the raising of one's heart from the everyday to the Eternal and Encompassing. It reaches a highpoint in the religious community of confession and forgiveness and in the *unio mystica* of the Eucharistic celebration.

Religion takes up Art into the expression of that relation in exterior form, the highest mission of Art. But Religion rises above images and isolated proclamations in the effort of Theology to secure a consistent view based upon the tradition. Philosophy, in turn, is the attempt to rise above that by taking proclamation, not, like Theology, as starting point, but as external guide to its own internal development. Philosophy attempts to ground its comprehensive claims in evidence. The three regions – Art, Religion, and Philosophy – constitute the realm of

Absolute Spirit, the fruit that transcends the matrix in Objective Spirit as the flowering that precedes the fruit. The history of their parallel development is correlated with the development of the political understanding of freedom

* * *

Art passes through several phases in its history determined by the view of the relation between the Now of sensory presence and the Beyond to which we are directed by our spiritual structure. The notion of Being that is the basis of the System is also the basis for the human spirit: from the beginning it relates us, although emptily, to the Totality. At first the Beyond appears as massive power and mysterious encompassment that gains expression in what Hegel calls *Symbolic Art*. Here the sensory surface is modified to give expression precisely to that notion of the Beyond. Eastern architecture is the main carrier of such expressiveness: the massiveness of Egyptian pyramids, the Indian temples teeming with life. The political matrix for such work was the Oriental empire in which only the emperor was free, and free only in the sense of being able to exercise arbitrary choice.

The Greeks attained to *Classical Art*, wherein the sensory form and intelligible content are proportionately related. They saw the Beyond, not as massive power empty of content, but determinately as Spirit. They hit upon the one natural form that is itself the expression of Spirit, the human body. Anthropomorphic presentation of the gods is an advance beyond the empty impersonalism of the Eastern view into a determinate spiritual view of the Beyond as Spirit, though bodily and finite and therefore plural. The Greeks developed what Hegel called a *Religion of Art*. It involved athletic cultivation, the production of temples to house the statues of the anthropomorphic divinities, epic vision, and liturgical drama that culminated in the great tragedies. Comedy as cultural criticism formed the transition to the critical work of Philosophy incarnate in Socratic irony. The political matrix for such developments, resting upon a slave substratum, was the notion of the free citizen who participated in the decisions of the political community.

In the concluding portion of the Encyclopaedia dealing with Religion, Hegel organizes his thought around the logical moments of Universal, Particular, and Individual. The *Universal* moment is God before Creation, Who eternally begets a Son and remains united with Him in the Spirit (§567). As Hegel said in the Logic, "God is eternally complete and eternally completing Himself." *Particularity* is the sphere of Creation, of the multiplicity of things that exist outside of God while internally rooted within Him. In the moment of *Individuality*, the eternal Son is "transplanted into the world of time, and in him wickedness is implicitly overcome" (§569). He appears among men and is put to death, remaining in His eternal nature, through whose mediation arises the witness of the Spirit in the religious community. "The Being of Beings ... through this mediation brings about its own indwelling in self-consciousness, and is the actual presence of the essential and self-subsisting Spirit who is all in all" (§570). This three-fold "syllogistic process" is "one syllogism of the absolute self-mediation of Spirit" (§571).

Christianity, as *Revealed Religion*, is the locus for the manifestation of the highest truth: the announcement of the identity of God and Man in Jesus. The history of religion as the history of the human spirit attains its end in principle: Christ is the Logos made flesh, a principle of otherness in God through Whom all things were made and Who, as such otherness, could alone enter into the otherness of Creation. On the part of Creation, that can only occur at that place where the finite is open to the Infinite: in Man. This entailed a Trinitarian God: Father as Ground, Son as Logos, and Spirit as the Love between them. Through the death, resurrection, and ascension of the Logos made flesh, the Spirit came to dwell in the community of worshippers. Such revelation involved the basic principle of Identity-in-Difference that allowed Hegel to overcome the traditional dualisms that plagued the history of philosophy.

With the Beyond clearly manifest in principle as infinite, eternal Trinity that comes to dwell in the human community, Art returns to the Symbolic mode because the infinity of the divine exceeds the finite proportionality of Greek art, so that the sensory is no longer adequate. But the Beyond is not empty; it is filled with the glory of the infinite divine Trinitarian Presence. We reach the stage of Art that Hegel calls *Romantic Art*. It belongs to Christianity as such and thus is not the same as the literary Romantic artform. It belongs to the Christian order, which, entering into the political, is based on the principle that all are free. With the infinite Beyond present here in the religious community, Art once again becomes symbolic and takes as its theme whatever interests artists and their audiences as the scene of theophany.

Coming now to Philosophy, in his *Lectures on the History of Philosophy*, Hegel traces the development of thought up to the point where it can be synthesized in his System. He maintains that each thinker has seen an aspect of the round of eternal truths underpinning human experience, "the thoughts of God before Creation"; but each has seen and expressed it in terms of the limitation of context determined by his times. The history of thought stumbles piecemeal, but roughly in logical sequence, through the categories that appear systematized in Hegel's own *Logic* and extended to both Nature and Spirit.

Parmenides opened the speculative tradition with the announcement of the identity of Thought and Being and with the isolation of the notion of Being as absolutely one and changeless, apart from multiple changing things as mixtures of Being and Non-being. Things are internally divided, other than each other, other than they were, and other than they will be. Heraclitus finds Being in Becoming by the unity of opposites accomplished through the Logos, while the Atomists located Being in a vast multiplicity of internally changeless things that combine and separate externally in the existent non-being of the Void. Aristotle presents for Hegel the broadest range of insights that were systematized together with Plato's work in the Neoplatonism that was the culmination of antiquity.

Then came Christian revelation. Hegel considered himself, on his own terms, a good Lutheran. He accepted Jesus as the God-Man, the core of Christian revelation, simultaneously involving the identity-in-difference of the Infinite and the Finite in human existence as well as the Trinitarian structure of God as "Creator of heaven and earth," "eternally complete" but also "eternally completing Himself" in creation. In Christian revelation the secret is out: through the manifestation of the God-Man, human existence at its deepest is identical with God, and Identity-in-Difference rather than strict identity is the basic representation. This does not mean the reverse, as Feuerbach and all too many of Hegel's commentators would have it, that man is God in the sense that humanity is the "Creator of heaven and earth." It means that man is the locus of the achievement of God through Creation. According to Christ's own words, he had to disappear so that the Spirit would come who would teach human beings to worship "in Spirit and truth," in inwardness and not simply in sensory presentation. Here Hegel appeals to Luther's "witness of the Spirit" that becomes rational inwardness post-Descartes – to Luther's horror, I'm sure, for he considered Reason "the whore of the devil."

Before Luther, the Church Fathers and the Scholastics strove to link together pagan reflection upon human experience and its possible implications with the piecemeal utterances of the Scriptures. Because revelation is addressed to human beings as carriers of Reason, faith inevitably gives rise to Theology as the attempt to interpret and render coherent the truths of faith. But as we noted, theology remains confined to taking the contents of revelation as given without trying to derive them from further rational grounds.

Hegel sees the witness of the Spirit as taking a new turn with Descartes in the *cogito* with its demand for indubitable evidence. Here, Hegel remarks, philosophy, after being buffeted in various ways by the sea of changing opinions, reaches land. Descartes points in the direction in which Revelation can be assimilated and surmounted by grasping conceptually its own deeper grounds. On the heels of Descartes, one observes in Spinoza the working of Hegel's central claim that "the Truth is the Whole"; but in Hegel this had to rise from the representation of the Whole as a single Substance in Spinoza to the representation of the Ground of all as Subject and the correlative representation of the free subjectivity of the human individual.

Kant explored the structures of subjectivity, but split the Whole into phenomena and noumena and the human being into self-determining rationality and law-governed inclination. But his late reintroduction of the representation of finality or the purpose-driven character of living systems – albeit in the mode of "as if" – pointed in the direction of a reintegration of the Whole in a systematic matter. Human goal projection is not a stranger in a strange land, but operates as living forms seem to operate, subsuming mechanisms under purposes. Following Fichte's attempt to deduce the list of Kant's categories from the activity of transcendental subjectivity rather than simply accepting them from logic as Kant did, Hegel developed the systematic co-implication of the categories from the activity of the self as the Concept entering into existence. He claimed that in his System he was able to bring philosophy beyond its traditional love of wisdom to a complete Science of Wisdom.

* * *

In his treatment of Art, Religion, and Philosophy at the end of the Encyclopaedia Hegel makes a most intriguing claim that he does not go on to develop or clarify: "Philosophy is the synthesis of Art and Religion." Let us attempt to clarify that idea.

As we have said, for Hegel the core of Religion is located in the heart, rising out of the everyday into the Eternal and Encompassing. He goes on to say that, without having this experience, one cannot know the essence of Religion. In the treatment of Subjective Spirit he claims that authentic existence is the unity of heart and head; their separation splits the person. The heart is what is radically individual, radically mine. Each of us has his or her own peculiar "magnetic field" of attracting and repelling factors. What we can come to know at the level of the universal, as is the case with all science, Philosophy included, leaves us fractured, split between the universality of reason and the radical individuality of the heart, unless I assimilate the universal into the way I live my life, the way my heart is engaged. The reverse is also the case: unless my heart has been measured by reason, it goes astray.

Hegel also said that art has a two-fold task: at its highest level, to display the Absolute in sensuous form, but also, as its perennial function, to heal the rift that intellectual operation creates between its abstractions and the sensory world in relation to which we live our lives.

If we put these things together, the philosopher qua philosopher is charged with the task of displaying the interlocking set of conditions of possibility, logical, anthropological, historical, and cosmic for rational existence and its maximum flourishing. But this is synthesis at the universal level of experience. For human wholeness, that synthesis has to be assimilated into the heart and linked via the arts to the sensory. In this way Philosophy involves "a synthesis of Art and Religion" and cannot properly exist without them.

* * *

Now that thought had reached its full maturity in the post-Kantian period, Hegel was able to work out all the systematically interrelated presuppositions involved in any rational activity. Hegel claims to have done that in the interlocking relations between Logic, Nature, and Spirit laid out in his *Encyclopaedia of the Philosophic Sciences*. The Philosophy of Spirit – the last part of the System – culminates in sketching the way in which the three interlocking domains can each be used as the starting point to mediate the other two in the *Realistic Synthesis* with Nature mediating between Spirit and Logic, in the *Idealist Synthesis* with Spirit mediating between Nature and Logic, and in the *Logical Synthesis*, with Logic mediating between Spirit and Nature (§575–7).

The keystone of the System is set in place by a final quote from Aristotle's *Metaphysics* presenting the ultimate Divinity as Self-Thinking Thought Who, as Absolute Spirit, completes the circle begun with the empty notion of Being. The En-cyclo-paedia presents the eternal circulation of Absolute Spirit. It culminates, he says, in Philosophy of Religion.

The System as a whole lays out the interlocking set of conditions of possibility for rational existence and flourishing. It lays the basis politically for the exercise of freedom in ongoing exploration in science and creativity in technology, art, and entrepreneurship, ultimately grounded in the depth relation, through Art, Religion, and Philosophy, to "the Being of Beings."

* * *

We chose as our focal point the texts from his Philosophy of Spirit that Hegel himself recommended as the best introduction to his System: the Phenomenology and Psychology, which mediate, in directly available experience, between Philosophy of Nature (in the Anthropology) and Logic (in the final domain of Psychology) and thus point us onwards towards those domains as their presuppositions.

Once inside the System, one can begin to appreciate the depth and power of Hegel's thought and realize, as Heidegger said, "It is not that Hegel's philosophy has broken down. Rather, his contemporaries and successors have not ever yet stood up so that they can be measured against his greatness."

Selected Bibliography

There are two principles for selection. First, since this book is an introduction to the System, I have included the pertinent books by Hegel in the first part and in the second a selection of works that either give a general orientation to Hegel or deal with a specific part of his work. The second principle operates in the third part of the bibliography, which includes those works that deal with the themes in Hegel's *Philosophy of Spirit/Mind*.

1. G.W.F. Hegel

Aesthetics: Lectures on Fine Art. Trans. T. Knox. Oxford: Clarendon Press, 1975.
Berlin Phenomenology. Ed. and trans. M. Inwood. Dordrecht: Reidel, 1981.
Elements of the Philosophy of Right. Ed. A. Wood, trans. H. Nisbet. Cambridge: Cambridge University Press, 1991.
Encyclopaedia of the Philosophical Sciences:
– *The Encyclopaedia Logic*. Trans. T. Geraets, W. Suchting, and H. Harris. Indianapolis: Hackett, 1991.
– *Encyclopaedia Philosophy of Mind*. Trans. W. Wallace. Oxford: Clarendon Press, 1971.
– *Hegel's Philosophy of Nature*. Trans. A.V. Miller. Oxford: Clarendon Press, 1970.
Lectures on the History of Philosophy. Trans. E. Haldane. Lincoln: University of Nebraska Press, 1995.
Lectures on the Philosophy of Religion. Ed. O. Hodgson. Berkeley: University of California Press, 1988.
Lectures on the Philosophy of Spirit: 1827–8. Trans. and intro. Robert Williams. Oxford: Oxford University Press, 2007.
Lectures on the Philosophy of World History. Trans. H. Nisbet. Cambridge: Cambridge University Press, 1975.

Phenomenology of Spirit. Trans. A. Miller. Oxford: Oxford University Press, 1977.
Philosophy of History. Trans. J. Sibree. New York: Dover, 1956.
The Science of Logic. Trans. A. Miller. London: George Allen and Unwin, 1969.

2. General Orientation or Particular Areas

Avineri, Schlomo. *Hegel's Theory of the Modern State*. Cambridge: Cambridge University Press, 1972.
Beiser, Frederick. *Hegel*. Cambridge: Cambridge University Press, 2006.
Beiser, Frederick, ed. *The Cambridge Companion to Hegel*. Cambridge: Cambridge University Press, 1993.
Bernstein, Richard. "Why Hegel Now?" *Review of Metaphysics* 31 (September 1977), 29–60.
Burbidge, John. *The Logic of Hegel's "Logic."* Peterborough, ON: Broadview Press, 2006.
– *On Hegel's Logic*. Atlantic Highlands, NJ: Humanities Press, 1981.
Dewey, John. "From Absolutism to Experimentalism." In *On Experience, Nature, and Freedom*, ed. R. Bernstein. Indianapolis: Bobbs-Merrill, 1960.
Fackenheim, Emil. *The Religious Dimension in Hegel's Thought*. Boston: Beacon Press, 1967.
Findlay, John. *Hegel: A Re-Examination*. New York: Collier Books, 1962.
Gadamer, Hans-Georg. *Hegel's Dialectic: Five Hermeneutical Studies*. Trans. P. Smith. New Haven: Yale University Press, 1976.
Gilson, Étienne, Thomas Langan, and Armand Maurer. *Recent Philosophy: Hegel to the Present*. New York: Random House, 1966.
Harris, Errol. *Cosmos and Anthropos*. Atlantic Heights, NJ: Humanities Press International, 1991.
– *Cosmos and Theos*. Atlantic Heights, NJ: Humanities Press International, 1992.
– *The Foundations of Metaphysics in* Science. Lanham, MD: University Press of America, 1983.
– *Hypothesis and Perception*. London: George Allen and Unwin, 1975.
– *Nature, Mind, and Modern Science*. London: George Allen and Unwin, 1954.
Houlgate, Stephen. *Freedom, Truth and History: An Introduction to Hegel's Philosophy*. London: Routledge, 1992.
– *The Opening of Hegel's* Logic. West Lafayette, IN: Purdue University Press, 2006.
Houlgate, Stephen, ed. *Hegel's Philosophy of Nature*. Albany: SUNY Press, 1999.
Houlgate, Stephen, and Michael Baur, eds. *A Companion to Hegel*. New York: Wiley-Blackwell, 2011.

Kojéve, Alexandre. *Introduction to the Reading of Hegel*. Ed. A. Bloom, trans. J. Nichols. Ithaca: Cornell University Press, 1969.

MacIntyre, Alasdair. *Hegel: A Collection of Critical Essays*. Garden City: Doubleday, 1972.

– *Three Rival Versions of Moral Inquiry*. Notre Dame: University of Notre Dame Press, 1990.

Maher, Chauncey. *The Pittsburgh School of Philosophy: Sellars, Brandom, and McDowell*. New York: Routledge, 2012.

Marcuse, Herbert. *Reason and Revolution: Hegel and the Rise of Social Theory*. Boston: Beacon Press, 1960.

McDowell, John. *Mind and World*, Cambridge, MA: Harvard University Press, 1996.

Merleau-Ponty, Maurice. *Sense and Non-Sense*. Trans. H. and P. Dreyfus. Evanston: Northwestern University Press, 1964.

Pinkard, Terry. *Hegel: A Biography*. Cambridge: Cambridge University Press, 2000.

– *Hegel's Dialectic: The Explanation of Possibility*. Philadelphia: Temple University Press, 1988.

Pippin, Robert. *Hegel's Idealism: The Satisfactions of Self-Consciousness*. Cambridge: Cambridge University Press, 1999.

Redding, Paul. *Analytic Philosophy and the Return of Hegelian Thought*. Cambridge: Cambridge University Press, 2010.

Russon, John, and Michael Baur, eds. *Hegel and the Tradition: Essays in Honor of H.S. Harris*. Toronto: University of Toronto Press, 1988.

Taylor, Charles. *Hegel*. Cambridge: Cambridge University Press, 1975.

Westphal, Merold. *Hegel, Freedom, and Modernity*. Albany: SUNY Press, 1992.

Williams, Robert. *Hegel's Ethics of Recognition*. Berkeley: University of California Press, 1997.

Wood, Allen. *Hegel's Ethical Thought*. Cambridge: Cambridge University Press, 1990.

Wood, Robert E. "Misunderstanding Hegel." *Epoché*, Fall 2012.

Wood, Robert E., and Charles Sullivan. "Rationality and Actuality: Hegel and the Prussian Reform Movement." *Existentia* 21, no. 1–2 (2011), 57–78.

3. Themes in the Encyclopaedia Philosophy of Spirit

Brandom, Robert. "Knowing and Representing: Reading (between the lines of) Hegel's Phenomenology." Munich Lectures, 2011. Available at http://www.pitt.edu/~brandom/currentwork.html#munich.

Chiavatta, David. *Spirit, Family, and the Unconscious in Hegel's Philosophy*. Albany: SUNY Press, 2010.

de Vries, Willem. *Hegel's Theory of Mental Activity*. Ithaca and London: Cornell University Press, 1988.

Greene, Murray. *Hegel on the Soul: A Speculative Anthropology*. The Hague: Martinus Nijhoff, 1972.

Harris, H.S. *Hegel's Ladder*. Vol. 1, *The Pilgrimage of Reason*; vol. 2, *The Odyssey of Spirit*. Indianapolis: Hackett, 1997.

Hyppolite, Jean. *Genesis and Structure of Hegel's Phenomenology of Spirit*. Trans. S. Cherniak and J. Heckman. Evanston: Northwestern University Press, 1974.

Inwood, Michael. *A Commentary on Hegel's* Philosophy of Mind. Oxford: Clarendon Press, 2007.

McCumber, John. *The Company of Words: Hegel, Language, and Systematic Philosophy*. Evanston: Northwestern University Press, 1993.

Mills, Jon. *The Unconscious Abyss*. Albany: SUNY Press, 2002.

Petry, Michael. *Hegel's Philosophy of Subjective Spirit*. Vol. 3, *Phenomenology and Psychology*. Dordrecht: Springer, 1977.

Russon, John. *Reading Hegel's Phenomenology of Spirit*. Bloomington: Indiana University Press, 2004.

Stillman, Peter, ed. *Hegel's Philosophy of Spirit*. Albany: SUNY Press, 1987.

Surber, Jere. *Hegel and Language*. Albany: SUNY Press, 2007.

Westphal, Kenneth. *Blackwell's Guide to Hegel's Phenomenology of Spirit*. Oxford: Wiley-Blackwell, 2009.

Index

www.ingramcontent.com/pod-product-compliance
Ingram Content Group UK Ltd.
Pitfield, Milton Keynes, MK11 3LW, UK
UKHW042110180325
456433UK00002B/98